T0159050

DREAMING OF CUPCAKES

A FOOD ADDICT'S SHAMANIC
JOURNEY INTO HEALING

JENNIFER ENGRÁCIO

BALBOA.
PRESS

A DIVISION OF HAY HOUSE

Note: Some names and places have been changed in the stories to preserve privacy.

"The Language of Emotions" quotes © 2010 Karla McLaren,
with permission from Sounds True, Inc.

Cover art by Jennifer Engrácio

Edited by Lyreen Dressel

Balboa Press books may be ordered through booksellers or by contacting:

Balboa Press
A Division of Hay House
1663 Liberty Drive
Bloomington, IN 47403
www.balboapress.com
1 (877) 407-4847

Because of the dynamic nature of the Internet, any web addresses or
links contained in this book may have changed since publication and
may no longer be valid. The views expressed in this work are solely those
of the author and do not necessarily reflect the views of the publisher,
and the publisher hereby disclaims any responsibility for them.

The author of this book does not dispense medical advice or prescribe the use
of any technique as a form of treatment for physical, emotional, or medical
problems without the advice of a physician, either directly or indirectly. The
intent of the author is only to offer information of a general nature to help you
in your quest for emotional and spiritual well-being. In the event you use any
of the information in this book for yourself, which is your constitutional right,
the author and the publisher assume no responsibility for your actions.

Any people depicted in stock imagery provided by Thinkstock are models,
and such images are being used for illustrative purposes only.
Certain stock imagery © Thinkstock.

Print information available on the last page.

ISBN: 978-1-5043-7261-9 (sc)
ISBN: 978-1-5043-7262-6 (hc)
ISBN: 978-1-5043-7270-1 (e)

Library of Congress Control Number: 2016921322

Balboa Press rev. date: 12/30/2016

"Healing may be defined as a miraculous unfolding of consciousness for one's being in the world. We learn who we are, what and who really matter to us, how to express ourselves fully and openly. Ultimately, the healing journey leads to an intimate union with God through the experience of the flow of God's spirit within. It is a...passage...unique for each individual, filled with danger and risk, triumph and joy, and finally, peace, trust, awe, reverence, love, tenderness."

- George L. Hogben from "Spiritual Aspects of the Healing Arts"

Dedication

....

This book is to all those–past, present and future–that struggled, struggle, and will struggle with addiction. My prayer to the living is that you find the strength inside yourself to heal and step into your shining. To my own ancestors: thanks for living so that I too could live and experience this Earth walk. To all my shamanic teachers: thanks for your compassion, expertise, and unconditional regard.

Disclaimer

The reader uses this material at his or her own risk. Many people have experienced the ceremonies, exercises, resources, and assignments presented herein. Great care has been taken in the preparation of the information contained in this book. The author is unaware of any harm having come to any individual who participated in any of the ceremonies, exercises and assignments in this book. However, as with any ceremonial self-growth work, uncomfortable, personal issues will inevitably arise for you to deal with.

If you have concerns about this, it is strongly recommended that you do not do these ceremonies in isolation, but rather with the support of people you trust. The ceremonies in this book are NOT designed as a substitute for therapy or work with a mental health practitioner or other professional advisor. If you have mental and emotional issues that require professional help, it is strongly recommended that you contact a mental health practitioner or your family physician.

It is important that you exercise good judgment and common sense in undertaking any ceremonies including the ceremonies in this book. Have care for your physical and emotional safety. Any application of the ceremonies, exercises and assignments in this book is undertaken at the reader's own risk. The author and publishers disclaim any liability, loss, injury damages, costs or expense (including legal fees and expenses) arising directly or indirectly from their use.

Although there are many resource suggestions in this book for exploring shamanic traditional healing technologies, it is highly recommended that readers work with certified and trained shamanic practitioners to support their healing journey in addition to working with healthcare professionals in their communities.

The author retains copyright, trademark and all other rights in all material contained herein, including all text and graphic images. No portion of this material may be used or reproduced, another than for personal use, or distributed, transmitted or "mirrored" in any form, or by any means, without the prior written permission of the author.

Contents

Introduction

··

"To put our art, our writing, our photography, our ideas
out into the world with no assurance of acceptance or
appreciation–that's...vulnerability."
                    -Brené Brown from "Daring Greatly:
               How the Courage to Be Vulnerable Transforms
                    the Way We Live, Love, Parent, and Lead"

This book is divided into nine sections that follow the energetic
themes of the medicine wheel. Medicine wheels are ancient maps
that have been found all over the world. The energies of the
directions differ according to what tradition the medicine wheel
comes from. Our ancestors knew that life was circular in nature
and that healing was an inside job. The medicine wheel shows us
all our inner aspects so we can examine them to see what might be
out of balance and make the changes necessary to return to health.
When all the elements around the wheel come into balance, our
sense of well being returns.

At the end of each medicine wheel direction's introduction,
you will find listed two ceremonies that you can do to solidify
your understanding of the teachings from the book "Shamanic
Ceremonies for a Changing World" by Marilyn Keffer and Gael Carter.
Although reading this book will likely be impactful, in shamanism,
learning through personal experience is where the deep learning
and transformation happens. You can find more information on
how to purchase a copy by looking at the Recommended Resources
section of the Appendix of this book.

One of my dear friends commented on how the repetition of certain themes (i.e. forgiveness) was tiring for him and he recommended I consider changing that. Trust me: I got sick of having to do the same things over and over in order to get good at them! Upon reflection, I decided to leave those repetitions in because they illustrate the diligence, awareness, and work needed in order to successfully heal an addiction. There is no one-time, magical solution when it comes to overcoming well-worn addictive patterns and so employing the same strategies over and over in different situations is the only way to begin to break down these insidious, destructive behaviour patterns.

I've also included e-mail entries from the year I worked actively with my teachers (Wolf Woman and Tiger's Breath) to heal my addiction. These provide examples of some of the themes I speak of while also lending some context to the challenges I faced. While reading, you will hear many "voices" in the forms of my teachers, many authors, and some information that came from my journeys into the spirit world. Engaging with all of these resources helped me and I share them here in the hope that they can also turn on some light bulbs in your own mind.

Although it is true that all books present challenges in the creation process, this was a tricky book to write for many different reasons. For one, the subject matter is deeply personal and I wrestled with how much to actually share with the public. In a world with instantaneous access to print material via the Internet, I worried about being misrepresented. Ultimately, however, I came to the conclusion that there will always be critics that misunderstand the intent of a piece of work. All I can do as an author is state the intent of this book clearly and offer it out from my heart with the deepest wishes that something I shared supports someone else in healing from addiction. I also hope that those who love addicts receive insights about addiction from reading this book that can help them support their family and friends in healthy ways.

I was deeply concerned about the reactions of family and friends. What I learned is that addiction often arises out of ancestral trauma that is handed down from generation to generation. These patterns are unconscious and the work of healing an addiction is to bring these out of the shadows so that they no longer usurp the person's ability to make healthy choices for themselves. Because addicts operate so much out of these patterns mostly as a way to numb out pain, the choices they make are anything but light.

They have a huge cost to themselves and to those around them that they are often not even aware of. Having done this huge piece of healing work myself, I have great compassion for where addicts are at when they are in the "unconscious" phase of their addiction. It is for this reason that I do not blame family or friends for my addiction. They did not cause my addiction; that is a choice I made on my own–however unconsciously. The healing of the food addiction was also a choice I made on my own. There are also new scientific findings that will be presented in this book that show how addiction works from a neurobiological perspective that will shed light on the societal issue of addiction.

Throughout the book, the reader will hear about interpersonal struggles I had with family members and friends. Learning to take command of my responses to others' behaviour as well as taking responsibility for my own part in relational issues with others was a big part of my healing. While addicted, I wandered around blaming others for my feelings and reactions to situations presented to me in the course of living. What I learned is that although I have minimal control over what life sends my way, I can *always* take command of how I respond to circumstances and people in my life.

I am grateful to my loved ones for the mirrors of reflection they provided during this process and for hanging in with me through all the changes I underwent in regaining balance. I know that my decisions had an impact on others. Looking back, I do not regret decisions that advanced my healing although some were hard to make (like my move to Calgary away from my blood relatives). The right decisions are often full of mixed blessings and take courage and faith to make. This book is all about this theme. I offer it to you without attachment.

I share my story not in a prescriptive way for everyone to follow step-by-step. I hope that telling my story opens up possible new pathways of healing for people. I believe each person is on a unique journey. Each person came into this life with karma and issues from previous lives needing healing as well as the healing of their own ancestral blood lineages. Each person is also here with a life purpose that involves sharing his or her gifts with the world. The healing process, therefore, will never be the same from person to person. I send out a prayer that each of you who read this book find and stay on your own unique pathways to healing, however that looks for you.

Jennifer Engrácio
Calgary, AB
2015

What is Shamanism?

"Shamanism is not a faith, but a wisdom tradition in which we learn purely from our own individual, collective and personal experience. It is not a religion and is dogma-free; indeed it supports any existing spiritual practice one already has. Many of us deeply desire a connection to our own 'soulfulness' and that of all other living beings in a free and natural way. This is the essence of Shamanism."

- John Cantwell

The etymology of the word "shaman" itself comes from the Siberian language and it was originally used to refer to a spiritual medicine healer in the community. In fact, shamanism itself is widespread among the indigenous people of the world today. In each area of the world, including Europe, earth-based spiritual practices can be traced back to specific groups of people who knew how to enter into communion with nature spirits through non-ordinary reality in order to obtain information that could aid in the healing of a person or a community. Although we don't tend to call urban shamanic practitioners "shamans" in the modern world, the skills indigenous shamans utilized are being used again by shamanic practitioners the world over.

Shamanic practitioners do not focus on what is "broken" in a person or even necessarily how the imbalance happened in the first place. Shamanism is concerned primarily with reminding an individual of their inherent wholeness. Shamanic practitioners see that when a person experiences trauma or illness, they are not in need of fixing; rather, parts of their being splinter or shatter away from the whole causing inner and outer dissonance. Because imbalances manifest in the spiritual energetic level of being first, this is also where practitioners travel to bring back these pieces to the afflicted person. In the case of a long-standing physical illness, the body can begin to heal only when the spiritual aspects that caused the illness to begin with are brought back into alignment with overall health and wellbeing.

Today, many of us have lost contact with these old ways. The traditional shaman has grown scarce in North America due to our colonial past. In the modern world, we've had to adapt ancient traditions to fit our hurried, busy lifestyles. Urban shamanic practitioners train in ancient shamanic technologies in order to heal themselves and to support healing in others in the community. Ancient tools are used by everyday people again with great success: drum journeys into the spirit world, vision quests for extended time out in nature, and other spiritual ceremonies. All of these strategies help us to quiet our inner world so we can hear the voice of Spirit and our inner wise one who knows what medicine we need to heal.

This may seem strange to people who were not brought up in shamanic cultures. However, because of their close proximity and dependence on the natural world, ancient peoples knew that the consensual reality we live in is not the only reality we can sense and participate within. It is not uncommon for shamanic practitioners to work with spirit guides, totem animals, and their ancestors in order to affect positive change in their own lives and in the world around them. In shamanic cultures, dreaming is not an idle activity without any useful function: it is the way people dream a new reality into being. This does not involve attempting to control anything outside the practitioner. What we put our attention on is what manifests. And so just like a journeyer can enter the spirit world for answers to problems, she can also enter the spirit world to lend energy to a different dream than the one she is currently living. In fact, both are needed in order for healing to be effective.

Shamanism may seem like magical thinking and there are definitely magical and mysterious moments in the practice as we learn to deepen our individual connections to Spirit. However, the truth is that there is substantial work needed on the physical plane of existence, putting our visions into action, if any change is to occur. As individuals on a growth and evolutionary edge, if we choose, we continue to heal until we die. Healing requires us to keep sensing the splintered parts of ourselves, working with the spirit world to bring them into wholeness again. This is a tremendous act of power that we are capable of as human beings. Unlike other living creatures, humans can consciously learn to direct their will to literally change the pathways available to them in the future. This is one of the benefits of being able to go back in time or travel into the future, whereas animals only live in the present. Shamanic practitioners learn to responsibly travel the spiritual realms to affect change.

If it is so easy, then why are there so many suffering people? Of course, this gift we have can also be a pitfall. Many of us get stuck in our ego minds. Or we refuse to let go of the past. Much of the pain of the human condition is caused by our lack of awareness and ability to direct our attention. This takes lots of practice and mentors who know how to teach these methods with skill and care. Many of these traditions have been lost and many have been revived. There are some modern-day shamanic practitioners that are charlatans, yet there are many more who are earnestly passing their teachings onto sincere and responsible individuals willing to learn these ancient ways of dreaming, healing, and creating. Many elders are passing on this wisdom for the benefit of humans as a species, regardless of cultural and societal barriers. Some of these reputable people and organizations appear in the back of this book.

A Sweatlodge Experience

"*Apprenticeship means seeking. Apprenticeship means spiritual training. It means learning the way. You must first find the spiritual teacher within. The true spiritual teacher will lift you with kindness and love—a love that burns through the universe.*"

- David Carson and Nina Sammons from "2013 Oracle: Ancient Keys to the 2012 Awakening"

I had a lot of good things going for me in life and I wasn't happy. I didn't know why I was so dissatisfied. I only knew that my life was not working and I was seriously depressed. I had healed a lot of destructive patterns in the first five years of practicing shamanism. I decided to take this issue into the sweatlodge ceremony to see what was going on with me on a spiritual level.

Archaeologists have discovered sweatlodges all around the world in many cultures. A sweatlodge is an ancient shamanic tradition of creating a sacred space inside a dome-shaped lodge made out of saplings and covered with blankets. Heated rocks are brought in and placed in a dug out pit inside the lodge where the ceremonialist says prayers over them thanking them for giving away their energy for the healing of the people inside the lodge. When the flap closes, the people inside are shrouded in darkness, save for the glowing of the hot rocks in the pit. The ceremonialist pours water over these rocks throughout the ceremony while people pray and "sweat."

I had sweat many times before this particular one. My intent this time was to find the source of my unhappiness. I had no idea that this one would be so life altering or challenging. I entered the doorway to the lodge after the ceremonialist blessed me in. I took my seat and worked at centering myself in the moment as I watched the other people, then the ceremonialist, and finally the rocks come into the lodge. I was unusually agitated–a sign for me before ceremony that there was something major about to shift inside me. When my time came to pray, I asked Spirit what was standing in the way of my being happy. Now, sweatlodges are magical places where time tends to stand still and where the inner voice sometimes gets *very* clear–sometimes painfully so. The things that are easy to ignore in our everyday lives tend to get highlighted so we can deal with them. Sometimes, images come as a part of my answer from Spirit. Sometimes, the answer comes in the form of a thought I've never had before falling into my head. This time, both happened.

For as long as I can remember, I've enjoyed singing. I spent many years performing in various choirs and ensembles in Vancouver. The beginning image was of me singing on stage in front of thousands of people in the audience. As this image came, the feeling I had inside me was of extreme anxiety and Spirit showed me that I was separated from the audience by a thick glass. I was unable to connect with them and they were unable to connect with me in an authentic way. I was frozen inside. I *knew* that feeling. I had experienced that many times on stage. I still didn't know what it had to do with my question, and then Spirit continued in words:

"Jen, there is something in your physical reality that is not in balance."

I searched my inner wisdom for what that might be: finances, house, roommates?

"No. Your relationship with food."

I felt the huge knot in my gut seize and then start to release. I felt a huge wave of relief and anxiety at the same time.

"You are addicted to food."

My mind resisted while everything in my being knew this message was true. My ego started railing with all sorts of thoughts:

"Isn't 'addiction' a bit of a strong term? It isn't like I am a crack addict or a smoker. Heck! I don't even eat unhealthy food. I exercise. This is crazy! I don't have a problem. I am not giving up food. No way!"

I was stunned for the rest of the ceremony. I don't even remember hearing anyone else's prayers. I came out of the lodge in shock and the next thing I remember, I was sitting in front of one of my teachers asking for support navigating the information I received. She looked at me compassionately like someone who'd been there; she had been an addict herself.

Without flinching and with absolutely no judgment, she asked, "Do you know why you eat?"

I connected with my inner wisdom, " To feel better; to soothe myself when I am anxious or stressed."

She nodded and continued, "Do you know what your trigger foods are–the ones you reach for most when you are in this state?"

I reflected for a moment, "Yes. Wheat and sugar–especially baked goods."

"Okay," she replied calmly, " I will work with you. I want to tell you upfront that it will be at least a year if not more of committed work to heal this."

"I understand," I replied, feeling deflated." I commit to that."

I met my life partner, Margaret, just two months after this sweatlodge experience. Over the last few years of being involved in spiritual healing together and separately, we've both seen the other transform in positive ways, revealing more of the essence of who we each are. We tend not to talk a lot about the spiritual ceremonies of specific things we are healing. In fact, I personally prefer to keep my journey to myself when I am working on healing my issues. The reasons for this are two-fold. First, I've noticed that talking about my experience dissipates the personal power I am recovering and that energy is essential to continue the healing in a good way. Second, because it saves me from having to field the concerns, questions, and comments of family and friends who, though well-intentioned, unwittingly draw energy away from my process with their worry and fear.

A while ago, I shared with Margaret that I was writing this book and she asked me a question that was impossible to answer simply: "How *did* you heal your addiction, anyway?" It was a journey of finding and restoring pieces of myself that were unique and personal to me. I convalesced about writing about the journey at all. I wondered if it was self-indulgent and if telling the story would reinforce the patterns I'd worked so hard to shift. I was hiking in my hometown at the river when my answer came loud and clear.

I was thinking about the history of addiction in my family after interviewing family members for a Family Tree Ceremony I was doing when I heard my grandpa's voice in my head. He gave me permission to tell his story based on the information I had and the information he gave me from his place in the spirit world. He was adamant that these stories would be of assistance to people in their own healing and must be told to stop the cycle of addiction from plaguing future generations. Reluctantly, I conceded.

Ancestors

"Being born into this world in a particular place is like having the signature of that place stamped upon you. The essence of your place of birth cloaks and protects your walk through this life, and whatever you do becomes registered in the ledger of that geography. You can end up thousands of miles away from your birthplace, and if you are involved in a healing ritual that is meant to work, you have to invoke the spirits that are at the place where you were born in addition to those who are natives of the place you are in. The spirits that witnessed your birth at that place are still there, and your calling them will awaken their attention to your direction. If you embrace this concept, you will find that human mobility does not remove a person's original connection to the birthplace. Your footprints still lead back to the place where you began."
-Malidoma Somé from "The Healing Wisdom of Africa:
Finding Life Purpose Through Nature,
Ritual, and Community"

In general, we tend to tell and remember stories of the dark side of human lives. When someone's shadow side is prevalent, few take the time to look deeper to see that person's true essence and shining. This was the case with my ancestors. I tell this forthcoming story from a light side not to excuse any addict's behaviour or to minimize the pain they cause themselves and others through their addiction but to shine attention on a different perspective. I do not blame my ancestors or hold any resentment toward them for the decisions they made. My own healing depended, in the end, in accepting all that had passed: I forgave others and myself.

People tend to treat addicts with everything from pity to disgust. All addicts are trying to soothe and cope with pain and emotional trauma of some sort. I want to highlight these people as survivors who have made choices that enabled them to keep living. I understand that we are each responsible for our own actions, thoughts, feelings, and words. I hope that this book shows the complexity of addiction and the inner world of an addicted person. I pray for a compassionate approach toward addicts and the people who live with them.

During the Family Tree Ceremony, I found out things about my family members that I didn't know. I found power stories inside places of abuse, addiction, and violence that I didn't expect to find. I saw my family members in a new way. Creating the draft of the family trees of both my parents' lineages made me realize how many people had to live their lives and go on their journey simply for me to be born. This was extremely humbling.

I wondered how many people came before my great grandparents that I didn't get to know that also contributed to my being here at this point in time in a body. It helped me to see that the way I live my life and the choices I make really *do* impact the generations ahead of me and behind me in a visceral way. The gifts my family passed on are of open-heartedness and care for one another–through all kinds of challenges as well as the good times. Seeing how all the generations worked together to make sure we all survived was really good for my heart. To know the conditions they were living in and that they all made it, however fragmented they were inside, is a testament to their strength and determination.

Another thing that struck me was how much courage it must have taken my relatives to move to other countries where they knew few, if any, people before the revolution in Portugal in 1974. It was also neat to see this new generation coming and leaving space for babies that have yet to be born and spouses that have yet to join our family thread. As I added the spouses, I could see that their family lineages were now joined to ours as well and that has been an interesting point of reflection. If we joined everyone's family trees in the world, would we all be connected somehow? It seems endless, the points of connection. Perhaps in a more real way than we think, we are indeed all relations and not separate at all. I share this next story here with permission from my grandpa's spirit.

Avô Vitalino's Story

I was working as a full time gardener some years ago when I smelled cherry tomatoes in a client's garden, or so I thought. I searched high and low for a vegetable patch in the area–even going so far as surveying neighbours' yards over fences. There were no cherry tomatoes in sight. Then it hit me: that was my Avô Vitalino's way of getting my attention. My paternal grandpa passed away in 1990 but has since then continued to communicate with me in dreams and in waking hours. I inherited his pruning shears and it was his way of nodding his approval at a passion we shared: gardening.

That night, I had a dream–the kind I get that comes with a message. In the dream, I was in a garden working when I felt a presence behind me. On a stone bench wearing his green landscaping suit sat my Avô under an arch of roses. His hands were neatly folded in his lap and he wore a radiant smile on his face as he watched me work. That was his cute way of confirming his presence from that day on.

I remember being in awe of my Avô when I was a kid; he could grow any plant and raise any animal to thrive. His garden was filled with edibles that we grandkids were allowed to pick and eat straight from the plant. Cherry tomatoes were his specialty and they lined the walls of his urban East Vancouver lot. Avô had a small sod runway where we could ride our bikes, but besides that, every inch of his yard was covered with plants. Nature was his passion and where he found peace.

This year when I was doing the Family Tree Ceremony from the shamanic ceremonial children's book I co-authored ("The Magic

Circle: Shamanic Ceremonies for the Child and the Child Within"),
I learned more about my ancestors' histories. Avô never spoke of
how he grew up. In fact, he didn't speak much at all. His own dad
died of an intestinal illness and shortly thereafter, his mom was
found dead at the bottom of the family water well. No one knows
for sure what happened to her but suicide is the cause of death
accepted by many family members.

At the age of seven, my Avô, an only child, was orphaned. At
first, he was sent to live with various aunts and uncles. However,
the financial strain of having an extra mouth to feed in Portugal, a
dictatorship with food rations, drove relatives who were struggling
to care for their own families to look for someone who could employ
and feed him. He was given away to a man who ran a hide business.
It was child labour and conditions were terrible. Given the wide
acceptance and use of corporal punishment, it's no stretch to
imagine how he was treated at that place and others after it.

Avô was addicted to alcohol. He was pretty reclusive. He spent
most of his time away from people with the plants or the animals
in his garden. We usually only saw him at mealtimes or then when
he fell asleep on the couch at the end of the day. I remember him
keeping a box beside his chair at the kitchen table where he had all
sorts of alcohol. He started his day with some kind of fruit juice and
poured in vodka. In the end, he died from multiple systems failure
at the age of sixty-seven. He was never an affectionate person. I
remember going to visit him in the hospital and when he saw me, he
looked at me pleadingly and stretched out his hand. At that point,
he was no longer able to speak. I took his hand and looked into his
eyes. It was the only intimate and open moment I'd ever had with
him. I was fifteen. He died the next day.

I once read the words of a First Nations Grandmother whose
name I now forget that have stuck with me to this day: "We were all
in our Grandmother's womb." I thought about that for a long while:
how could that be? Then it occurred to me: my mom and all of her
eggs were in my grandma's womb when she carried her for nine
months. One of those eggs became me. In teasing out the trauma
that is handed down in cellular memory, it started to make sense

to me how I could still experience the traumas of my ancestors and the role my own addiction to food played in toning down that pain. It started to dawn on me that everything my ancestors did impacted me as well. And everything I did, as an ancestor of the future, would impact my nieces, nephews, and children's children. This was a huge motivation for me to heal this aspect of myself. Each time I do ceremony, I am aware that I am not only healing myself but the seven generations behind me and the seven ahead. This is extremely humbling and empowering.

Chapter 1

THE WEST

West Introduction: Satisfying the Body

"Our bodies link directly to Father Sky. This is just one of the profound lessons emerging from today's cosmology. Science has now demonstrated that our bodies are formed of the 'stuff of stars'...60 percent of the atoms of our bodies are hydrogen and helium atoms, which were birthed in the original fireball 13.7 billion years ago. The other 40 percent of our bodies' atoms were birthed in supernova explosions about 5 billion years ago. We are made of ancient stuff...Consider: we couldn't run, jump, walk, swim, skate, embrace, kiss, wrestle, make love, eat, sing, dance, paint, sleep, write, or think without our body. All we do we do with our body. And that includes pray and communicate with the divine: body and Soul, body and consciousness, go hand in glove. Our bodies also contain the DNA of our ancestors, all of them, so each one is a meeting place for the entire human race."
- Matthew Fox from "The Hidden Spirituality of Men"

Does it change something inside of you when you hear that every cell of your body is made of stars? I hope so. I know how life changing that was for me when I first learned this scientific fact. And it really brought home that I was destroying the only physical container my spirit had available to it in this lifetime. If I am made of light, why am I insisting on behaving as if there were only darkness?

There is a long history in the Western world of denying the pleasures of the body as if they were evil, lustful, and wrong. This is a belief worth scrapping from our minds. Why? Because our bodies contain the innate wisdom of what they need to survive and thrive. When we ignore its messages, we do so at the peril of our health and wellbeing. Coming back to our bodies and to an awareness of what we are sensing, feeling, and needing at any given moment is what brings us into the present moment. If we are truly present in this moment, unless we are in immediate physical danger, there is no stress. There is no past or future in the picture. It is easier to appreciate life and to become conscious of patterns that need to heal when we are present in our bodies.

An addict's body is often very imbalanced chemically and energetically because of abusive and unsustainable addictive patterns that have often spanned unchecked for many years. All addictive behaviour numbs out our ability to feel our bodies, therefore blocking the messages for rest, sex, exercise, healthy food, pleasure, and water that our bodies naturally give us that help us to maintain our overall wellness and vitality. Our bodies do not lie and tend to get louder in the form of disease and illness if we don't take care of them. Our bodies are sacred vessels that carry our spirits through this lifetime. Healing an addiction means having to recover that knowing inside of us that Matthew Fox speaks of in the above quote. Good self-care and body-awareness are cornerstones of any recovery program. Illness and disease are not inevitable outcomes of living–they are signs of imbalances that begin in the spiritual realm as warning whispers and are exacerbated by the choices we make in our lives. If we can make poor choices, we can also learn to make better ones that are in alignment with our spirit knowing.

In North America, many of us are caught up in the rat race of competition, climbing never-ending corporate ladders, and accumulating as much "stuff" as possible as a way of proving our worthiness and status. The thing that we've forgotten is that worthiness is an inside job–it doesn't come from outer markers of what others think of as "success." This way of living is simply not conducive to what our bodies need to build and maintain health and overall wellbeing. It's a breeding ground for addiction and illness. Workaholics spend so many hours at work that they don't receive the down time needed for their bodies to recover from the amount of stress they are under. This addiction is often coupled with cocaine, sugar, caffeine, and other stimulants that keep a person's energy revved high. With this stunning amount of energy loss, it becomes impossible for the body to maintain homeostasis.

The West of the inner medicine wheel is the place of the body and the physical world. In the West, we get a chance to look at our relationship to our physical world. This includes our bodies, how we use and care for them. This also includes our finances, our ability to meet the many needs of living in a physical body, the condition of our homes, the environment, and the communities we live in. In the following chapters, I discuss how I regained balance in the West of the medicine wheel. This includes a commitment I renewed to living from a place of pleasure and body awareness.

In order to consolidate your understanding of this direction from your personal, experiential and embodied perspective, I recommend doing the following ceremonies from "Shamanic Ceremonies for a Changing World" by Marilyn Keffer and Gael Carter. You can find more information on how to purchase a copy by looking at the Recommended Resources section of the Appendix of this book.

Breath of Life Assignment 0-18
The Conservation of Energy Ritual 1-2

Zoning Out

> *"Dissociation is natural...and happens as a result of a stress response. It's a floating, absent feeling. It can last a long time, especially if you were traumatized as an infant, when you didn't have the option to fight or run away. Checking out would have been the only strategy you had in your earliest days...When people reach the limits of their terror, their survival brain throws the circuit breaker on their mind, and they check out. They no longer feel sensations in their body. If you check out repeatedly, then over time, you will lose the awareness of how your body feels...The purpose of the freeze response...[is] not to change the situation but to help you survive the situation."*
> *-Kim Barthel from "Conversations with a Rattlesnake"*

I will always remember my first assignment from my teacher. It seemed simple enough: eat all your meals with your eyes closed. I thought this would be easy and had no idea why she was having me do this exercise. Boy was I dead wrong! The following excerpt is taken from an e-mail I wrote to my teacher, Wolf Woman, in May 2010:

Breakfast: I did my first session of eating in my room by myself with my eyes closed. I discovered that it is hard for me to eat more slowly. It is like the flavours of the food are really hard for me to take in. Like too much information in a way. Flooded with sadness for all the times I missed noticing those flavours in my life and allowing them to nourish my body and spirit. Then

coffee with my eyes closed. Immediate comfort and memories of being a kid and drinking coffee in the morning with relatives before school. Good times. Remembering the mix of coffee and milk in my bottle as a toddler. Tears as I write this realizing that connection I've made between coffee and family. I am not sure I completely understand what they are about. The feeling is a mixture of sadness and longing that I can't quite place. Boiled potatoes, salmon, and mixed greens for dinner. Memories flood back of summers in a relative's backyard with cousins exploring the creek and picking watercress. I didn't know I had such connections between food and memories–that they were so linked. They can be a blessing, but often times, they are a curse. Not all those memories were good ones.

It was a real epiphany to me that I didn't notice the flavours of what I was eating. I later discovered through my own experience that sugar numbs out the taste buds when consumed in large quantities, making it more challenging to get the full sensory experience that food can offer. Eating, for me, was an automatic response to stress. It didn't really matter *what* something tasted like, it was that full feeling that I was after and I ate as fast as I could to get it over with. I was after a feeling of satiation and satisfaction. Needless to say, it was always fleeting. Despite feeling full, I still felt empty inside and this distressed me. I didn't know what that emptiness was and I was too scared at first to go into it to find out.

Social eating was challenging. Indeed, food is everywhere and it is perhaps the most socially accepted addiction out there. Many friends I later shared my struggles with around food tended to minimize it as if everyone has some kind of addiction that they are unwilling to give up (caffeine, sugar, shopping, or watching TV) and that it is not a big deal. Loved ones often unwittingly enabled my addiction by putting food in front of me even if I didn't ask for it or then attempting to shame me into eating food they had "lovingly" prepared for me.

Food, unlike cocaine for instance, is impossible to avoid so I knew that I had to learn how to master all the situations where food was accessible and where I'd likely be experiencing stress: at staff meetings, during family dinners, at parties, and during hard conversations with people I love. It was not easy to stay conscious while eating when I first began this exercise–even when there was no one around. Over time, I was able to notice I'd zoned out and was able to bring myself back in less time. For this first year, results were inconsistent, as you can see below. One day, I'd have an easy time staying present in social situations and then the next day, it felt hopeless. Persistence was a necessary trait for me to develop because I knew I would not get it right every time. Even today, this pattern is still there and that is okay. I use it as information and will question why I checked out instead of beating myself up about it.

Another thing I practiced was not multi-tasking. In a world where multi-tasking is touted as a desirable workplace skill, this was a tough one to overcome. When I was eating, that is all I did. I didn't read a book, surf the Internet, or look at my phone. All my attention was in what I was doing. I learned that multi-tasking is not conducive to developing mindfulness and so I was really conscious around meal times of this tendency. I won't lie; it was excruciatingly painful at first to just sit with food, sensation, and feeling. With practice, it became a source of pleasure and wonder. Just learning to observe was really an education because I got to see what my patterns were. Awareness is the first step to making any transformation, I've found.

May 11, 2010

Starting to notice more changes in my body (i.e. improved posture). My body seems to be going through subtle shifts without my really trying. Voices still there but more faded in the background now. Something is changing. Goddaughter is here staying with me for two days. We had pasta last night for dinner with steamed broccoli thrown in. It was exquisite. Another dinner with family tonight. Connection with food while socializing has gotten better. Even with eyes open, I find

I am able to focus and pick out flavours in what I am eating; that is different than before when I'd be so caught up in what was happening that I'd miss that. So that's a victory. Again turned down cake. I was worried that I wouldn't keep up my practices with a relative visiting but it was totally fine.

May 18, 2010

Well, I bought something called Mana "Bread" which is high in fiber and has raisins and carrots in it. And although supposedly "healthy," I noticed that I had the same response to eating it as I had with other baked goods: I was super excited and it soothed me right away. Never noticed before how certain foods just bring my anxiety level down. I looked at the package and it contained sugar too. Shit!

May 24, 2010

Visited with friends and ate dinner with them. As soon as I got there, the friend I've been in conflict with left the table. Kept eating but noticed immediate disconnection with the food and myself. By the time I caught myself, I was totally distracted... getting up and eating while I was walking to the kitchen to clean my plate. I forgave myself for a bunch of stuff including not "feeding" myself when things get hairy around me. And being hard on myself for mistakes made. More victories: still staying away from the baked goods.

All of this zoning out made me begin to wonder why I did it. When did this start? Why did I begin this pattern? What was its purpose? One night at a family dinner, this became clear.

Jun 2, 2010

Woke up this morning guilt-wracked. The other night at a family gathering, I watched an adult hit a toddler and did nothing. It did occur to me to do or say something on his behalf but my intuition told me not to. I knew that I would be of more use to him in the long run if I stayed in good standing with his parents. This whole thing is a paradox that I am having a hard time accepting. I have been in this adult's place. He's doing what he has been taught to discipline his son. I forgave myself. However, my values are just not lining up. If that had been a kid on the street that that happened to, I would probably have interjected somehow. And logically, I know that this is a different circumstance, and yet I feel like I went against my integrity. I don't condone beating people into submission and yet there I was doing nothing. After it happened, he was sitting in his high chair sobbing while his mom was forcing him to eat his food (that is what the power struggle was about in the first place). I went up to him and tried to make eye contact but he was not in his body. I called him back by saying his name and looking into his eyes and holding his hands and communicating with my energy that he was okay–said hello to his spirit. I guess I could see it as a victory that I understood that his choice of taking back his power by choosing not to eat (a pattern he has) was not something I could support. So I reframed this for him after he came back into his body: "You know this food (as opposed to a popsicle which is what he wanted) has magic in it. You know all the things you like doing like sliding and playing on the swings? This kind of food makes your body strong so you can do all those things." Some kind of recognition went off inside him and he started eating. That is something I wouldn't have known unless I had done this work with food addiction so far. I realized this morning as I was trying to eat my breakfast over the tears that it is really hard for me to feed myself when I feel guilty. It was all I could do to eat my breakfast (even though I was hungry). I punish myself by not eating when I am feeling guilty.

Jun 10, 2010

Although my body's sore, it feels a lot lighter this morning after yesterday's dance. Still watching my tendency to zone out while eating or standing in front of the mirror. I also tend to still rush these. Impatient with the process. Lots of forgiveness again this morning as I stood in front of the mirror: for being impatient and for being unconscious. Recently, I've noticed my tendency to slip out of my body while I am eating. I don't know how long I've been doing this but I think it's been a long time. That day looking into that toddler's eyes after the eating incident provided a good reflection for me. I was not sure what it had to do with me for a while but now I do. It is one of the ways I block nurturing myself. So been working on receiving–a weak point of mine. Eating is a noticeably different experience when I stay in my body where I am present and can feel the pleasure in my body. I had this moment of bliss a few days ago that reminded me of watching a relative eat when he was a baby. When the food was coming, he would watch it in excitement and his whole body would shake and he'd let out this squeal of joy. I had an inside moment like that. I want to develop (or go back to) that kind of relationship with food.

Jun 18, 2010

Drifting in and out of connection as I eat. So this morning I decided (instead of a blindfold) to load up my fork and put it in my mouth eyes closed. When I am done chewing, opening up my eyes and loading my fork again. This worked and it slowed me down. Realized I was forcing myself to eat after a while and all these memories flooded back of adults force-feeding me when I was a kid. It was hard to fight the impulse to eat the rest; I felt super nauseous. Lots of tears. Lots of forgiving myself for allowing them to do that, for not fighting back, for losing connection with food and myself. Now I see why the force-feeding with the toddler triggered me so much.

Jun 19, 2010

Continued with the eating with eyes closed and loading up spoon only when bite was done for breakfast. That seems to work. Still feeling myself trying to rush through eating and "get it over with." Wondered as I ate where that came from and then I got pictures of this force-feeding and the overwhelming feeling of just wanting it to be over. Associating it with wanting to get away from that tyranting energy. Lots of forgiveness around allowing myself to be tyranted like that and doing the victim thing. Planned to eat lunch before going to visit a relative this afternoon. Didn't want to show up hungry and be prone to temptation. The first thing Portuguese people do is offer food and drink to visitors; it is considered an insult not to accept something "of theirs." So I prepared myself to accept coffee. Told my relative I wanted 1 tsp. of honey and she put in 2. I drank it but made a note to myself to put in my own next time.

Force-feeding and controlling how much and what kids eat is such a common part of parenting culture in some circles that no one questions what this might do to a developing child. Food is not love. Food is energy our bodies need to survive. It's wise not to confuse the two. Force-feeding taught me that I had no control over my body, what I wanted to eat, or how much. It taught me that if I tried to fight for what my body wanted, I would be punished in some way so it was better to just zone out. Although I now know that this helped me to survive these early interactions with adults who were more physically powerful than I was, it was not a good strategy to continue long term. I stopped blaming myself for my freeze response when I learned more about how the brain copes with stressful situations. The online source Wikipedia states: "implicit memory is a type of long-term memory in which previous experiences aid the performance of a task without conscious awareness of these previous experiences." So when this memory is triggered, it needs to be tended to consciously in order for new patterns to emerge.

This is what I learned to undo in the process of healing. I had to train myself to be in my body, to listen to my body, and to trust that my body knew what it needed. I had to learn that it was safe to be in my body at all! I learned to give my body what it needed regardless of the social pressures around me. I learned that bodies are always changing in order to maintain homeostasis and so it stands to reason that they won't always want the same things. During days where I worked out hard, my body naturally wanted protein. Other days, I could go without meat and feel well. Making food a control issue between parents and kids means that no one wins. The parents are stressed that their kids might not be eating enough and the kids develop unhealthy behaviours around eating– sometimes avoiding food altogether so they don't have to deal with the power struggle that ensues.

At a school I once worked at with young children, I got to see a new way of doing things. These kids were obviously going through growing spurts throughout the year. The three meals a day thing was not working for them and so we decided as a community of teachers, parents, and kids to make sure there was a tray of healthy snacks that kids had access to the whole day they were at school. The community decided to set guidelines around the kinds of foods offered: organic, refined sugar free, raw, vegetarian, and balance of nutrients. Some kids paired up with an adult two times a day to prepare the healthy snacks–once in the morning and another time in the afternoon. The kids were like deer grazing! They naturally ate in very small amounts several times throughout the day. And I noticed that they mostly ate in balanced ways. The only kids we supported nutritionally in a more hands-on way were those with sensory processing issues that were only able to eat foods with certain textures and tastes. Otherwise, most kids were naturally really good at listening to their bodies. It was so healing for me to see this because it showed me that I too could trust my body to know what it needed.

Jun 20, 2010

Was at a Solstice Celebration yesterday where one of the elders was speaking about his work with healing plants. In order to work with these plants, he had to fast from certain foods–one of which was sugar. He said something that stood out for me: "I learned that sugar is about slavery." And right then it hit me: I don't want to be a slave to sugar. So I've decided to cut out the honey in my coffee and make sure to buy granola that is not sweetened with honey from now on. Dinner again with my family tonight. Despite it being hard to connect with myself due to the energy that shoots around the dinner table, I managed to stay connected most of the time. Took coffee without honey today and it was just fine.

Jan 9, 2011

Found myself eating absently today. When I realized that, I stopped and figured out what was going on. Struggling again with the big empty space inside of me and all the solitude. Just took today one moment at a time. Blustery outside and 20 below so went for short walks and that helped. Also did a couple of hours of meditation. Mantra for today: everything passes.

Body Awareness

....

"*To trust children we must first learn to trust ourselves...
and most of us were taught as children that we could not be
trusted.*"

-John Holt

After working for nearly two decades with children in structured
and unstructured learning environments, I've come to see that
many primary-aged children are naturally connected to their
bodies and can give themselves the food, rest, exercise, and
stimulation levels needed at any given time. Unless, of course, they
are forced into a situation where they are not allowed to give their
bodies what they need, when they need it. This is the case in most
conventional schools today where kids are punished for following
their bodies' needs (i.e. moving around, stretching, going to the
washroom, and eating in class). Children and adults who have such
rigidly scheduled lives often have no idea what they need or when.
This is a real problem in a world where efficiency seems to be more
important than balance and it comes at the cost of our health. In
Japan, the people are so overworked that the risk of cardiovascular
illness has increased exponentially. This is such a chronic problem
that the Japanese now have a name for workaholism: karoshi, which
means "death from work." Thankfully, listening to our bodies is a
skill that can be re-learned with practice and support.

In my case, it was my move from the public school classrooms to
working online from home that really helped me begin to make the
switch to living in alignment with my body and its needs. I realized

at first that I had no idea how to move through my days without some external schedule telling me when to eat, when to teach, and when to sleep. I began to play with my own circadian rhythms and I realized that I have a natural sleep cycle that works well for me (from 11 pm to 7am or midnight to 8 am). I can survive off of seven hours' sleep but I do better with eight. I also played with when to eat, how long to sit at the computer, when to interject exercise into my day, and when to rest. I got a pedometer to track how many steps I was getting in a day and made sure to get 10,000 steps (the recommended daily amount for high cardio fitness levels). I learned Qigong, yoga, and meditation techniques and practiced them daily to relax and stretch my body.

In shamanism, we learn to talk to our bodies and to listen to the messages our bodies give us. In shamanic cultures, the body is considered a being with its own wisdom. I would routinely ask my body what it needed when I felt like reaching out for food. I started to see a pattern of eating when I was tired, when I was irritable, when I was too energetically stimulated, and when I was emotional about something. I also began to identify when I was legitimately hungry and ask my body what it wanted for nourishment. One method I'd use to make sure that my cunning mind was not getting in the way of this process was to hold food up to my belly and see how my body responded. If I had sensation in my belly, then the food was a go. If I felt nothing, I didn't eat it. I even did this in the grocery store! This is a variation of a type of muscle testing that I learned from a friend who is a Traditional Chinese Medicine Doctor.

Because I have a tendency to push my energy in order to accomplish tasks, I had to learn how to pace myself better so I wouldn't burn out. I have a strong body so I can do that, but it comes at a price and it takes a long time for me to recover. It also tends to increase the risk of physical injury. My body changes every day and some days my energy is higher than others. On those high-energy days, I can do more if I go at a slow and steady pace. I know my body type is not built for speed so I really capitalize on my high endurance levels. On low energy days or ones where my body is feeling sore, I do more stretching, resting, and swimming. These varied exercises give my body the movement it craves at the level of intensity it can handle from day to day. Today, I continue to incorporate new types of exercise into my life to keep my fitness levels from plateauing.

May 6, 2010

Made another smoothie this morning and added kale. What I noticed was how "alive" the food was and how it immediately raised the vibration of my body. It was the first time I made the link between that feeling and food. I'd felt it before while making love. I didn't know that food could do that too. Had coffee in the afternoon instead. Noticed that I use it as a pick me up. Especially when I am feeling sluggish. Quite a difference between that and smoothies.

Sept 4, 2010

I'm not a big alcohol fan so I don't drink very often and when I do it is usually just a little bit of wine or single malt scotch. The other day at the restaurant, I had a glass of wine and it went down REALLY nice and I wanted more. That is pretty unusual as I am usually good with just 4 oz worth. Turns out that there is sugar in wine. Never thought about that and it makes sense—especially since I have cut out the sugar completely, I really notice when something is "off" in my diet.

Oct 7, 2010

Did the eating with eyes closed exercise today after not having done it for a while. Noticed that I really like and appreciate simple food that has not been processed much. Today I was eating raw cucumber and prunes and could just enjoy the flavours. Six months ago when I started this process, that wasn't the case.

Dec 10, 2010

Swimming.

On Goals: I learned that I make "rules" and set routines up. My body said that that is unnecessary. To go with how my body is feeling that day. So although good to track progress, not good to force certain outcomes. So today I swam 32 laps in 30 minutes (8 more than last time). My swimming is becoming more smooth and quick.

On Obstacles: I learned that when I am stuck or scared, my breathing slows and my body freezes. My body told me to get moving in those instances to swim/walk/move around those obstacles. Move through obstacles instead of allowing them to stop me.

Dec 16, 2010

Went swimming today. Only did 18 laps but did them without stopping–the most I have done without stopping yet. Then my body said it was done. I am learning how to push myself a bit but not to the point of exhaustion. This was good balance today. Body also told me to stretch before I start–haven't been doing that. Was disappointed at first I couldn't do more laps but it seems that it is my body and spirit's way of training me in how to accomplish small goals instead of wanting or expecting the big picture somehow. Today was about: how many can you do without stopping? Other days it is about: how can you pace yourself to do more? All useful cross-training for working on the book and other projects because all these different modes seem to be required at different times. Interesting how it is coming through being physical with my body.

Dec 22, 2010

Well, today was about pacing. Got lots done and walked a ton (about an hour and a half including all my errands). But I noticed myself pushing my body just that little bit too much and half way through the day was losing some steam. Been feeling lately like lots of stuff I try to do is like molasses. I realize from working with the mesa for the book that I am pushing the timing on things too. No wonder the universe is trying to slow me down. So again, lots of obstacles and yet I am taking it in stride. Doing good with humour. Doing good with not going into overwhelm and frustration.

Jan 25, 2011

My day intent today was to take care of my body. I am now in the midst of writing seasonal reviews for my kids and so that means lots of time on the computer. So today I took lots of breaks–went for a swim, walked to do errands, walked to the library, did some drumming and singing. This seems to help break up all the work and my body is happier. Another thing I have been noticing is my body asking for more raw veg so have been incorporating that too. Noticed myself rushing my eating because I had so much to do. Forgiveness after.

Jan 26 and 27, 2011

Been exhausted the last few days and needing more naps than usual. Was glad I went to drumming last night despite that because it lifted the fatigue. I think I overdid the walking around downtown yesterday; was out there too many hours. Went swimming and was at first frustrated at my slow pace. I realized that faster is not always the most efficient. This lesson also carried on throughout the day where slower is better. I do have moments where I need to move quickly on something but they are not as many as I think they are.

Feb 27, 2011

It was four below today and the sun was shining. I went out for a long walk in the afternoon and it felt good. I noticed myself going really fast off the bat because I was itchy to move some of that stagnant energy out of my body. I listened to my body and it had me slow down to warm up. After that, I was walking at a fast clip–not so much that I was having a hard time breathing, but I could feel my body working. Had a hot bath too. Body is happy today. I saw lots of flickers and heard them banging away on the trees. This is my south animal that works with my heart. I have been singing and drumming every day and this feels good too. Those medicine signs told me I was on the right track.

Feb 28, 2011

Went dancing tonight for the first time in three weeks or so and did it ever feel good. My body was sore from two weeks of only walking as exercise. I notice that swimming and dancing works all my muscles and tends to even out my workout weekly. Today I was particularly fascinated with how such small movements were more effective at releasing tension than the big ones I normally do to release tension. It was so pleasurable that I stayed in this mode most of the two-hour class and I could feel the life force moving up my body. Did some stretching at the end of class and walked the 20 minutes home in the snow. It felt great!

Mar 1, 2011

Went swimming today. My body was a bit achy after yesterday so I stretched first. The slow movement thing continued today as my first 10 laps ended up being a warm up. I started out going fast but my body said the big NO to that right away. It felt good using the resistance from the water to warm up my muscles as I went. Also walked around quite a bit to run errands even though the 30 below is challenging when the wind kicks up. Brrr...

April 30, 2011

When I woke up this morning, I remembered something my sexual qigong teacher told me about the moontime: it is a ceremonial time in and of itself. Women in ancient times used to rest during this time to allow the transition to occur smoothly as well as to honour their bodies. So with that in mind, I followed my body's messages today: no kickboxing. My body simply didn't want those kinds of movements today. Instead, took a hot bath, stretched, went for a walk, meditated. Spread these out throughout the day in a fluid way just by listening. All the stuff that I needed to do got done. I am really feeling the wisdom of simplicity in my life the last week. When I take the effort out of something, it seems to move easier and, more importantly, where it needs to go instead of where I want it to go, which are not always the same thing.

May 20, 2011

I continue to work out. I really love the kickboxing circuit, which sort of surprises me. It is just the right amount of challenge and I find that if I pace myself, I feel really great during and after. When I first started, I was pacing according to what my trainer was suggesting. Listening to my own body is working well. And the best part is that it is so empowering. Who knew?

Accountability

....

*"A source of refuge must…have all the attributes of altruism—
those attainments which are necessary for achieving others'
welfare. For it is doubtful that anyone lacking these two
prerequisites can bestow refuge; it would be like falling into a
ditch and asking another who is in it to help you out. You need
to ask someone who is standing outside the ditch for help; it
is senseless to ask another who is in the same predicament."*
-His Holiness the 14ᵗʰ Dalai Lama of Tibet

While I was learning to really listen to my body, I had to be really
careful to stay out of my cunning mind that liked to make excuses
for why I should eat a particular thing. It was so easy to slip into
former patterns unconsciously until I had practiced and built
in enough new ones to tip that critical mass scale. Wolf Woman
suggested an accountability measure of recording my food intake
and sending it to her daily along with my e-mails early on in my
journey. I gratefully accepted. As you will see in the following
journal entries, she acted as a sort of rudder steering me in the
direction of my intent when I could not see that I'd veered off the
path. This was especially helpful to me when I was going through
stressful events like conferences, parties, or traveling in unknown
lands–physically, spiritually, and metaphorically.

My teacher advised me not to quit eating sugar cold turkey. I
took her advice. It was already overwhelming going through this
process, at the beginning especially. I can't even imagine what
it would have been like to go through sugar withdrawal at the

same time! Wolf Woman always set me up for success. Over the course of a month or so, I gradually reduced and cut out sugar. I scrutinized all the labels on all the foods I bought and learned to read the data on the backs of these packages in order to apply this to my food planning, which I talk more in depth about in another chapter. I also learned not to implicitly trust the advertising on food packages because many of them are misleading and do not provide accurate information. For example, carbohydrates turn into sugars in the body so just because something doesn't have any added sugar in it doesn't mean it is low on the glycemic index. This index measures the effect foods have on blood sugar levels and is used by doctors often. Folks who are diabetic are often advised to learn more about this scale and how they can use it in food planning.

Portions were also another area that needed attention. Wolf Woman helped me to see when I was eating amounts that were likely over-the-top for my daily calorie intake (around 2,000 a day for someone my weight and height). These calculators can be found online easily. I just plugged in my information and it gave me a rough estimate. I also discovered that my body didn't need a ton of protein per day in order to function well. This may not be so for everyone's body, but it certainly was true for me. I learned to limit the amount of protein I ate in one day unless I had exercised intensely.

At restaurants, which I ate at infrequently since I was cooking at home so much, I asked a lot of questions of servers. I practiced asking for exactly what I needed and had them double-check with the chefs to make sure there was no sugar or wheat in food. When they asked if I was allergic, I said that I wasn't but was on a pretty strict medical diet. Most folks were happy to accommodate and with those who were grumpy, I learned to hold my boundaries. I was also really careful with the restaurants I ate at, making sure they served whole foods that were not processed or filled with chemicals. When this was not possible during travels, I chose the healthiest choice available to me.

May 30, 2010

In the middle of this emotional storm inside me, I went out for something to eat and ordered a turkey pot pie and a salad. I was into the turkey pot "pie" when that familiar feeling of soothing came over me and I went, "Uh oh. My cunning is at work again." Today was another tough day and I noticed that I had to keep reminding myself that feeling confused, angry, hurt, or despairing is okay and that everything passes. Clarity comes when I wade through the discontent.

Food for the Day:

8:30 am: smoothie and cup of oatmeal

11:00 am: two eggs in 1 tsp. butter and a cup of corn tortillas.

1:00 pm: the turkey pot pie and a salad. Coffee with soy and a teaspoon of sugar.

4:30 pm: 6 oz. steak, 2 cups mashed potatoes and steamed broccoli and cauliflower.

6:00 pm: strawberries and grapes and a cup of earl grey tea with milk and 1 tsp. honey.

8:00 pm: banana.

1.5 L water

July 4, 2010

Thanks for your e-mail, Wolf Woman:

Just an FYI: careful about your pasta intake. 3 times in the last 2 days according to your food list. Pasta is a comfort and spike food.

Aug 27, 2010

I am here at the training for work and the energy is pretty chaotic. I don't like the fact that because of the chaos, I am required to have meetings with my mentorship group over meals but I am working with it. It's been challenging to keep connected to myself, my food, and follow along the stream of conversation. Definitely not something I'd want to do on a regular basis. So...learning experience. We only really see each other in person once or twice a year so often our impressions of each other are based on the "last year versions of ourselves." So I was also thrown off centre yesterday a few times by comments some folks made in my direction that were carry-overs from last year. I noticed that although I was slightly off kilter most of the day, I was able to keep on track mostly through sneaking out when I could to go outside or get some perspective. Also called in some of my animal totems to help me through some rough bits. Also not working on a lot of sleep so that's an extra challenge. Will find bits of time to rest and do some qigong today.

Breakfast: eggs, bacon, a sausage, hash browns, latte

Lunch: mixed greens, turkey, beef soup and raw veg, nectarine

Dinner: mixed greens, roast beef, roast potatoes, banana

2L Water

Aug 28, 2010

Decided to take meals alone yesterday and reschedule my meetings during chunks of time during the day. This worked well. Also going out for quick walks in the woods whenever I can to keep perspective. Lots of past pictures and stories about how I have done/seen my role as a teacher being left behind in order to carry on in a new way. Lots of self-forgiveness. Workin' it....

Just an FYI,
Watch your intake of food
eggs bacon sausage and hash browns is quite a bit of food along with the rest of the food you ate that day. Check with your body, Wolf Woman

Thanks for that. I was actually feeling a bit protein overloaded. When I went to check in with my body at dinner, it didn't want any so I stuck to rice and veg.

Food for the Day:

9:00 am: granola, a banana and milk.

1:00 pm: a wrap with 3 bean salad, sprouts, hummus, olive spread, antipasto and cheese. Cup of coffee with milk

5:00 pm: 2 cups basmati rice with steamed broccoli and cauliflower, seafood mix and fruit for dessert. Cup of coffee with milk.

1.5 L Water

Living from Pleasure

....

"Pleasure is so essential to our wellbeing that without it we get distressed and eventually may fall ill... psychologically, physically, or both. When we awaken our erotic energy (Eros) and marry it with our evolving emotional/psychological self (Psyche), we literally birth more pleasure which in turn sustains our aliveness keeping us youthful and vibrantly healthy! When we can learn to trust ourselves and the wisdom of our body, all of our neurosis around pleasure will surface and have a chance to be loved into wholeness. And if we are willing to embrace ourselves in our totality, free of judgement, we can begin to live from a truly shameless and pleasureful place."

-Saida Désilets from the article "Shameless Pleasure: What it is and why you need it."

I will be forever grateful to Saida for the sexual qigong teachings she imparted to me in 2004 that laid the foundation for this piece of allowing pleasure to fall into place in my life. Back then, I had just come out of a passionate and stormy relationship with a lot of questions about my own sexuality and my relationship with myself. I'd begun seeing a pattern in myself of sexual neediness in all the relationships I'd been in and I became curious about that. I was studying energy healing at the time in Vancouver when a fellow healer recommended Saida's Jade Goddess course to me.

I showed up in a beautiful old house to find about twenty-four women of all ages and ethnicities. Saida greeted each of us warmly in turn and blessed us into the space where we seated ourselves in a circle. I remember crying as I was being blessed because I'd never been honoured like that as a woman. I started to see that my pattern of neediness in relationship with others came from not understanding this feminine energy that resided naturally within me. I'd never been taught to look for what I needed within me. This was a huge paradigm shift that happened inside me that weekend. I left feeling alive and ready to put the ancient qigong exercises we were taught into practice in my life. I can never thank Saida enough for the gifts she passed along to me!

Traditionally, rites of passage ceremonies were done for young girls in cultures around the world teaching them about women's mysteries. Ceremonies were also done for young boys initiating them into men's magic. I've always seen Saida as a Taoist medicine woman for women guiding them in remembering these ancient ways. We are sorely in need of bringing these ways back to the people. I am glad Saida is doing this work. I highly recommend her book "Emergence of the Sensual Woman: Awakening Our Erotic Innocence" to readers. Her partner, Sol Sebastian, offers this work for men. Both of these resources appear in the Recommended Resources of this book.

I grew up in a Catholic culture so self-pleasuring was not something we talked about though I did wonder about it. In fact, I don't remember any adult talking to me about sex at all until high school when it was compulsory to learn in grade ten. I learned not to bring this subject up at all because it seemed so highly charged in my family. I am really grateful to one of my older relatives, for guiding me through sexual education in a non-judgmental way when I was a teenager.

I was well into my twenties before I even tried self-pleasuring because there was so much shame around it. I practiced self-pleasuring for years. It was not fun at first because I had so much inner dialogue to overcome. I didn't go blind, become sterile, or any of the other myths I heard about masturbation! The wrath of God did not come down on me. Quite the opposite: I felt blessed and empowered in a way I had not before. Don't get me wrong:

I'd enjoyed sex as a teenager and have never regretted it. I was really fortunate to have a loving partner back then to have my first experiences with. It's just that being able to pleasure yourself is so important as a piece of self-care and staying vital. I love this quote by Freya Watson because she describes what I was discovering at this time in my life:

> "Just remember that the wonderful feelings are coming from inside yourself and not from outside. You have generated them, by focusing your attention on something you desire, and you always have the power to generate them, even without an external catalyst."

I also did dancing meditation several times a week to inspire me and to feel pleasure in my body. Now, all this pleasure is quite natural, but it took some time of listening and experimenting to see what worked. And because the human body is a dynamic system, I continue to tweak and add new things to my Pleasure List even today.

I want to share with you some of what I've learned about sexual energy since then as well as why pleasure is so important in life. I grew up believing that I had to work hard and that play was a waste of time and energy. I really thought that if I gave pleasure any free reign in my life, that I would never get anything done. How wrong I was! It turned out that pleasure made my body feel good, it made me feel excited about living, and it made my everyday work flow more easily than ever before. Sexual energy is what keeps us young and energized. Pleasure that stokes up our sexual energy can come from many experiences: a good nap, eating wonderful food, moving the body in ways that feel good, listening to inspiring music, or watching a sunset.

I worked a lot with my sexual totem animal by journeying to the spirit world in order to learn more about things that could bring me pleasure. I will speak more about shamanic journeys and working with animal totems in a later chapter. During my healing process, I began keeping a Pleasure List that I could refer to and made a commitment to do some of the things that spoke to me from that list each day. When I was feeling uninspired or grumpy, doing something from the list changed my outlook and brought me back to feeling good in my skin again. The following journal entries give some clues as to some of the challenges I came up with when I was practicing living life from a place of pleasure as well as highlighting some a-has and victories I had.

May 13, 2010

Still don't love the standing in front of the mirror exercise. However, it is useful just for me to see how my thoughts change. So working on not rushing through it to "get it over with." Forgave myself for the criticism. Noticed an interesting thing while self-pleasuring today: for the first time in a long time, I didn't flip into fantasy in order to juice myself up. Forgave myself for doing that for so long. My experience was very much focused on finding that juice within me. It's quite a different feeling from bringing it from "outside" like I do when I imagine I am with a partner, for instance. I felt filled up and so calm afterward. I usually feel good after but this "filled up" feeling from the inside is new. I can now see the pattern of codependence in relationships and with food. I can also see how important this connection with myself from the inside is. I think this is the first time I've felt that power and strength extending from the inside through my body to the outside besides in ceremony. Victory: knowing how it feels to fill myself up from the inside.

Jun 8, 2010

The variety in my smoothie this morning was really awesome. Noticed during lunch that I was experiencing pleasure during eating–was really present to how the food tasted and my eyes were open. The feeling of pleasure was surprisingly similar to a sensation I get when making love. Different from that "craving"

feeling. So a victory that I am noticing these nuances. It was a challenging day where things did not really flow all that well. Noticed my tendency to want to fill in those uncomfortable times with something. Victory is noticing that I was not giving myself the yin or receiving time after I ate my food. I would just get up after the last bite and go. That integration time is having a good effect on me and keeping me connected to my food. After reading about our connection with the earth through food, it helped me to see how important it was for me to give thanks before I eat. All these things seem to be helping my connection to myself.

Jun 12, 2010

My sexual animal is a black puma. She showed me how she runs energy from the earth through her body as she eats her prey. She purred with delight. I think there is something there for me to learn; she was in bliss. My body feels powerful and clean after so much breath work today.

Jun 13, 2010

Well, today was a bit of a blur with the end of the workshop and the travel home. Lots of energy running through my body. I felt every vibration on the ferry in my first chakra. LOL! I am off to bed but I did want to say that I noticed that my ability to notice the exquisite flavours in my food increased. The fruit I ate today actually made my whole body quiver when I put it in my mouth. That was really pretty cool!

Aug 17, 2010

I've now been working on self-pleasuring without going into a fantasy of seeing myself through a lover's eyes. I've been working on staying connected with myself throughout and when I lose that connection, I stop and then start again when it is back. I realized this week that until I am able to do that, I will likely keep making decisions in my life based on how others see me and my decisions sexually won't all be healing ones for me. So it was challenging yesterday and although I wasn't able to stay connected the whole time, I was able to make it through the exercise anyway.

Nov 23, 2010

Feeling a bit stir crazy inside for so long during the 30 belows and not feeling so hot the last few days and sleeping a lot. It was sunny today, 30 below and no wind so I went exploring. Found out that there is a trail I can follow in snowshoes along the river. I wouldn't do it in 30 below necessarily, but it is good to know. And it was good to get out there and walk. Tomorrow, swimming.

Dec 26, 2010

Learning today in the sexual realm: I am responsible for my own body and pleasure. Some things have not been feeling too great and I have not spoken up. When I looked at this, there were some beliefs there that had to go so I worked with my shadow animal to transform them. It is clear: I need to tell Ewan what I like instead of hoping he figures it out or picks up enough clues. LOL! We had a good talk about this last night together. A whole new world for me so I am also aware of being patient with myself during the learning curve. And as you put it...FLOW.

Feb 23, 2011

Woke up this morning from a really bad dream. In my dream, I was married to a huge and violent man who was trying to destroy me. At one point in the dream, he strapped an explosive device to my leg. I managed to get it off and throw it away (even though it took some of my skin with it) and run to safety. After waking and recalling my energy from this dream, I went into the spirit world to my power spot to see what was going on. My shadow animal told me I had a belief that pleasure came from outside me. I now know that I create my own pleasure. My skunk also did a restoration and brought me my own inner authority. I asked why I gave it away and he said that it was easier to conform than to assert myself so I gave it away. Turns out, I was doing a good job of destroying myself. Lots of forgiveness for sabotaging my healing and my life.

You have been through a lot of change since you have been in Vancouver. Eating is a sign of your accepting or not accepting your true nature.
Wolf Woman

Mar 7 and 8, 2011

Started my moontime and lots has been rolling around inside of me. Spent the whole day at home working with menstrual cramps in bed and hot baths. I figured it was better self-care to stay home and be with what was happening in my body/mind than to medicate myself and go out and do stuff to keep myself busy. I didn't write yesterday because I didn't even know how to articulate it. Lots is on the move–things that no longer serve me. Some of it hard to let go of nonetheless because of how well-worn the stories are.

Restoring Ruthlessness

....

"Stalking is used in dreaming to find the mental and emotional images that prevent us from being free."
-Don José Luis (Toltec Nagual)

"Don Juan explained to me that ruthlessness, cunning, patience, and sweetness were the essence of stalking. They were the basics that with all their ramifications had to be taught in careful, meticulous steps...The very first principle of stalking is that a warrior stalks himself...He stalks himself ruthlessly, cunningly, patiently, and sweetly...Very succinctly he defined stalking as the art of using behavior in novel ways for specific purposes."
-Carlos Castaneda from "The Power of Silence: Further Lessons of Don Juan"

The Toltec culture arose in what is today Central Mexico. Carlos Castaneda was a graduate student in anthropology at the University of California when he met a Yaqui man named Don Juan. Castaneda ended up apprenticing with this skilled Yaqui sorcerer for many years and then wrote a series of books detailing what he learned. The sorcerers of Don Juan's lineage were master cartographers of the inner worlds of reality. They were interested mostly in ways to conserve as much energy as possible in order to go after their dreaming. They knew that energy was required in order to accomplish their life's purpose and they systematically worked at plugging their internal energy leaks. This process is called "stalking."

When a human declares a healing intent to the universe like I did to heal my addiction, stalking is required in order to close the internal gaps that are keeping the person from accomplishing sobriety; it does not happen magically without effort by the person who prayed for healing. Healing is a collaboration between the human and Great Spirit. Spirit leads the way and we do the work. Stalking in the shamanic sense of the word does not mean to follow another person in a creepy way with malicious intent. It means that there is a requirement that the person who wants to heal stalk or hunt down the habits, stuck trauma, thoughts, and other energy drains that are causing the behaviour to take place and stop the leaks inside of themselves by essentially changing their inner world one step at a time. Although I am not going to talk a lot about the other basics of stalking (sweetness, cunning, and patience), I highly recommend reading Carlos Castaneda's book "Power of Silence" to learn more about these strategies.

Ruthless energy can be used in a dark way that is cruel and merciless. This is not the kind of energy I am talking about here. The Merriam-Webster dictionary defines ruthlessness as "having no pity or compassion." Ruthless has no pity because shamans know that feeling sorry for someone or yourself is a waste of energy because we already have all the tools inside of us to accomplish our goals if we go looking. Ruthlessness is not without compassion, however. Sometimes, the most compassionate thing someone can do is to give us a truthful reflection–even if that hurts temporarily. My teacher, Tiger's Breath, did that for me when she pointed out addictive behaviours she saw me engaging in before I even knew that is what I was doing. Was I ever mad at her at first! But you know what? When I reflected on her words, I felt deep down that she was right and that she told me because she cared about my wellbeing. She knew that I was not seeing this pattern and that it was causing me pain. This was such a gift she gave me that I will always be grateful for.

I still remember the day I learned that I had no ruthless skills. We were in a workshop engaging with our teachers in an exercise designed to show us which basics of stalking we were masterful in and which we were weak in. Wolf Woman came up to me and shoved me lightly at first all around the room. I did nothing in return. Then she started shoving me harder to see what I would do. I was so angry I was crying–even my tears were hot! Finally, she shoved me onto the couch and returned to humour: "You have no ruthless, dear. Time to build that up." My anger dissipated into bewilderment. I wanted nothing to do with ruthless and I told her so. I had always seen it used so unkindly and inhumanely; I didn't know there was another way or why it was so important. Wolf Woman said that ruthlessness was the key to freedom and that unless I could learn to use it wisely, I would never be able to stand in the center of my own personal power.

Wolf Woman is a great teacher of ruthlessness. She can cut through the bullshit in a room with just a few measured, neutral words. This has the effect of bringing everyone back to their original healing intent and away from posturing and other behaviours that zap our precious life force energy that we need to stalk our dreams. I observed her intently for years to see how she used this energy so well. I learned from her and am grateful to have an image-maker for ruthless in the light.

Wolf Woman gave me an assignment: to relate to others only with ruthless every day. It took me a whole year to master this and it wasn't always pretty. At the beginning, my emotions overtook me–especially anger. I was too harsh and instead of clearing communication, the directness cut like a knife. There were a few messes I needed to clean up that year. However, sometimes, that kind of harshness was appropriate when someone was overstepping my boundaries–especially when they were threatening my physical body and safety. I learned to stick up for myself using my body when necessary. I recovered natural survival instincts that I gave away during years of abuse.

I share the following journal entries to highlight the kinds of opportunities that Spirit put in front of me to show me why ruthlessness was important. It is often the case that the people we love the most are our best mirrors of reflection and are the hardest folks to be ruthless with. So I actually give a lot of thanks to my family, lovers, and friends for providing me with a practice space, even if they didn't know that's what I was doing! Today, I still test how I am doing with my ruthless by how neutral I can be with family and friends in challenging situations. If I can do ruthless compassion with good boundaries with them, I can do this with anyone!

May 29, 2010

Another victory: dinner at a relative's house. She made a "special dessert" for me. Was visibly disappointed when I turned it down and went for the fruit instead but she accepted that and we moved on. I told her I was on a cleanse. I don't like to lie but I guess that just seemed the more healing thing for me to do without telling her about the addiction. I don't think having any more of her "worried" energy coming my way would be helpful to my process. She later called all worried that I just didn't seem like myself at dinner. I was so tired of pretending to be happy in my life to prevent that worried energy from infecting my energetic space. I said, "You know what? The truth is that I am not happy 100% of the time. And you know what else? I don't know anyone that is." She balked a little and got defensive but I just didn't have the energy to care. And the victory is that I was ruthless with my truth with her–something that has pretty often been hard for me to do in my life.

June 22, 2010

When I went to a relative's house today, she offered me food. I declined. She asked again if I wanted cake. I declined and said I wanted coffee. Got my coffee and she put a piece of cake down in front of me. When I didn't eat it she said, "Eat your cake, it is melting. (It was some kind of mousse thing)." I said, "I told you I didn't want any" in a firm way. She backed off. I was proud of myself.

Oct 27, 2010

Went to drop off some stuff at a relative's today and she was pretty mopey. I was fierce. She started picking at me. I was fierce. I saw that she just doesn't know how to cope with the grief and that is how she is doing it. This gave me a compassionate stance. When I drove away, I felt a lot of sadness but I also felt good about taking a more neutral stance.

Nov 10, 2010

Tough day. The start to life here in Calgary is not what I'd hoped and there were a lot of moments today that I wondered whether I can really make it here. Despite that, I also sense this new part of me coming to the surface at surprising times. It is a ruthless part of me that I really like; she comes out to protect my energy and my creative space. All of this journey with Ewan, my family, and healing my relationship with food has shown me what I am actually made of. I am a lot stronger and resourceful than I gave myself credit for when I began. I feel free here. And so I am going to take advantage of not having to be anywhere, see anyone, do anything. Been spending lots of time working on the book, doing some art, singing, setting up my place. Stuff that is feeding my spirit. Keeping me sane, really. Along with the exercise.

Nov 17, 2010

Today was the first day where I was able to put things into perspective: this will all be okay. Nothing stays the same forever–everything passes in time. Also notice that all the practice I've had with Ewan has really helped me in being ruthless with others–like the banker I talked to today to open an account. He was doing all that smooth talking business and I was able to be assertive and non-negotiable when he was trying to push other products on me. Backed off right away. It was good. No nastiness required.

Nov 25 +26, 2010

Was on a really full bus today standing by the exit doors when I felt a small shove, which turned into a big one. This old man was pushing me and yelling at me because I was standing over the yellow line. By the time I turned around to face him, my first instinct was to either hit him or break his arm. I was livid that someone would do that to me. But in a split second, I thought about the consequences of that and instead told him loudly to keep his hands off of me. The whole bus was quiet and he was stunned. I moved away and continued seething. In the end, I told the bus driver what happened and all she said was, "He's one of my regulars." Not necessarily supportive. I got off the bus and went swimming (the original reason I was on the bus). I used the anger to swim laps and I did the same amount of laps I did Wednesday in half the time! But as I swam, I realized I was mad at myself. Mad for not following my original instinct to stay away from him (I felt his energy was off as soon as I stepped onto the bus). Mad for not responding after the first shove and mad that I didn't choose a more impactful response. I was still confused by my feelings around the whole thing when I headed into the steam room–hot, angry tears streaming down my face and then a cascade of memories of all the times I was hit as a child by adult family members. And how angry I was at myself for being a victim. When I went to lean against a tree after the swim, the tree told me that I made the right choice not hitting that man and that I stuck up for myself–something I didn't do when I was a kid mostly because I'd get in trouble every time I stuck up for myself. This was considered to be back talk or disrespectful to my elders. Children were not allowed to have a voice. I realized that learning to just take it was probably a good option as a kid because there was not a lot of recourse. I know I have more self-forgiveness to do around this. Will do more work tonight.

Nov 28, 2010

Been seeing how much energy I expend picking up on peoples' judgments of me and then trying to "prove" that I am not what or who they think I am. I remember doing this from the time I was really young. I've always been sensitive to that sort of thing and I think this is why I don't always give an authentic response to something–like that occurrence on the bus the other day. It stops me from speaking my mind, always thinking about the consequences of everything. And although it is good in a way because I have been able to control my impulse to just spew stuff out, it is obviously not helping me in other ways. On the bus that day, part of my concern was for how the other people on the bus would feel if I just spouted off. I could already sense folks were uncomfortable with what was happening between me and the guy. Always a peacekeeper and mediator in my family growing up–the rescuer. Living in Calgary is a new start for me and I gave away that pattern today as I walked in the snow. Forgave myself. I imagined what I could do with all that energy and figured it would probably be enough to fuel my Sacred Dream–that is incentive enough. Lots of traveling in my dreams lately and figuring out how to get from one place to the next. That is sorta what my life feels like at the moment– navigating from the known to the unknown constantly.

Dec 15, 2010

My shadow animal is teaching me how to be ruthless. It is WAY more straight ahead than I am used to and I am seeing all the ways I cushion things and pad them to spare the impact for people. I guess I just saw the way adults used to tear me another asshole so often for things at the drop of a dime when I was a kid and I never thought that was fair or just taking their stuff out on me. I've also had my center power animal tear me another asshole to get me to see and move through my shit to heal and it was a totally different energetic. So I know that it is valuable to be able to do sometimes. I just pray to Spirit that I can learn to use it well and with care for life the way my horse knows how. My skunk showed me that I had a belief that I had to be a certain way in the world (peacekeeper role I held in my family).

I really value the skills I learned in this area and they have served me well in many ways–and then not in others. So there was a feeling of loss letting go of this belief cuz it is actually something I value (mediation). I see now that ruthless is a type of mediation too–the kind that cuts to the heart of the matter; I want to incorporate it into my repertoire this year in a good way. I am glad I know about these beliefs I've held; being ruthless in letting them go is really speeding up healing in interesting ways.

Jan 23, 2011

Had an interesting incident today at a Scottish ceilidh dance I went to. There was a lady there that was new to ceilidh dancing and sitting by herself. I was sitting by myself too, happily. Another lady introduced us and we had some small talk. I was going back to my seat when she said, "Sit here, Jennifer." I don't know if it is my conditioning of how to be around elders from my culture, but I sat beside her despite hating her commanding tone. She was complaining about how clique-like the club was and how she can never make friends there. I sat there thinking, "Why did I do this?" Was ruthless with her during her complaining fest and went and sat in my original seat. I don't know if it was because of all the older folks there (between 60-80) but some of them were fond of bossing me. I stood out, I guess being the only participant there in my age bracket. Anyhow, interesting learning of how I give my power away with elders. I sometimes notice this with Ewan too, which is weird considering our relationship. I notice myself defaulting to his "experience" sometimes and then I catch myself later when it doesn't feel right to me.

Feb 10, 2011

Well, I knew that this was going to be a ruthless in the light kind of trip with my family. I was stunned at how much I had to say and how much I'd kept inside because I felt my family never "got" me. What I learned is that I can be open, honest, and ruthless and say what is true for me and that that act in itself helps clear up misunderstandings. I don't imagine that it will bring acceptance of how I live or parts of who I am and I don't care. That's new for me. I was in integrity with myself and it felt great after I stopped feeling bad for letting it all out there. I was in alignment with the light aspect of ruthlessness–it just felt so raw and I could tell my relative was hurt by some of the things I said. Realized that speaking what is true for me will sometimes be hurtful to others and it doesn't mean I shouldn't say it or that I am responsible for how they are feeling. It cost me a lot not standing for myself with my family most of my life. I spoke in "I" statements pretty much the whole time–no blaming anyone. Forgiveness after for breaking my crazy rules that weren't serving me.

Feb 12, 2011

My intent today was ruthless compassion; I knew I was going to be seeing my a relative. It was hard to see her in so much pain and yet I realized as I listened to her that I can't save her from the natural consequences of her choices. And it was sad for me not to have a relationship that I wanted with her. But it was not because I didn't care. We are different people. I love her and I can't be who she wants me to be just so she can feel more comfortable around me. I have to be me." Also told her: "We can't change the past and now I am in Calgary so our options are more limited to Skype and phone." I invited her to form a new kind of relationship with me from now on. She said she needed to think about it. And that is where we left it. It was good to know that I felt complete and proud of what I'd done in the past; I had really thought things through consciously.

Feb 13, 2011

More hurdles today with family. I knew I'd need my warrior animal today and the way the ruthless in the light appeared was surprising to me. I knew my relative was mad that I didn't stay with her this trip and I didn't call her right away when I got here. My relative was doing a lot of passive aggressive stuff today and I usually call her out on what is going on to get rid of the tension. I didn't do that today and thought I was just wimping out or something; I just rode it out. I thought this was a failure on my part. When I asked my wolf why I did that the answer was: "It is futile to waste your energy on a fight with her; you can't fix her problem. And it isn't even about you anyway."

May 3, 2011

Another interesting thing happened today. I was walking through the park when a drunk guy and his friend came up to me and started walking along beside me. The friend looked uncomfortable and was urging his friend (who was trying to hit on me) to leave me alone. I called my warrior animal and my inner man and kept walking. He persisted alongside me and I was alert and waiting to see what needed to be done. I didn't speak to him or even look at him. I was not scared. I was calm and preparing to fight if I had to. A lady in the distance called his name and he stopped pursuing me and backed off. At first, I was berating myself: why didn't you run? Why weren't you more assertive? But the moment was perfect. It taught me how far I'd come. I didn't run because I wasn't scared and I didn't feel it was the right thing to do. I was totally in my instincts. If he'd touched me, I would have fought him–no questions asked. That was so clear to me in the moment. The old me would have probably frozen in the moment and allowed him to hurt me. It is a huge victory that the natural instinct to protect myself with my body has returned.

Chapter 2

THE NORTH WEST

North West Introduction: Telling the Truth

···

"Have patience with all things, but chiefly have patience with yourself. Do not lose courage in considering your own imperfections, but instantly set about remedying them–every day begin the task anew."

-Saint Francis de Sales

Being honest with myself about what was really going on in my inner world was not a simple task after so many years of denial, being overly harsh with myself, and blaming my despair on others. I was so angry at myself for covering up my pain and adding more layers of suffering to it that didn't need to be there! I didn't know how to look at the truth about my situation without beating myself up at first. I had to train myself to look at the choices I'd made and the consequences they had (both positive and negative) in neutral ways so that I could make better decisions in the present. Like a scientist, I learned to accept what was so: the fact that I'd spent a long time practicing negativity and it would take time to turn that around. In the meantime, all I could do was clean up the messes that developed out of this pessimistic thinking and replace old patterns with new ones that brought me closer to my goal of healing.

One thing, for example, that I had to come to terms with was the fact that I was simply not in a good financial state due to addictive patterns. How could I learn to save money and curb spending when I had no self-regard and wanted everything yesterday? Today, I am forty-years-old and just coming out of debt that I've been in my entire adult life. I could be depressed about it, and I was for a while as I watched friends my age pay off their houses, for instance. But I've chosen to see it as an opportunity to learn new skills. As I recovered, I took a bookkeeping course, made a budget, tracked all of my spending on spreadsheets, and worked toward my financial goals one month at a time. This was a sobering activity–to see where my money was actually going.

One of the things I learned is that not all of my spending was fruitless. I invested a lot of money on my healing and growth in my 30s that is paying off today. In fact, if I hadn't made that choice, it is very likely that I wouldn't be here today considering the suicidal thoughts I had in my 20s. Working through depression was a huge victory! So I took command of my spending and I am mindful of everything I spend my money on today. I am not financially rich and that is not my goal. As long as I have the funds to keep working on my life's purpose without going into major debt, I am content. I am looking forward to a different financial reality for the next half of my life. The emphasis here is on effort. We can't expect magical things to happen without it.

The path to healing my addiction was like a rollercoaster ride; one day I'd experience so much joy I was bursting at the seams and the next day, another piece would be uncovered and I'd find myself sinking into sorrow as deep as the ocean. Healing was like peeling off layers of an onion to get to the true me. Just as one layer came off, another was revealed. It helped to train my mind to stay focused on the victories while acknowledging the unhealthy mind states in order to move past them. Addicts often want the quick fix but that is not how changing years worth of neurological patterns works. When someone has a chemical addiction, there are very real physiological as well as psychological pieces that need to come back to balance.

Depending on the kinds of addictions and how many someone has, routing out addiction from one's life can take many years. I have friends who I've watched come out of chemical addiction only to begin healing food addiction, sex addiction, spending addiction and many others. In order to heal one addiction, it is common to take up another that is the lesser of the evils (like smoking) simply to keep being able to work on challenging issues. Sometimes, one chemical must replace another so the healing work will not stall and the person will have the energy to keep going. I look up to these folks because I know how hard it was to heal one major addiction; I can't imagine the perseverance, patience, courage, and determination it must take to go after all of them one at a time!

In the North West of the medicine wheel, sit the cycles of life. Everything we've ever been, done, thought, felt, and experienced throughout lifetimes is available to us here in a cyclical nature. In shamanism, reincarnation is considered a part of the cycles of life. If there is a pattern that needs to change, we get many opportunities in our lives to heal them. Often, going into past lives to find patterns that have been repeating throughout lifetimes is necessary. The truth is that all addictions–no matter how small– cost us life force energy that we could be using to live our dreams. As long as that energy has a hold of us, we cannot move forward. Believing in past lives or reincarnation is not necessary in order for one to work to change these patterns. Thankfully, it's never too late to go after our healing. I've watched a lot of elders go through this process and they've inspired me to keep going! In this chapter, I speak about some of the challenges I faced in the North West as well as my victories.

In order to consolidate your understanding of this direction from your personal, experiential and embodied perspective, I recommend doing the following ceremonies from "Shamanic Ceremonies for a Changing World" by Marilyn Keffer and Gael Carter. You can find more information on how to purchase a copy by looking at the Recommended Resources section of the Appendix of this book.

The Burden Basket Ceremony 1-5
Law of Karma Ceremony 1-6

Flat on my Back

"Truth is that which does not contaminate you, but empowers you. Therefore, there are degrees of truth, but, generically, truth is that which can do no harm. It cannot harm."
-Gary Zukav from "Seat Of The Soul"

The truth, by nature, is not necessarily comfortable. Learning to sit with discomfort, allow information to sink in, and sort out what is true for us takes practice and infinite patience. Our bodies have a natural way of showing us the truth, sometimes in dramatic ways when we have not paid attention to the other more minor cues in the form of light knocks, minor aches and pains, omens, and synchronicities. For a shamanic practitioner, life is speaking to us all the time in many different ways. The universe actively tries to pull our attention to things that are out of balance in order to rectify them. Our job is to notice the messages, decipher them, and put them into action to regain equilibrium. When we repeatedly ignore these messages, things get uncomfortable and loud so that we will be more likely to be forced by necessity to do something about them.

This is what happened to me in preparation for my move to Calgary. There were a lot of little things niggling at me for weeks that I chose to ignore amidst the overwhelmed energy of preparing for a big move. If I had slowed down and dealt with them, I'd likely not have had to be stuck lying on my back for a whole week! However, everything can be a learning experience if we re-frame it and so that is what I chose to do: learn.

In her book, "Hands of Light: A Guide to Healing Through the Human Energy Field," Barbara Ann Brennan adds her experience as a NASA research scientist in the area of atmospheric physics as well as her studies with indigenous healers to describe the original five energetic body types (originally pioneered by Wilhelm Reich) and their effect on humans in deeper ways. I highly recommend her book. The five body types are energetic armourings that humans choose on the spiritual level of being that will help to protect them in their most vulnerable time: childhood. Dr. Brennan provides information about each of these body types in handy charts and speaks about how to identify them in depth in her book.

While working as a psychoanalyst in the 1920s, Reich first discovered these body types by studying people who came to work with him. He noticed visible and categorical patterns between character traits, posture, physiological issues, and even the ways people breathed! Today, the field of quantum physics has scientifically revealed the existence of electromagnetic fields (known as auras in spiritual terms) that surround all living things that shamans have been able to see energetically for a long time. Indeed, our bodies are made up of atoms that respond to the laws of nature–this is basic physics. All our thoughts, beliefs, feelings, habits, and actions shape the messages our bodies receive (chemically and energetically) and our bodies respond accordingly.

Reich noticed how these protective energy patterns (known as "body types") shape our life experiences as well as our bodies. In shamanic terms, although our spirits choose these armourings consciously, our human selves are often unconscious of them. Learning about them has helped me to navigate the world with more ease because I began to accept them in order to bring awareness to their natural tendencies. Now, when I seem to be on autopilot with an issue, it is a clue that my armouring might be at work and I can choose my actions with more awareness. When I was unconscious of them, they wreaked havoc in my life and I was very reactive, giving knee-jerk comments or taking rash actions to any perceived danger–real or imagined.

There is also a process of de-armouring that I did to release that patterning so I had more freedom and energy available to me. Through the Body Power Program at the Institute of Shamanic Medicine, I utilized breathing techniques, sound, and body movements in a specific way to literally blast away that armour. This gave me much more fluidity in my body and in my available responses to life. More information on the Body Power Program is available on ISM's website (see Recommended Resources at the back of this book).

In this next section, my journal entries reveal the sorts of habits I'd developed out of my body armouring that were no longer working for me. The entries also show how I went about using body pain to teach me about them and what needed to change within me in order to come back to a state of balance.

Oct 14 + 15, 2010

Been a busy couple of days with work stuff. I threw my back out today. I thought it was fine after massage therapy on Wednesday but apparently not. I can barely move at the moment. It started as a tweak on Tuesday. I have never had this happen to me before and so the pain and experience in my body is totally new. I have an appreciation and new compassion for folks who have back pain. And am learning how to move around in a smart way without taking dumb risks.

Oct 16, 2010

The last 24 hours has been basically one long ceremony to heal my body armouring structures. Last night after I wrote the e-mail, I got up to go to the toilet and couldn't. I managed to get myself onto the floor in our living room and grab some blankets to put around me. I lay flat on my back for about two hours until one of my roommates came home. At first, I panicked: What if something happens to me when I live in Calgary and no one is there to help? Then my stalker kicked in.

This was interesting because I couldn't move and I associate stalker energy with being physically active. I learned a whole new way to use that energy while I was lying there. When Kay came home, I had a plan. I asked her if she would go get me muscle relaxants and she did. When Jane came home, she did some energy work on me and I asked her to get me cloth menstrual pads from the washroom and towels because I figured I was in for a long night on the floor and wanted to be prepared in case I couldn't get to the washroom. I also had my cell phone beside me and asked if I could ring her if I needed help through the night. This was really healing for me because I was able to ask for help and have humour about it and I also knew exactly what I wanted so I could delegate to people. Excruciating pain throughout the night and so I got pretty much no sleep but it was an interesting process. Journeyed to my spirit world and my healing and warrior animals took me on a healing process that night. A lot around healing my particular body armouring tendency to collapse and give up instead of taking action. My goal was to go pee. Simple. It took me from 10 pm until 6 am to finally get to the point where I was ready physically and psychologically to make my way over there but I did it. I went to stay in Kay's bed for the rest of the day where my animals taught me about my other armouring structure. Basically, my way of hunkering down and barreling through is not going to work in my body any more. Today, I have more mobility but I am seeing the places where I push when my body is telling me not to. I used my stalker to help me figure out ways to get to where I needed to go while also listening to my body: rest when I need to, go when it is time, and not to torque my body that way...etc. I am still lying in bed but I feel better and I learned a lot of new things to take into my new life in Calgary. My roommate is concerned and keeps asking me if I am sure I don't want to see a doctor but when I check in with my Higher Self, I really don't feel like that will be necessary. So it is challenging me to stay in my truth. My intention tonight is to heal my back.

Oct 17, 2010

Lots of gifts coming out of being immobile. Namely seeing all the places where I push that I don't have to. And how much of an energy drain that has been. Learning to be more efficient with my energy. I have much more mobility today. It forces me to stay tuned in to my body. When my thoughts wander, I pay for it because I usually tweak something. So I need to be totally engaged with what my body needs at all times in order to feel good. What I learned is how much I check out and the price that comes with not checking in to what my body needs and wants. Lots of good changes to make now to support that. And renewing my commitment to healing my relationship with my body. I now know that my body really does have a consciousness and intelligence. I am interested to tap into this now in a different way.

Oct 18, 2010

Even more mobile today. Woke up with the idea to use my own energy to heal my body while doing the breathing technique you taught me and it seems to have gotten through a lot of the energy blocks in my body. Today was an integration day of all I learned. Was able to shower, dress myself, feed myself, make food, and do my work on the computer (standing and lying down). The trick was to listen to my body and rest when it said to rest. When I was lying down, I did the breath and sent my energy through my body. I managed to stand for pretty much an hour this morning before my body had enough and then to make meals and work at the computer in half hour stints. Not bad considering where I started from Friday night.

Oct 19, 2010

Much more mobile today. Was even able to put on my socks all by myself! Still took a lot of lying down breaks. I was lying there today and feeling restless. I realized that there was a time in my life when lying in bed for days would have been appealing. That was when I was depressed, unmotivated, and living someone else's life. Although it was annoying to be in bed for that long, it connected me with how much I have grown. I wake up in the morning interested in what the day holds and I have a lot of projects and things I am doing that I am stoked about. And my pending move to Calgary is getting really exciting now that the moving plans are mostly sorted. I was also able to keep my humour most of the time. I actually found myself laughing at my predicament a lot–roommates cracking jokes about being my personal assistant. So it was a good experience–excruciating pain notwithstanding. Most of all, I have a new relationship with my body. I can "hear" it now and I am more in touch with the way it speaks to me. Now it is just walking out what I learned.

Oct 20, 2010

Now up and mobile. Drove a car this morning. A bit painful but it was for a short time and it showed me how to work with pain in that kind of situation (BREATHE! Relax!) Been noticing lately how much I plan ahead and seeing how that keeps me stuck in terms of how I allow myself to respond to unknown things that come into my scape. Since I was a kid, I would think out all the possible scenarios that could happen in the future and think about how I would respond to them. Although that is a good thing in some ways, in my case, I see that I do it because I don't fully trust that I will know what to do in the moment and I want to avoid making mistakes for a whole cascade of reasons, not the least of which is public humiliation. What my body taught me the last few days as I was lying on my back is that everything changes. What worked yesterday in terms of a way to get into bed with minimal pain was not exactly true for today. I saw how I was planning so far ahead in the future with so many things that it drained my energy to respond creatively in the moment. My body forced me to pay attention to the present and I noticed how much wisdom it had. Dancing improvised forms for a few years came in handy because there were a lot of times where I had to yield to the floor or roll along surfaces to get to where I needed to go or to decrease pain. This surprised me–this body knowledge and memory. And I learned that I can trust it and that I actually liked those surprises that it showed me. Including how to get through excruciating pain.

Being with What Is

....

"You have to know suffering in order to have the joy, and that has to do with not resisting what's happening to you... Instead of being resigned to your fate, you could get curious about what's going on. You could take an interest in the irritation that's rising up in you, and you could be curious about how other people are reacting. One of the main things I work with personally is saying to myself...: 'This is how I am right now. I have a very short fuse and I'm losing it.' Then I ask myself, 'Do I want to strengthen this habit so that a year from now my fuse is even shorter?... Did I want to strengthen it or find a way to shake it up, weaken it, and infiltrate it in some kind of way?'"
-Pema Chödrön
from the article "The Wondrous Path of Difficulties"

One of the hardest things to learn was how to put my ideals on the shelf in order to truly live in the moment. I have values that I really treasure and if the world worked according to them, it would likely be my version of Utopia. My problem was not that the world is filled with folks that have different values from one another but that I was constantly trying to force change so that I could feel more comfortable in the world.

In Buddhism, there are three personality types, which Jack Kornfield goes over in his book "The Wise Heart: A Guide to the Universal Teachings of Buddhist Psychology:" grasping, aversive, and deluded. These are sort of the lenses that we see the world through. In my case, mine were rose coloured glasses! His book describes the differences between these types and gives a guide for how to identify which category individuals fit into. Kornfield says that "[t]he unhealthy patterns of our personality can be recognized and transformed into a healthy expression of our natural temperament." For the purposes of this book, I will describe each of them briefly complete with their light aspects and their shadow ones.

Aversive Types are survival oriented. They tend not to be terribly politically correct and they don't care much whether their views are unpopular. They are on alert for any danger or problems that might be in the space they are in. Because they are mainly interested in survival, they are very interested in energy conservation. They can be aggressive in their approach when they are operating in the dark side of their characters. In the light, they are assertive and direct. Their shining is that they know how to survive and they can be fantastic leaders who know how to delegate to people who are skilled in various areas in order to bring a goal to fruition.

Deluded Types have a natural connection with the spirit world. They are quirky and dance to the beat of their own drummer. They are often artistic and creative and they put their attention on beauty. Their strength is their ability to tap into the world of Spirit to pull down a vision. Their weakness is that they can get caught up in that world and forget about the physical and human laws that govern their existence here on Earth. They are often late to events and can become easily overwhelmed and confused. When under stress, they tend to check out and visit their dream worlds so they do not have to deal with the discomfort they feel in the physical world. In the light, they can be true beacons showing people the way into new ways to be in the world that are more life-giving.

Grasping Types have a vision for how the world "should" be. They like to help– even when it means overriding their own needs. They are natural mediators with a healthy dose of diplomacy. Their shining is that they can often come up with creative solutions to the world's problems. They are the worker bees who will put their energy toward a dream that benefits the global community. Their pitfall is that they can sometimes get so caught up with their vision that they refuse to accept the reality of the situation or world where it is in the moment. Presence can be hard for them. There is also a tendency towards "right" and "wrong" thinking–making things into a dichotomy.

I am a Grasping Type. Learning that this is just the lens I see life through really helped me to ease up on myself and on the universals I lived by (always/never) that were simply not true. I know I am not positive all the time and that used to be unacceptable to me. However, it is the truth in the moment. It is authentic. Learning to accept that and also accept that the negative states offer a window into the shadow part of my nature gives me a unique opportunity to see what needs to be healed or shifted. In that way, negativity is essential to my evolution.

I used to think that I had to get rid of my ego to become enlightened. I am not sure I would want to do that now. I know that probably sounds weird considering all the folks out there who are trying to cut theirs away from their being. To me, the ego is part of being human and learning to live with vulnerability. It's been useful to me to hear what my ego is saying and to differentiate that from the voice of my essential mind. Often, my ego is simply trying to protect me in the best way it knows how. Unfortunately, it is usually programmed with old stories and does not always make the best choices based on the information available in the present. Learning to co-exist with it has been a gift; it has been training for accepting all parts of me. It's taught me compassion.

Similarly, I am happy to know my shadow so I can keep it in check. I have found that if I am willing to look in there, it has less of a tendency to be like an untrained puppy peeing and jumping all over the place. The beauty of getting to know my shadow nature is that I also get to uncover all the stuff I threw in there that I didn't know what to do with–including my shining. Sometimes, I sent gifts into my shadow because my family, society, and friends did not value them growing up. I assumed they were a liability. And maybe they were at the time. Maybe that was a good survival strategy back then.

Peering into my shadow now is not as overwhelming as it once was. I am curious when I go in there now and much less judgmental of what I find. I used to fear that if I went in there, I would discover that all my worst fears about myself and my essential nature were true. Although I still get scared when I am going in there at times, I no longer believe that I am a horrible, bad, evil person. I no longer wonder whether I am worthy of living and the gifts that come with it. This fact alone makes all those anxiety-ridden journeys to the dark side of my personal moon more than worthwhile. I am able to enjoy my life more often without guilt, doubt, or undue shame. I have my inner joy back. I have more space for myself in all my humanness and because of that, I can also give others more space in theirs. Perhaps that is really the root of peace.

The road to accepting myself has been a very long one. My journal entries below show some of the issues I ran up against while learning to sit with the truth in any given moment. You can see how my beliefs about how life was "supposed" to be made me feel miserable. It was hard at first to fix nothing, but that one task really helped me recover from my grasping-itis.

Jun 15, 2010

My appetite has not been the same since the course. That happened last time too. It was a while before I felt back to normal. I felt really tired today during the day and had a bunch of stuff to do. The temptation to grab a coffee was pretty strong. Inner man helped me to pick out my cunning while at a coffee shop with a friend. I was going to order a coffee but I was exhausted and I didn't want to deal with that exhaustion while I was with my friend. I ordered a mint tea and had a glass of water and just stayed in the authentic tired state. It went fine. I wasn't as peppy as usual but I was still able to stay present. When I got home, I had a nap and in my dream, I was at a party and there was this lovely cake with white icing. I went into it

all sneaky like and dipped my finger in. I managed to not eat any more but it was clear that the craving for it was still there. Then in my dream I ended up at a friend's house and she had all this cooked food that had been donated to her from local restaurants. I stayed away from the fast food and went to the grilled fish and stuff. It was a real feeling of gaining control over these cravings and choosing myself.

Apr 17, 2011

I went up to the park for a walk in the snow with Margaret today. I forgot my sunglasses and I could not believe how brilliant the snow was; it took a while for my eyes to adjust. This was a good teaching about snow and it was a good example of how radiant it is without apology. I read a quote today: "Experience is the hardest teacher. You get the test first and the lesson later." This is what my life feels like lately. And an interesting thing is happening–I actually don't mind this. It is helping me to relax actually knowing that jumping in, screwing up, learning and jumping in again is the way it is meant to go.

April 19, 2011

I have an interesting task for you. For one week change nothing. No recapitulation, no ceremony, no forgiveness, no releasing, no fixing anything. Just accept what is.
Wolf Woman

My first response to this e-mail was NO- RESISTANCE- RESISTANCE- FUCK YOU- NO WAY-MORE RESISTANCE. So I guess it would be a good idea to do it. She says through gritted teeth.

April 21, 2011

Went swimming today and used the steam room and hot tub to stretch my muscles. Was not as sore from kickboxing as I thought I'd be. Then walked home (45 minutes). Felt really energized today. Also starting to see that by just letting things be, they transform anyway–nothing is static.

April 23, 2011

I had a dream last night that I was looking out my kitchen window watching a robin in its nest. Robins to me mean new growth and spring. The robin had laid two of its beautiful powder blue eggs and was rolling them into the proper position so it could sit on them simultaneously to nurture them. Later, when I was outside, I saw a dead robin in another nest and when I rolled it over with a stick, I could see that it was sitting on a faded blue egg that never made it. For a moment, I thought about putting the egg in the other robin's nest in the hopes it would make it, but then didn't want to endanger the other two bright blue ones in case the mother abandoned them. Something shifted inside me yesterday when I was with my relatives. I could let everything be without fixing it and I was also aware of all the gains I'd made (bright blue eggs) and being firm about not wanting to go back to the old ways (dead blue egg).

April 25, 2011

I had the entire day free today and when I went to check in about an intention for the day, I remembered an exercise you recommended: live as if it is your last day on Earth. At first, I found myself planning the day and then I started to really think about how I would want to spend my last day. What surprised me most is that the things I really wanted to do were things I do all the time: be out in nature, eat, sing, dance, self-pleasure, move my body, be in community. I did these things and noticed how different the experience was doing it as if it were my last time. I was present in my body and when I found myself thinking about tomorrow or things to do, I reminded myself: there is no tomorrow. What a humbling perspective. I spend so much of my time trying to prepare for future things that it robs me of the beauty of the moment. And there is so much beauty. All of the little things that don't matter fell away. And I felt sad at how much time I'd spent focusing on all these things.

April 26, 2011

I am doing a parenting course with my kindergarten parents this week. I came across this quote and I get why not changing anything for a week was good practice for me:

> *"We have legitimacy in our very being, and even though we may desire to increase our competence of physical perfection or relational skills in order to feel more confirmed, we are really quite perfect in this moment, even as we experience what we think of as our imperfections... If we are focused on moving away from the negative, we are essentially starting from a single point of the thing we don't want and then dispersing our energy by looking for all the ways we can avoid or eliminate it. In this scattering of energy, our focus becomes diffused and we limit the possibilities of obtaining our goals. We lose our wholeness and coherence or integrity."*
>
> *-River Meyer*

I've spent my life trying to fix myself as if I was broken. I'm not. Others aren't either. So learning to stay present.

Being Honest with Myself

....

"Dzigar Kongtrul Rinpoche, the teacher I am studying with right now, says that in order to progress along the spiritual path, you need to be able to self-reflect, to really look at yourself honestly. He says that's where most Western people get stopped right away. They sit down, they start to meditate, then they begin to self-reflect and to see clearly their habitual patterns, thoughts, and emotions. Then everything is immediately twisted into self-loathing, self-disapproval, or self-denigration. Consequently, he teaches a lot about guiltlessness. He discusses the poison of guilt and how it never lets you grow. When you are guilty, you can never go any further. Somehow, for self-reflection to work, there has to be a lot of emphasis on loving-kindness and friendliness toward yourself. But that doesn't mean self-indulgence."

-Pema Chödrön
from the article "The Wondrous Path of Difficulties"

I worked with Wolf Woman to learn how to be neutral with myself. This meant that no matter what feelings, judgments, or problems I was experiencing internally, I could employ the strategy of detaching myself to look at them as a neutral observer. This helped me to self-reflect and to see my patterns for what they were without going into blaming and shaming myself. However, the shame was intense and it didn't evaporate for a long time. It took effort and awareness.

I had guilt in spades and I was the Queen of Self-indulgence at the beginning of my journey. Sometimes my cunning was so thick that being honest was not an easy task. I would never talk to someone else the way I talked to myself in my own head, which added to my guilt and shame feelings. I had a belief that unless I was hard on myself (insert cruel), then I would simply not grow. I speak more about the specific pattern of being hard on myself in the chapter by the same name. I can't say that I became proficient in loving kindness toward myself during my healing journey with addiction, but I did learn this in the years afterwards when I began studying Hawaiian Traditional Medicine.

> *"[People] soon realize that aloha is not just a word but a concept that is multi-dimensional, that it encompasses random acts of kindness, that it means giving love or affection to both close ones and strangers, and that it represents an attitude, a way of thinking, a spirit of living, a philosophy."*
> *– Mutual Publishing of Honolulu from "The Book of Aloha: A Collection of Hawaiian Proverbs and Inspirational Wisdom"*

Giving others aloha was always a strength of mine. However, it never occurred to me that giving myself aloha was just as important, if not more so, to my ability to impact the world positively. The practice of giving myself aloha transformed my relationship with honest self-reflection. In its pure form, aloha is the unconditional love of Spirit. This is an energy that runs through everything and can be tapped into by humans. I had disconnected myself from this energy because I felt unworthy of it. My kumu ("teacher" in Hawaiian) taught me to breathe this energy into my body consciously using my intent and my imagination. Every time I realized I was being harsh with myself, I'd stop and do this breath. I practiced this for a long time and it required a lot of mindfulness because those thoughts had become so automatic that sometimes I didn't even notice I was having them.

Thankfully, my body was my alarm system. When I felt myself tensing up or getting stressed, I'd immediately go into my mind to monitor my self-talk. Usually, it had begun getting nasty. According to the online Collins English Dictionary, self-talk is a term psychologists use to describe "the act or practice of talking to oneself, either aloud or silently and mentally." I found that it didn't do much good to listen to the thoughts or analyze them because that just seemed to feed them more energy and I had already decided I wasn't giving them any more of my time. So I'd just start the breath and put my attention on feeling that aloha run through my body. By the time I felt calm again, the voices were gone and I could go on with what I was doing. I started to see that I was not a bad person; I just had some bad behaviours I needed to change.

Rather than indulging these patterns as a way of taking the edge off of the inner harshness I was experiencing, I learned to give myself love, which began to chip away at the patterns of inner cruelty I was running. That aloha fortified the value I held for my own life. When I began to value living, running harmful behaviour patterns was simply not okay with me any longer. I began drawing different bottom lines that I refused to cross.

Honouring myself bled into my relationships with others. I was able say what I needed to say in neutral ways while finding solutions that worked for everyone involved. This, in turn, also kept me in integrity with myself. At its heart, addiction is an inability to be intimate with oneself. The following journal entries demonstrate the transformation I had in just a few months.

Sep 1, 2010

Dreamed last night again that I was eating sugary foods uncontrollably but I didn't care. I have noticed in waking hours the tendency with foods that are okay for me to be eating to sometimes indulge (like the other day with the protein) as a way of filling myself up. I support my decision by rationalizing: This is challenging what I am going through with all the transitions and I need this to help me through this hump. But of course, that is the whole thing with addiction. So I am noticing these times and although I sometimes cave (like last

night eating my dried mango because I was uncomfortable), I have been recommitting and then doing forgiveness. I have not been using my inner man as much as I did at the beginning to point out the cunning. I did this today and it was helpful.

May 2, 2011

Went on a walk in the woods today with Margaret. It was good to get away from the city and out in the forest. I noticed beauty. Took photos. Enjoyed myself. As I become more direct with Margaret, our relationship works better. At one point, she was trying to get me to go into a rough terrain that I really didn't want to scale. Before, I would have ignored my needs and instincts and would have gone along. Instead, I found a win-win; I suggested she go and I would meet her at the bottom of the trail. That way, we could both get what we wanted. There was still some tension throughout the day as I could tell she really wanted to get off the trails and I just didn't feel comfortable with that–not knowing the area and all. I was proud of myself for sticking to my instincts.

Breaking Codependent Patterns

"A codependent person is one who has let another person's behavior affect him or her, and who is obsessed with controlling that person's behavior... Codependent behaviors or habits are self-destructive. We frequently react to people who are destroying themselves; we react by learning to destroy ourselves. These habits can lead us into, or keep us in, destructive relationships, relationships that don't work. These behaviors can prevent us from finding peace and happiness with the most important person in our lives–ourselves. These behaviors belong to the only person each of us can control–the only person we can change–ourselves."
        -Melody Beattie from "Codependent No More: How to Stop Controlling Others and Start Caring for Yourself"

I didn't realize I was a separate person from others in my family with my own needs, wants, desires, values, and beliefs until I was twenty-seven. This epiphany came to me in a flash and it changed the trajectory of my life. Since I was a kid, I always tried to make others happy at the expense of my own happiness because I thought that would keep me safe and it would make me more lovable. I realize this a-ha moment of mine may seem utterly senseless to someone who has never been in an enmeshed relationship, but I've talked to a lot of other people since that moment that had a hard time figuring out if what they were feeling was "theirs" or belonged to another. I had developed an extreme sensitivity to how others were feeling to the point that I could actually feel their feelings in my body.

The accuracy of what I was picking up much of the time has been validated by many people in my life. I needed to start drawing a line between my energy and that of others without necessarily losing sensitivity to their boundaries. Over the years of traveling and meeting people from all over the world, I've noticed that his tendency seems to be more prevalent in cultures that value community over individuality–not that one is better than the other. In fact, we need both, and this line can sometimes be tricky when we speak about human relationships. When do we put our needs first? When do the needs of another person take priority? Both have their place; it's a question of balance.

I used to get codependence and interdependence mixed up and that is understandable when I look at the definition of 'interdependence' in the online Merriam-Webster Dictionary: "related in such a way that each needs or depends on the other: mutually dependent." So what is the difference between the two anyway? Perhaps the best analogy comes from the natural world. In nature, species are interdependent and often cooperate with one another in order to survive. For instance, certain kinds of fish feed on bacteria that live on the skins of sharks. Although sharks are carnivores, they don't eat the fish because they know the fish provide a much-needed service that keeps them disease-free. If the shark were to refuse to allow the fish to feed one day for whatever reason, the fish would likely just move on to another food source. The fish would not hold a grudge and try to force the shark to comply. The latter would be codependence. Nature adapts instead of forcing control over anything. There is no doubt that the actions that a living thing takes impact other living things around it either in positive or negative ways. Other species are good at maintaining balance and supporting the continuation of life. Humans can learn a lot about healthy relationships from observing nature.

One of the hardest tasks that Wolf Woman gave me was not to help or offer help to anyone unless they asked for it first. If they asked, I could not immediately say yes. I had to ask my inner wise one if that was for me to do or not. This was a serious challenge to my Grasping Personality because she was used to feeling good about herself by helping others. My self-worth was tied up in a lot of ways to how helpful I was. If I wasn't helping, I didn't feel useful or worthy of love and affection and my inner wise one tested me in effective ways! I was in the grocery store one day when a lady dropped a bag of oranges. I watched as they went rolling all around the store! I was about to help her when my inner wise one stopped me. My inner dialogue was brutal as I sat and watched helplessly: "You are so selfish. What kind of a person just watches someone struggle and doesn't help them?" When I started to pay attention to my self-talk, I realized that it was a bag of oranges–not life or death. That person may have felt embarrassed but she was certainly not in any danger!

This may seem like a silly example but I would agonize over these sorts of things that happened every day as if they had something to do with me and my worth as a human being. Now, I am not saying that I stopped helping everyone in every situation. I was also in situations where it was clear that I just had to act, like when a kid made a break for it on a busy street; you bet I am on the move without thinking in those sorts of situations. Most of the situations we come across each day involving others are not life and death and I realized that by helping and offering advice incessantly, I was not only depleting my life force energy, but I was also disempowering others in attempting to solve their problems *for* them. First of all, this is impossible because ultimately, the person I was trying to help needs to learn that skill on their own and the universe will keep sending them situations so they can master it. Secondly, if I was so involved in rescuing all these people from themselves, who was over there in my life solving my problems and taking care of me? No one. That was *my* problem.

This enmeshment was mirrored in all of my relationships with friends, loved ones, strangers, and, of course with food. When I was in a situation where I was feeling like I wanted to eat, help, or people-please, I developed the strategy of asking myself: "What do you really need right now, Jen?" The answers often surprised me and I saw that all the unhealthy behaviours were standing in for real needs that I simply hadn't acknowledged. Sometimes, as in the examples below, I needed space to myself. Other times, my spirit yearned to be as I was authentically in the moment even if it meant that I was less than stellar. Yet other times, I had to stick with what I knew was right for me even if others disagreed or thought I was over-reacting. I also learned to live with the discomfort that comes with other people's reactions to my self-care, which were not terribly positive or supportive much of the time.

May 9, 2010

Mother's Day. In front of the mirror, the words came: pretending to be happy. I've been pretending to be happy with my body but when I really am truthful, I am not. And it is not about wanting to be skinny, necessarily. I listened to a podcast the other day of a lady speaking about food addiction. The focus was on "skinny" for most of those women: if I am skinny, I will be acceptable and lovable. I've not been obsessed with being a certain weight nor have I dieted. I really am clear that I just want to find a place with my body where I feel good about it. The "skinny" model doesn't work for me. And it also doesn't work for me to be stuck in an illusion that just because my body type is desirable to some folks "out there" that it is working for me. I used that attention to prop up my ego. Really, it's just another codependent behaviour. What I really want is to consistently feel good in my own skin—even on bad days. So I've decided to start today rather than waiting for when I "look" a certain way. To be honest, I am not sure I am even conscious about how I want myself to "look" although I sense there is a picture there. Don't feel that it is about how I look but more about how I feel. So it's a bit nebulous right now. Forgave myself for being caught in the illusion of happiness about my body.

May 31, 2010.

This has been a hard stretch. Truth is that I have a lot to forgive myself for. I stand in front of the mirror and get a

bunch of images to describe what I am feeling. It is all so confusing: What is hunger? What is craving? How can I tell the difference? It is all a jumble sometimes. So forgave myself for lying to myself, for not taking ownership. I feel shaky and unmotivated.

Jun 3, 2010

In my dreams last night, I was living in a crumbling building. The people I was living with wanted to stay there but I insisted we be proactive and design a new building that had strong foundations. I went to speak to the elders in the community about how to do that. My dream intent last night was to let go of all the guilt I feel about taking care of myself first. For example, unless I am at my family's house or I've been invited to someone's house for dinner, I have been taking most of my meals in my room. I find that there are less distractions for me that way and I can focus on eating and connecting with my food and myself. Roommates are concerned and I haven't had the extra energy to communicate with them about what is going on. Really, I think I just have to tell them: I am working through my stuff. It is not personal, it's just all I have the energy for at the moment. I am certainly no social star as of late. I've been writing a lot and reflecting; I just don't feel like sharing anything much with the outside world–including most of my friends. At least not yet. Besides, I don't know what I'd say: I am a mess. Well, they can see that. They ask: "Are you okay?" I say: "No. But I will be." That's all I got and that part of me that used to comfort people or try to make things okay is simply out of commission at the moment. I want that part of me to come back in a healthy way–that part that is sensitive to the needs of others. It's the codependency of taking inappropriate responsibility for others and fixing, solving, making okay that needs to change. I am learning to become my own best advocate.

Jun 16, 2010

In the dance tonight I realized that I am feeling kind of cramped in this new relationship. I want to be with him so it was perplexing. I realized further that I just need to let him know that I like space and time to myself. While I was dancing, I figured out a way to say that that kept me in integrity without blaming him. It really has nothing to do with him. Just more of me not slipping into codependent patterns from the past.

Jun 23, 2010

Thanks for this e-mail, Wolf Woman; it resonates with me. I have set that intent. I think that will be good for me because one of my fears is losing myself in the other person like I used to.

Regarding engagement with a man give yourself an intent to be able to get a sense of your energy and how it engages with another energy. Keep it simple.
Wolf Woman

Jun 25, 2010

I am so glad I said yes to making love to this man. It's been such a fun adventure. At the beginning the codependent patterns from my past were really evident but I was able to work them out that first night after I took some space to figure out what was going on. The fact that I took space is a victory, as I would never have done that before! I have pushed lots of edges in a good way in the last two days while still staying in my integrity.

Oct 13, 2010

Mostly what is up and what I've been working with is my relationship with Ewan. Cleaning up codependent tendencies I have. I am not sure Ewan believes that the food addiction is an issue for me. He looks at me and says: "you look great." Looks at what I eat and says: "you eat good food. You should give yourself a break." I find myself sometimes getting sucked into his cunning. So talking to him is helping me clarify what is true for me and also teaching me how to stay in my integrity because it is so tempting to just fall into the old role of allowing my value to come from outside me. And I am weary of letting my guard down with the healing but also trying to find a balance between being too serious and letting my own cunning get in the way of my wellness. I found myself at Thanksgiving dinner the other night at a friend's (who is an awesome cook and uses all organic food from his garden mostly) looking at the home-made pies and actually considering eating some and rationalizing that with: but it is organic and made with love. I had some tea and put some whipped cream (with real vanilla bean) on top to make it feel like I was having dessert and that worked. But man was my cunning part convincing and seductive!

Boundaries and Agreements

> *"[Boundaries are]...crucial...for healthy human development... Without adequate boundaries people are vulnerable and frightened. It is this fear that underlies our compulsive, addictive, and self-destructive urges and behaviors...While growing up, we are indoctrinated into the culture with phrases like 'Be polite to others,' 'Mind your manners,' 'Don't let the other guy get you down,' and 'Put on a happy face,' all of which send a direct message to deny our instincts, intuition, and feelings for the sake of looking good or coming out ahead."*
> *-Megan LeBoutillier from "'No' is a Complete Sentence: Learning the Sacredness of Personal Boundaries"*

We live in a world where children's boundaries and rights are not recognized or respected in many parts of the world. I've made it part of my life's work to ensure that children have a voice in their own education in order to guide their own life's journey in the direction that is right for them. As a teacher, I advocate for a child's right to be who they are and to study the things they are passionate about. A large part of this work entails supporting parents in learning how to work with their children's boundaries as well as their own in order to build mutual respect and loving kindness in the relationship between parent and child. The way we treat children when they are young and looking to us for models of acceptable behaviour is the way they will treat others when they grow up.

In her book "'No' is a Complete Sentence: Learning the Sacredness of Personal Boundaries," Megan LeBoutillier speaks about different kinds of boundaries: physical, emotional, spiritual, and intellectual. A physical boundary is one where the child decides who touches them and when, if at all. This includes the child's parents. We all have times when we don't want physical touch for whatever reasons. For some kids with sensory processing issues, for example, physical touch can be very painful. When parents honour their child's right to set these sorts of boundaries, they are telling the child that it is okay to set boundaries and that their parents will support them if they don't want to kiss a family member, for instance. Another kind of physical boundary kids can be honoured in setting is in regards to food, rest, and exercise. Children have the right to listen to what their bodies need and to follow their body's natural instincts as long as this does no harm to others. Unless, of course, the child is fending off a physical attacker.

An emotional boundary is one where the child is allowed to have feelings and express them in a safe environment. This is only possible when the child feels they will not be shut down, blamed, or shamed for having those feelings. Parents who open space for feelings give their child the message that feelings are a natural part of living and learning. These parents are able to hold space for their child's feelings while dealing with their own emotional triggers as they occur. I saw a beautiful example of this the other day in a grocery store. The toddler in the shopping cart was obviously tired and I am sure the grocery store was the last place he wanted to be in that moment. His mom was busy shopping and so she didn't notice that an emotional meltdown was about to occur. When it did, it was full on. All the people in the aisle were looking at the scene and a sense of judgment was palpable in the air. I expected the mom to respond like most stressed out parents do: yell at the kid and tell him to be quiet, maybe add shame and guilt into the mix to get him to comply and stop the embarrassing scene. However, she didn't do that. She stopped shopping and gave her son her full attention. She was calm and this helped him to calm down too. She negotiated with him and told him that she just had a few more things to put in the cart, they would pay, and go home to do something relaxing. As soon as her son felt heard, he was able to hang in there. It was amazing how quickly a potentially explosive situation can de-escalate with compassion and care.

An intellectual boundary is one where the child's own unique values and thoughts are recognized and welcomed into discussions with others. Critical thinking and new ideas are a regular part of family and school discussions. Children are not outcast or shamed because they have a different point of view on topics than their loved ones do. Parents ask what the child thinks about this and that rather than imposing their own belief systems on their child. These parents still share their own beliefs, values, and thoughts with their children but do not demand that their children adopt the same stance in life. In these families, members learn to listen to one another and consider different perspectives–even if they disagree with them.

A spiritual boundary is one where the child is encouraged to develop his or her own connection to the spiritual energy of the universe. Parents may have their own spiritual practices and beliefs that they share with their children, but they also support their children in exploring different ways to be in their spiritual selves. Parents are curious about how their children experience the divine in their lives instead of using the threat of the wrath of God to keep their children in line. In these families, spirituality is not used as a tool of guilt and shame in order to extract obedience from their children. It is rather used as a way to help children feel connected to the universal web of energy they are a part of. Spirituality is a way that we can learn that we are never really alone. Like many parents of previous generations, the adults in my extended family misinterpreted boundaries as "acting out" or defiance.

Authoritarian parenting was the kind of parenting my relatives grew up with so it makes sense that this is the kind of parenting that's been passed down in my family. Authoritarian parents take children's boundaries personally instead of seeing them as a natural and healthy part of development. Authoritarian parents walk over their children's boundaries in order to keep their own boundaries intact. In her book, "Kids Are Worth It!" Barbara Coloroso describes three type of parenting styles: jellyfish, brick wall, and backbone.

My relatives mostly used the "brick wall" type of parenting where there is no negotiating and no agreements made. It's the parent's way or the highway.

On the other end of this extreme is the permissive or "jelly fish" style of parenting. These parents are very wishy-washy with their boundaries–if they have any at all. Often, these parents grew up either in homes where they were in the position of parenting their parents because of substance abuse issues, for example. Permissive parents might also have been raised in an authoritarian household where their boundaries were severely compromised and might be unwilling to submit their own children to that treatment. Although this is noble, this sort of parenting does not engender a sense of security in children. Children look to their parents to take the lead and set healthy boundaries. When parents allow children to make major decisions and do not set healthy limits, children tend to develop high levels of anxiety and begin to act out in many ways. Interestingly, in this situation, it is the parents who give up their personal boundaries in favour of their children's.

Some parents may find themselves moving all along the brick wall to jellyfish continuum in their parenting depending on the situation they are faced with. What I've learned by working with parents is that the "category" is not as important as being aware of these energetics when they are coming up so that parents can make a conscious decision of how to respond instead of reacting in their habituated ways.

At this point, I'd like to reinforce that there is no such thing as a perfect parent; this creature simply doesn't exist. Parents are human and they make mistakes. Children are human and they make mistakes too. Even "backbone" parents who do not fall into authoritarian and permissive parenting styles make mistakes they must then figure out how to resolve with their children. However, that is the key: they do it *with* their children. This involves conversation, negotiation, and making agreements that work for everyone within the boundaries they feel comfortable with. These agreements are not written in stone: they change as family members and life situations do. Every step along the way, family members communicate with one another when something is not working for them and then something different is attempted in order to accommodate this new way of being.

The journey toward creating healthy boundaries was a long and rocky one for me; imprinting that occurs in childhood can be difficult to override. I still have to be conscious today about making sure I know what my boundaries are and stay true to them in different situations. It's not an exact science, but I am much better at knowing when something is off and correcting it than I used to be.

These journal entries describe some of the boundary situations I found myself in during my healing journey as well as how I worked at building up personal boundaries in order to experience more freedom inside my world. It wasn't always a pretty scene. At first, I set "brick wall" boundaries. "Jelly fish" boundaries endangered my life sometimes. I had to learn to know what I would or wouldn't do while also making space for the other person's boundaries. This required me to get really good at creative problem solving.

> *"[I]f you are a warrior or a martial artist, you draw a circle in the sand and you stand in the center of that circle...You know the truth of that boundary, and if anyone advances across that boundary, you have the right to do whatever is necessary to get that person out of your circle of power."*
> *-Lynn V. Andrews from "Writing Spirit:*
> *Finding your Creative Soul"*

May 21, 2010

Been in a conflict with a friend lately that's got me feeling a bit sad. I told the truth about how I was feeling about something (albeit in a clunky way) and friend was offended. After a day or so of getting the silent treatment and uncomfortable energy, I approached this friend and took ownership for the clunky-ness and explained that I was working through some things and the intent was to set clear boundaries and come up with a

solution to the problem that worked for everyone. The intense energy lessened and I feel good about cleaning up my end, yet friend is still avoiding me. Now, this is a pattern that is familiar with me as a relative used to do the same thing when I was a kid. I'd apologize and she wouldn't speak to me sometimes for weeks. This was relevant because it came up today as I looked in the mirror. My relationship with my body is a reflection of that pattern of punishing myself for mistakes and of not letting go and forgiving unless that forgiveness happens from the outside. Well, in the case of my relationship with my body, no one is going to forgive me from the outside. I am the one making the choices and the mistakes so that forgiveness has to come from inside me. I woke up with this realization at 3 am after a dream so did the work of forgiving myself then.

Jun 6, 2010

I danced for almost 4 hours today. Did 2 hours of dancing in the morning and then went back in the evening for another almost 2 hours. I am spent and it felt really great. I continue to dance my inner man and I enjoyed dancing with several men today at the same time and individually. I am doing that purposely so that I can practice being interdependent instead of codependent since I seem to have the hardest time with men in this regard. I found that I could hold my boundaries better while still remaining open when I engage my inner man. My inner woman is still there too, it is just that she seems to be holding her own "role." I am reading Matthew Fox's book. Part of recovering body awareness, he says, is recovering a sense of boundaries. I see that my work with dance all these years and shamanism has really helped me to build this sense because I didn't know how to do this most of my life. John Conger says, "Without a clear no, we cannot have a clear yes...To keep the world at arm's length, to push people away with our arms, is a critical aspect of our healthy development...By learning our boundaries, we can then truly welcome others in."

Now I read this after my dance class and I realized that I was doing a lot of pushing away with partners and then jumping back in to play again. Sometimes it was to maintain a boundary, but other times it was simply to see what the other person would come up with–part of the creative process in dance. It felt really good to be decisive and change my mind when and if I was ready. My body, I am starting to see, is a wonder and I am continually amazed the more I dance how many new things I discover about myself and what my body can do. Five years ago, I would never have left a dance with someone–even if I felt "done." I would have been too scared of hurting their feelings. Today, I leave when it is time to go. And if people leave me before I am "ready," as sometimes happens, that's okay too. I just go back to my own dance. Dance is so healing right now specifically because it is helping me to learn in my body how to break those codependent patterns.

June 22, 2010.

Ewan and I have decided to make love and have made agreements around that. I am excited and nervous to spend time with him on Thursday. I guess my fears are coming through in my dreams because last night, I had a nightmare. These are rare for me so when they come up, I know it has something to do with a big fear. I dreamed that I was forced to work in a factory that cut up human bodies for parts. There was blood everywhere and I couldn't find a way to escape so I woke myself up and recalled my energy back from the dream. After I felt more like myself, I asked my Dreamer what all that was about and it turns out that it is a fear of the carnal and that primal energy that I feel when I am with new guy. Scared of losing control somehow. Made a resolution with myself to keep saying yes to whatever felt good during the process.

Aug 3, 2010

I realized today that when anger comes up for me, it is often because someone is encroaching on my space and I need to stand for myself. As soon as I stand for myself, the anger goes away. This is an epiphany because in my family, anger was not allowed unless it was coming from adults. I see why I suppressed it and let go of that coping strategy to welcome it as a sign to take care of myself.

Oct 1, 2010

Spent the afternoon and evening with Ewan. He invited me over for dinner and I was pretty hesitant about it–mostly because I still feel the attraction between us and didn't know if that was a good idea considering that my inner guidance was telling me not to have sex with him. But it felt important for me to go. So I did. When we got there, I could feel the sexual tension so I just told him, "I just want you to know that I am not going to have sex with you tonight." He was a bit taken aback and said that that was not his intent in bringing me to his house. I just let it sit. And then I said, "I said that for my healing." I was proud of myself because it was a really challenging evening. I could tell he was disappointed and he was a bit mopey for a while but I just rode the waves and stayed in my heart.

Dec 24, 2010

Remember how I went for STD testing in September and then had to wait until December to do the last HIV test? Well, all results are in and all is clear. I was not worried. However, it has made things more clear to me in terms of my boundaries sexually and I now have a reverence for my life that I didn't have before. I wouldn't have unprotected sex again with someone unless they are willing to get tested. Feels good to know that

I can set that boundary. Now that I know the consequences, I won't go back there.

Jan 24, 2011

Been humming and hawing about whether or not to stay with family members during my upcoming trip to Vancouver. Went through the: "well, I really should because I don't see them very often anymore..."

Then I was talking to a relative. She invited me to stay on the couch. I felt a big 'NO' inside me and realized why. I am a private person in some ways. This privacy was never respected or understood by my family when I was growing up (we were not allowed to close our bedroom doors or have locks on them). Privacy with equated with secrecy. They used to force me to socialize with people who were visiting–even if I didn't like them or get a good feeling from them. As a kid, I found my privacy outdoors–my favourite place was at the top of a favourite climbing tree in my neighbourhood. So imagining myself in that condition again when I know that I need my own space and privacy when I am staying with others and feeling the inner NO was great because I never realized that about myself before. I am an adult now, though, and I figure, why not just claim that and give them the real reason I am not staying with them? No more convolutions.

Chapter 3

THE NORTH EAST

North East Introduction: New Patterns

"What man actually needs is not a tensionless state but rather the striving and struggling for some goal worthy of him. What he needs is not the discharge of tension at any cost, but the call of a potential meaning waiting to be fulfilled by him."
- Viktor Frankl from "Man's Search for Meaning"

It's hard, if not impossible, to live a better life if we don't have good strategies for dealing with life's ups and downs. Because of the way an addict's brain is wired neurologically, they are notoriously challenged with developing new patterns and healthy strategies for working through difficulties life throws at them. Addicts are often in a state of fight or flight, and that survival stance is not conducive to innovative thinking. It was truly an epiphany to me that I could and should develop and employ strategies in order to begin to shift away from addictive patterns toward life-giving ones.

This may sound like a common-sense statement to those folks reading this book who have never struggled with addiction, but it is nonetheless true. Viktor Frankl saw this pattern in the European concentration camps as an inmate during the Nazi rule. He saw that some people were able to endure the horrific situations they were living in without losing hope and others descended into misery. I am not sure how many of these people already had addictive patterns wired into their brains before they were sent to concentration camps, but it would be interesting information to gather if that were possible.

When I was deep in my addiction, I had very few coping strategies for working through tough emotions, life's curveballs, interpersonal conflicts, and even challenges to my dream. Denial was prevalent. My go-to strategies were all soothing, temporary ones involving food that did nothing to improve my overall health and wellbeing long-term, although they did ease suffering for brief moments of time. The addict lives for these reprieves from deep pain that s/he cannot even usually really identify. All of my strategies revolved around soothing. It never occurred to me that I could utilize the resources around me and within me (my imagination, my totem animals, experts, and the natural world) to develop new strategies that countered addictive patterns of behaviour.

What I also didn't know then was that life is full of discomfort and that the goal was not to feel comfortable all the time but to learn how to lean into the discomfort and ride the learning edges that were being provided during those times. One strategy that helped me most of all to develop new inner and outer patterns of behaviour was to become curious about the messages that life and my Dreamer were sending me. What did that thing that happened today have to do with me? What was it trying to teach me about myself? If I didn't like the reflection that life was mirroring back to me, I learned that I could change my outer world by working on shifting my inner world.

Now, this doesn't mean necessarily that we have control of anything outside of ourselves. However, there were major patterns that needed changing inside of me and that was the only thing I actually had 100% control of. One pattern was the way I talked to myself in my head; my self-talk was generally abusive, cruel, and self-deprecating. In my bad moments, it could sound like: "You fucked up again. Can't you ever do anything right? You are so useless. No wonder your life is a mess." I honestly thought that without this inner bully, I would never accomplish my goals or improve myself. How wrong I was!

Along with that came the constant negative thought patterns that I followed all the way into serious depression in my 20s. It was a revelation when I started practicing meditation and I learned how often I follow these negative thought streams. Bigger still, was the huge a-ha that I could actually *choose* consciously not to follow the thought and to switch to positive and solution-oriented thinking. I felt a surge of power every time I took command of my mind's direction and learned to harness the energy of my mind to wire in new neurological brain pathways that were healthy and produced better biochemistry in my body.

We now know that thinking–even unconscious thoughts and beliefs–produces emotions and what we put our attention on is what tends to grow. Our bodies respond by creating chemicals that either produce wellbeing or begin to create physical imbalances that lead to disease, illness, and suffering. Dr. Bruce Lipton's "Biology of Belief" is a great book to read on the topic. Addicts tend to have low dopamine and endorphin levels in their brain chemistry. These are feel-good hormones that neuro-typical brains produce in balanced ways. When addicts use substances or enact the behaviour that soothes pain, they also experience a surge of those feel-good chemicals in their bodies. Even though they may not be aware of the science of what they are doing, this is actually why addicts engage in these self-destructive patterns. Unfortunately for addicts, this is tough on the body and there are better ways to increase one's biochemistry that are not so taxing to their biological systems.

In the North East of the medicine wheel, we learn how to change the ways we choreograph our lives. The North East provides us with the energetic and action-based movements needed for inner transformation to occur. Another way to think of the North East energy is to think of an alchemist turning lead into gold. In the following chapters, you will see how I worked new strategies into the fabric of my everyday living in order to stack the deck in my favour and to limit the use of food as a coping mechanism. In this direction, I also learned ways to produce more dopamine and endorphins naturally in ways that contributed to healthy living.

In order to consolidate your understanding of this direction from your personal, experiential and embodied perspective, I recommend doing the following ceremonies from "Shamanic

Ceremonies for a Changing World" by Marilyn Keffer and Gael Carter. You can find more information on how to purchase a copy by looking at the Recommended Resources section of the Appendix of this book.

Ceremony for Stalking your Attitudes 2-13
The Petty/Pity Tyrants 2-4

Scotland Trip

"Each morning, we are born again. What we do today is what matters most."

-Buddha

In 2000, I lived in Glasgow, Scotland for six months while I was finishing my undergrad. I had no idea how much I would love Scotland, the culture, the land, and its people when I left Canada. I met lifelong friends there and the spiritual energy of the place left a deep impact on me. Of course, now that I know that about twenty-five percent of my ancestors were from Great Britain, that makes sense to me.

In 2009, I began feeling a strong pull from within to go back to Scotland on a pilgrimage. As a busy student, I didn't get a chance to travel the country extensively in 2000. This was my chance to go back and visit sacred sites. Although I was excited about the prospect of this trip and had sold and given up many of my worldly possessions in order to save up for a whole year, I was really nervous too. Not about traveling–I'd done a lot of solo trips as an adult and felt confident about that. I was nervous about keeping up with my addiction healing and food planning while I was on the move constantly in another country.

I wondered how I would fare considering ritualized Scottish traditions of "High Tea," of which baked goods and sugar were an integral part. Wolf Woman prepared me by encouraging me to develop strategies such as taking food with me on planes, trains, and bus trips so that I would not be tempted to buy fast food loaded with sugar and carbs when I was hungry. I continued to e-mail her every day with my reflections, victories, and challenges. Traveling is an unpredictable venture in the best of times. Trying to learn new strategies in the midst of so much unknown, seriously upped the ante on my ability to adapt to new circumstances without losing my intent to heal my addiction.

As you will see in my journal entries from this trip, I faced many challenges that were not all food related that I had to figure out on my own in the moment. Although I didn't know it at the time, what I really embarked on was a type of modern vision quest. In shamanic traditions, vision quests are ceremonies that usually involve prolonged stretches of solitary time in nature where one connects with nature spirits, their ancestors, and spiritual guides (known and unknown) in order to gain perspective and direction in their life.

This trip was a month long ceremony that showed me what I was really made of. I was able to draw on resources within me and on the power of my spirit that I never knew before. I was stretched to the maximum, as you will see in the next few sections, and I made it. I learned to trust Spirit in a whole new way too. Even though I was alone, I was never alone, as the synchronicities below show.

Jun 28, 2010

Last day in Calgary and getting ready for my flight by drinking a ton of water. Starting to notice that I am really eating only when I am hungry. The rest of the time seems to be caught up in doing the things I need to do in terms of my dream. At first I would check in a lot to see if my body was getting enough food as it seemed too little to eat but it turns out that it is okay. Who knew? I feel stronger on the inside especially after these past few days in Calgary. I have pushed a LOT of edges and it's been healing. I am ready for my pilgrimage to Scotland tomorrow.

Jun 30, 2010

Okay. So I am now here in Glasgow and I skipped a day in transit so I will write my reflections for both days here. It was an interesting stalking experience because I was spanning 3 countries–all with their different "healthy" food options. I really loaded up on water as soon as I was past customs and drank that like crazy, which helped to keep me hydrated and feeling more full. I found that I didn't need a lot of food and I had brought some snacks with me from Calgary like apples, bananas, rice chips, and nuts to tide me over in case the meals they were offering were not ones I could partake in and that seemed to go well. At the airports, I stalked out food I could eat. I flew with an American airline and the food reflected the "fast" culture. There was one food place with "Healthy" in the title and I walked up skeptically (remembering our conversation from before) but figuring there must be something there I could eat. Although a lot of the things were coated in cheese still, there were Mediterranean options that I chose from. I didn't realize they'd let me bring on my own food so when I go home, I will load up with snacks before I go. Other than that, I just stretched as best I could and rested on the plane–meditating and breathing when my body felt uncomfortable. On layovers, I did some qigong and a good stretch of my legs and back. It was a long 24 hours and there were moments where I felt exhausted and on the verge of collapsing but I called on my inner man and it got me through. All in all, I am pretty proud of that accomplishment and I learned that I can make anything work in any circumstance. There was only one thing I compromised on because there was no other option and I was hungry: honey nut cheerios with milk. But I skipped all of the other baked items.

July 1, 2010.

Today was a day of stalking out my food for the next two days of travel on the train. I decided that instead of buying my meals at restaurants or cafes, it would probably be more cost effective to buy from groceries and I'd have more options. Turns out I was right. The grocery chain here did indeed have a salad/fruit bar and other foods that are snacky to eat. I'll go out for dinner tomorrow night when I return and I am having breakfast here at the hostel before I go tomorrow. I carry water with me wherever I go. Taking food along with me today eased my anxiety around finding suitable options so I think I will do that for the rest of my trip as much as possible.

July 2, 2010

Well, here in Scotland, when you ask for a cup of tea with milk, they bring a biscuit or some other treat on the side of the dish. I have resisted fine but noticed the strong pull. When I feel that, I have been asking what it is about and inevitably it is because I feel uncomfortable. Like today I was in a café in quite a conservative town and was picking up the vibe of disapproval coming from the folks around me. Okay. So I know I stand out like a sore thumb and I am not exactly conservative in the way I present myself. Once I figured that out, I was able to relax and the feeling went away when I realized it was just their judgments I was picking up and it had nothing to do with me. This was an epiphany; I've been doing this for a long time. I just didn't know what it was costing me until today sitting here in a different country with all strangers who I am pretty sure I will never see again. Tomorrow is a travel day. I went out today and bought all my food and snacks until dinner.

July 6, 2010

I have discovered everything oats: oatmeal and oatcakes and managed to find both in their raw form without sugar. Making my meals at the hostel in between sightseeing boughts is working well for me. All the walking whips up my appetite. Lots of exploring the island of Iona on foot.

July 8, 2010

Still noticing my tendency to jump in and out of connection with my food. Especially since staying in hostels where the eating is communal. I have been eating with eyes closed when I can. Went outside today to eat my lunch and found myself distracted by the landscape. It has been raining a lot and today was the first sunny day so I was trying to fit everything in. I ended up eating fast and running down to the beach for a swim. Forgave myself for being hard on myself. Really, I am quite proud of what I have accomplished since leaving home. It has been tempting to go for Cream Tea (with scones and such at 4pm) to "have the experience" but have resisted that as I feel like it is a slippery slope at this time in my journey with healing. My body is now used to eating for energy and I feel good. I don't want to screw that up. I do find myself missing desserts and so when I get back to Canada, I will start looking for recipes that I can make myself that don't involve sugar or wheat. I have decided to take it easy on the tea as I was finding myself using it for comfort (i.e. when I am cold, when I want dessert, etc.).

July 9, 2010

I did better with mindfulness and connecting today. Took one of my meals outside by myself and the others I ate in the kitchen. I am finding that I am really enjoying food. I look forward to it and I can take in a lot more of the pleasure than when I first started this process. Got loads of exercise today as I walked from the Northern tip of the island to the southern. Going out again now to walk to the Abbey for night service. Been really enjoying all the time outside in nature and yesterday I went for a swim in the Atlantic. Today, I was led to do a ceremony at the ocean. I realized that I did not have heart space for myself. I cried as my heart expanded to take me in. Then I threw a little heart stone I had in my hand into the ocean. I think my journey will be a lot easier now somehow.

Planning and Strategies

....

"Awakening does not mean an end to difficulty: it means a change in the way those difficulties are met."
-Mark Epstein from "The Trauma of Everyday Life"

I admit that at first the idea of planning and strategies made me twitchy. I was irritated and grouchy at having to practice this. In my mind, I prided myself on being a free, dreamy spirit and all that planning was putting a serious kink in my ego's style! Over time, I ended up breaking through various veils of illusion about the physical world and how it really worked. The problem with illusions is that they are not based in the reality of what is so in the present moment. My ego was happy but my life was not working because I was not willing to look at the truth of my situation: I did not have command of my inner world and so my physical world was falling apart.

During the course of my dancing meditation studies through dancing, I came across a quote that laid many of my illusions bare in front of me. In her article "The Spiritual Power of Dance," pioneer creatrix of 5Rhythms Gabrielle Roth explains the need for inner command:

As a young dancer, I made the transition from the world of steps and structures to the world of transformation and trance by exposure to live drumming.

Being young, wild and free, it didn't dawn on me that in order to go into deep ecstatic places, I would have to be willing to transform absolutely everything that got in my way. That included every form of inertia: the physical inertia of tight and stressed muscles; the emotional baggage of depressed, repressed feelings; the mental baggage of dogmas, attitudes and philosophies. In other words, I'd have to let it all go - everything.

The question I ask myself and everyone else is, "Do you have the discipline to be a free spirit?" Can we be free of all that binds and bends us into a shape of consciousness that has nothing to do with who we are from moment to moment, from breath to breath?

It never occurred to me that discipline was the way to freedom. And by that, I don't mean some external force that tells me what to do and how to behave, but really being a warrior on the inside finding all the spaces and places where I was holding myself back so I could transform them. Dancing taught me a lot about my blocks, fantasies, and illusions. It turned out that my body was my best guide because it simply does not lie. Learning to pay attention to what my body needed and to give it that was a simple, key strategy for me.

I was fortunate to grow up in a culture and family that valued dance. Every weekend, the whole extended family would get together at a relative's house, eat together, socialize, and dance. After everyone had had time to chat and digest their food, we'd all pitch in to help move the furniture to the outskirts of the room, thereby creating a dance floor. The record player belted out top 40 hits, world music, dance music, and all sorts of other eclectic beats and sounds; we'd easily go from Michael Jackson to Julio Iglesias in an evening! Although I confess, I was never much of a Julio fan, the adults in the group certainly loved him. That leads me to the other brilliant thing about these evenings: they were multi-generational. The kids danced with the adults, teens, and elders. Everyone was included.

As an adult, I found myself attracted to non-choreographed dance modalities such as belly dance, rave, and trance dance. I've been dancing since 2005 and it is a practice that has supported and moved me through some serious transitions in my life. I've danced through tremendous grief, exhaustion, fear, sadness, joy, rocky love relationships, moving away from my family, and healing an addiction. When I come to dance an issue in my life, my body tells me exactly what is going on as I move the way it wants me to. My body tells the story of what is out of balance and gives me clues for what I need to do to regain my center. It does not use words so I've learned to understand the somatic language of feeling throughout years of practice to uncover its messages.

Going to class isn't a competitive reality TV show sort of atmosphere. It is the polar opposite of competition, showing off my steps, or learning rigid dance moves. It is a spiritual experience and practice where my body literally moves and heals me. All I have to do is follow my feet and my instincts. Often, I can feel burdens lifting off my shoulders and emotions leaving the hidden caves they've been trapped in–sometimes for years. I never know what is going to happen and that unpredictability is a part of the attraction for me. The unknown is where we heal, learn, and grow. They body knows how to move us in that direction if we surrender to its non-linear intelligence.

Jun 11, 2010

On my way to Gabriola this morning and last night as I was packing, I noticed my resistance to planning my food. I realized that on trips, I am used to sort of "coasting." And my diet is a part of that. I would grab a sandwich or something on the boat. The eating on the go is not the issue; I can make healthy choices. However, last night I thought, "Well, I can go for the greasy breakfast on the boat or I can plan something different." So I made a smoothie last night, which I had this morning. And then on the boat I had other things I packed.

Jun 21, 2010

Was a busy day today with lots of running around to prep for my trip. I wanted to see today how I did scoping out good food while on the move in preparation for my trip (I work from home usually so everything food-wise is planned in advance). I noticed my tendency to put off eating when I am busy. I was pretty hungry (too much of a time gap between meals) after one appointment but found a place to duck in and have something to eat.

Aug 29, 2010

Had a dream last night that I was eating bread and didn't realize it. I've had other dreams like this. The other morning at the coffee shop, I actually considered the pros and cons of eating a croissant. My "pro" cunning went like: the owners are from the Netherlands and this is authentic European baking. I've been good so...But I put a stop to that because obviously rewarding myself with food is not a great strategy for accomplishing my victories so far. So I was just fierce about my healing and that was that.

Dec 9, 2010

Between a new life in a new city that I am getting to know, writing the kids book, and learning how to play the stock market, I am feeling overwhelmed on and off. The baths help as do hanging off the bed headfirst with the crown of my head touching the floor, and doing physical exercise, however, they are helping me manage it at the moment. This morning, my power animal told me to self-pleasure that energy away instead of letting it "get" me. I gained energy after so I think I will do that strategy more often–feels good and works!

Mar 4, 2011

Went swimming today and was kicked out of the lane after only 8 laps. I was really looking forward to swimming today and was livid. This has happened twice now where the schedule the pool has online is not accurate and they book groups at whim. I managed to calm myself down enough to inquire what was going on with the lifeguard. Turns out, groups have priority even if it is a public lane swim so I will now go at lunch time (noon) when they don't schedule groups. I sat in the steam room meditating to get out of my mental spin, then stretched, sat in the hot tub, and walked home instead to make up for the cardio. This response is happening to me with other things–I get really angry when things aren't going the way I expect them to. I manage to find creative solutions once I calm down. What a waste of energy though! Been watching the pattern.

Mar 5 and 6, 2011

Stayed over at Margaret's last night and then we went snowshoeing today up in Kananaskis for half a day. It was brilliant. I really needed that extended time in nature. My body feels well worked. Had a bath and a nap when I came home. I love Margaret; we have fun together and it was challenging being with her for pretty much 24 hours. I am not used to hanging with someone who talks much of the time without many breaks. When I did take some time away, she often broke my silence by knocking on my door or trying to grab my attention back. My boundaries were shitty. What I needed was space and quiet. I found it hard to keep up my energy level and state my needs when some decisions were made for me without checking first that I didn't necessarily like. I immediately got triggered. Lots of forgiveness work before I went to bed. What I did well was I planned all my meals and caught myself eating a banana to de-stress. Today was much better in the sense that I was able to state my needs, negotiate with her, and have a good day together. I've changed a lot and this situation gave me a chance to learn new coping skills and see these patterns and change them.

Celebrating Victories

....

"Are you all in? Can you value your own vulnerability as much as you can value it in others? Answering yes to these questions is not weakness: It's courage beyond measure. It's daring greatly. And often the result of daring greatly isn't a victory march as much as it is a quiet sense of freedom mixed with a little battle fatigue."

-Brené Brown from "Daring Greatly: How the Courage to Be Vulnerable Transforms the Way We Live, Love, Parent, and Lead"

It's safe to say that more than any other practice, celebrating my victories daily was the most transformative for me. I had learned as a kid to focus on the negative and it came as such a relief that even if I'd had a shitty day and made a lot of mistakes, I could and should still focus on one thing–however small–that went right. Sometimes, those victories came out of my mistakes: I'd catch myself eating absently and stop immediately and re-route. Every time an addict interrupts a habitual pattern, it's a massive cause for celebration! This means will power is returning and impulse control is being rewired into the brain.

I like Dr. Brown's quote because it also emphasizes that recognizing victories is not for the purpose of ego inflation. It's important to learn to give ourselves positive feedback so we begin to notice the things that are working in our lives and the things that are not. Awareness is the first step to change. Once we are aware, we are in a better position to change patterns that are not supporting us in life. I was proud of myself and I also felt a bit beat up on the inside–raw and vulnerable. That's how I knew I was doing it right. The ego doesn't like anything it perceives as weakness; it likes certainty. It wants to stay firmly in place so it naturally resists anything that changes its rigid patterns. Learning to know my ego's tricks was a natural outcome of this victory practice.

Every day was about taking one step at a time. I couldn't think of the big picture otherwise I'd get overwhelmed and that would lead to stress, which led to eating; I wanted to avoid that chain of events at all costs. Early on, my teacher was really clear that losing weight wasn't the goal. She knew society encourages women to hyper focus on looks and so she kept leading me back to my own intent for myself. My personal intent was to heal my relationships with food, my body, and myself. She worked with my intent–not one she made for me. This is so rare among professionals in the "helping" professions who often act like they know what's best for you and don't even acknowledge that people have the answers to their problems inside them. They just need support to find it.

Wolf Woman honoured me and my sovereignty and for that, I am deeply grateful. She believed I could heal myself and was there to guide me along. No matter what, I knew she would not give up on me and that was important because I had already mastered giving up on myself. In shamanism, intent is everything. Once we make an intent, the universe jumps into action to help us achieve our goals. Our job then is to stay awake to the opportunities for healing that come our way and to grab them when they arrive. When a hurtful memory comes to the surface, we have a chance to use our tools to heal and release pain from our bodies, minds, and hearts.

As the days went on, more epiphanies revealed themselves. Each night for a whole year, I e-mailed my teacher to tell her what I'd learned that day and what my victory was. She said to *always* count the victories–no matter how small. Some days, even small victories were hard to find. On those days, I asked my Higher Self to find the victories and drop them into my mind for me to consider. Sometimes, my Higher Self would choose things that, because of my filters, I didn't see as victories so that in and of itself was a victory.

For example, I remember one day I was walking through a park at night when a bunch of drunk folks started harassing me. I immediately got calm and brought my attention to everything around me. By staying present, I was able to stave off a physical confrontation. You might be thinking: "Wow Jen. That was a huge victory!" Do you know what I thought? "You are always so passive. You just didn't want to fight them. You are such a wimp." I went home that day feeling like a loser instead of a victor and it wasn't until my Higher Self showed me that avoiding physical confrontation when possible is an energy saving, smart move that I began to see how warped my thinking had become.

This, it turned out, was a key to healing. This was completely new to me. I realized how negative my thinking was toward myself. I spent so much time putting myself down that I never thought to look for the things I'd done well on any given day. My mind was programmed to find fault with anything I did. I was relentlessly trying to be perfect. I thought that being infallible, or at least appearing that way, would lead to more love from the outside. Of course, this is not where love really originates.

May 15, 2010

Victories: really wanted to have a coffee and a piece of chocolate this afternoon when I was feeling tired and still had work to do. And I didn't. I worked with that feeling of being tired and negotiated with myself: I don't have to always feel peppy to do the work. Found myself whining inside: I'm tired, I don't want to, etc. More victories: no baked goods and continued reduced sugar. Found myself at a baby shower this afternoon eating unconsciously. Realized that it was partly because I was hungry, as I didn't make time to eat before going. That is an old pattern I know well. I haven't done that for a while. Forgave myself for that. And also forgave myself for riding myself so hard lately.

May 25, 2010

Victory: was full at lunch so I stopped eating and saved the rest for later. Felt bad about taking a "to go" container (environmental reasons) and that would have stopped me usually from not finishing. Noticed that having a smoothie in the morning helps balance out my blood sugar throughout the day and gives me a lot of energy. I ran out of stuff to make smoothies so had coffee this morning and noticed a big difference. Another victory: felt the energy crash after dinner and was tempted to make a cup of caffeinated tea or have a square of dark chocolate but went for the black currants instead. This craving persisted throughout the evening so I just drank water and went to bed.

Aug 3, 2010

Something has shifted with my relationship with food where I am able to stay connected with it while eating with others. I am conscious when I am preparing it and I give thanks before my meals. I think living in this ritualized way in Scotland for those 10 days helped me shift this pattern of checking out. The cravings for sugar and cakes have diminished a lot. When I do feel this way now, I ask myself if I am hungry or if I am uncomfortable then I make my decision about whether or not to eat something after swinging it by my inner man to make sure I am not fooling myself. I am proud of the fact that I ate really well in Scotland. I never once had a scone or cake or sugary treat even though they were literally everywhere and often came served free with my tea even if I didn't order them. I feel I did a really great job of stalking out my food and making peace with choices when I wasn't happy with the options (i.e. eating pasta for a week and eating cereal on the plane). I didn't find a conflict with these choices because I was making them consciously. So that is a victory that I didn't beat myself up or then fall off the wagon.

May 3, 2011

Today is my year anniversary of the journey of beginning the healing of my addiction. I can hardly believe it's been 365 days! As I sat with my mesa this morning, it was clear that looking at all my victories would be a good way to celebrate. I wrote a whole, packed page of things in my journal of things I've accomplished: losing almost 30 pounds, moving to Calgary, leaving my family, getting pregnant, grieving the loss of my baby while traveling alone in Scotland, my relationship with Ewan (and all the learning I did in that relationship), learning to be a leader, and learning to take care of myself–to name but a few. When I finished making the list, I couldn't believe what I'd done this year. I could not have imagined a year ago that I would be where I am at right now. God knows there have been plenty of times during this process I've wanted to pack it in and I am glad I kept re-committing.

Self Love

....

Jack Kornfield on self-hatred from the article "The Wondrous Path of Difficulties:"

"It is definitely something I've wrestled with in my spiritual life. It's so painful, and yet it is a place where a tremendous turning can happen. One of the instructions I've loved offering to people over the past decade or two is to suggest that they do a year of loving-kindness for themselves as a practice. All of a sudden, people find out how difficult it is to do that. People feel unworthy and that they shouldn't be directing such kindness toward themselves. They cannot wish themselves happiness. So, initially, it's very painful. But after a while it does start to change people, and it also starts to change their relationship to their lovers, their family, and their community. We do have this capacity to care for ourselves and we are worthy of it, and when we discover that, it immediately translates into generosity toward others.

"You have to love yourself because no amount of love from others is sufficient to fill the yearning that your soul requires from you."

-Dodinsky

What I didn't know then was that the love comes from the inside, not the other way around. This would take another two years for me to really understand in an "inner knowing" way, where it was not just a nice concept in my mind but integrated into my whole being. Lomilomi Kahuna, Uncle Harry Uhane Jim also says, " I am enough." Those simple words encapsulate the piece I had been missing. I kept thinking that the love was somewhere out there and that if only I could find someone to give it to me, I'd be happy. This simply was not the case, as it turned out. I was following a persistent illusion like a dog chasing its tail. I eventually came to understand that this was at the root of my suffering.

Similar to Jack Kornfield's quote, I was really wandering around thinking that I was unworthy of love and that I was too broken to be loved. There were a few things I experienced in the context of ceremony that flipped a switch in my mind and shattered the concept that I was unlovable. In his seminal book "The Way of the Shaman," anthropologist and shamanic practitioner, Michael Harner describes the importance of experiential ways of going after knowledge in shamanic cultures:

> *"The shaman is an empiricist. One of the definitions of empiricism is 'the practice of emphasizing experience, especially of the senses'...And indeed the shaman depends primarily on firsthand experience...Why...is shamanic knowledge basically consistent in different parts of the... world? I suggest that the answer is, simply, because it works... The master shaman never says that what you experienced is a fantasy. That is one of the differences between shamanism and science. Yet there are similarities between the shaman and the scientist...Both are in awe of the complexity and magnificence of the universe and of Nature, and realize that during their own lifetimes they will only come to observe and understand only a small portion of what is going on...And neither master shaman nor master scientists allow the dogmas of ecclesiastical and political authorities to interfere with their explorations."*

Shamans over time have been able to change their perception of ordinary reality (also called consensual reality sometimes because it is a reality most of us "agree" upon) to enter into non-ordinary states of consciousness. The shaman knows that problems, illnesses, and disease manifest in the physical world only after they've been present in the spirit world for some time. Shamans all over the world enter into non-ordinary states of consciousness to travel into the spirit world in order to find the root of problems people are having in the physical world. One of the ways shamans get their brains and bodies ready for travel is through drumming. Drumming induces a trance state that deeply relaxes the body and mind. When scientists measure the brain waves of people in trance states, they move from alpha to theta waves. Drum journeys can be a really powerful way to bypass the ego so we can have a truthful conversation with our Higher Selves and spirit guides.

Meeting my Higher Self during a drum journey was a life-altering experience. She was not anything that I expected. I thought I'd find some world weary, beaten up warrior but that is not the essence of her. She is strong and centered, certainly. More stunningly, she is all light, filled with beauty, and unshakable. When she spoke to me, there was an unconditional love and benevolence that disarmed me. She was truthful without being cruel. She was supportive without laying blame. She provided context and perspective where all I saw were mistakes. Whereas my ego's voice is consistently mean (and that is how I know it's ego when it appears in my mind), my Higher Self's voice is calm, firm, and kind. I feel with every fiber of my being that she is absolutely on my side. There is nothing broken about my spirit and so I started going to my spirit when I knew I was stuck in negativity. I bypassed my ego to go to the place where I could count on the truth coming forth in ways that would not re-traumatize me.

The second ceremony that impacted me was the sweatlodge. This was shocking to me because I'd been attending sweats for years but it wasn't until I had the experience with my Higher Self that I started putting all the pieces of the sweatlodge ceremony together in a new way. When I go into a sweat to heal, I bring in all my ancestors with me. I call them and they always come. It doesn't matter what mistakes I've made, Great Spirit always gives me the chance to heal in the sweat and my ancestors stand by me. Great Spirit made me and so I am part of Great Spirit. This means that at my core, I am the unconditional love of God. All those years of sweating and I never put that together until that moment, and this led to another ceremony in this self love chain reaction...

The third ceremony that changed my relationship to loving myself was receiving the Hawaiian lomilomi ceremony for the first time. I describe my experience on my website:

> *"Lomilomi is one of the most ancient, sacred art forms in Hawaiian Medicine. Although lomilomi is commonly recognized as a massage, to Hawaiians, lomilomi is much more. Lomilomi is a spiritual ceremony that opens up the physical body to allow more of the person's spirit's energy to shine through, therefore, increasing their ability to walk out their life's purpose. Lomilomi is a way of showing reverence for the body by connecting with the spirit of aloha–the breath and unconditional love of Spirit. Lomilomi restores the body's natural state of relaxation by reminding it how to release stuck energy. Lomilomi teaches the receiver and giver both how to live in a state of aloha where the energy of Spirit moves through the body with ease and grace."*

I showed up feeling extremely nervous for my first lomilomi. Although I like being touched by people I know and already feel safe with, going to a new person is usually scary for me. I called my Higher Self to guide me and I eventually relaxed into the session. When the lomilomi giver instructed me to imagine breathing aloha from my spirit into my body, it felt like a tsunami of unconditional love went through me. It was simultaneously touching and incomprehensible to me. I realized in that moment that it was I who had put up that barrier by feeling unworthy. When the dam finally broke, I could see the illusion I was living with. Great Spirit had never left me; I had abandoned myself.

May 27, 2010

Also stood in front of the mirror this morning with hands on chest offering up love to myself. It is still hard for me to stand there naked in front of myself but not as much as it was at the beginning of this process. I am grateful for that.

Jun 1, 2010

Today was a good day. My meltdown over the weekend was fruitful–as I knew it would be it is just hard for me to see the light from that state. It was about giving myself love and giving myself compassion, or being my own best protector, as my inner man puts it. I found a crab shell on the beach today when I went for a power walk to blow off some steam. It stood out because my birthday is July 12 so I am a cancer (sign of the crab) on the zodiac and the shell protecting the soft interior has never been a metaphor I've liked much probably because I have spent much of my time in that state. But this shell was open on one side. I realized I can protect myself *and* be open. Somehow, the eyes closed eating exercise was easier today knowing that my primary responsibility is to care and feed myself. I wasn't rushing through my food as much and I got more enjoyment out of eating today than I have in this whole process so far. So that's a victory for today. Yesterday, Tiger's Breath told me that this is good work to be doing at my age. I find myself grateful that I get to do this at a young age and I recommitted myself to my healing today at the beach with a mini-on-the-spot ceremony where I wrote "committed to me" in the sand and threw my shell into the water as a promise. I am aware that I might have to recommit myself to the process several times in the coming months and it is work I want to do. I think this is the first thing I have done in my life that is for me.

Choosing My Attitude

···

"Do or do not. There is no try."

-Yoda, Jedi Knight

This quote from Star Wars captured my attention for years but took me a long time to really understand. It was confusing to me at first: I mean, if you are trying, aren't you doing? In the scene from the movie, "Star Wars: The Empire Strikes Back," Luke Skywalker is having what I call a "shitty attitude moment." He is whining about a task in front of him that seems impossible and he tells Yoda that he will "try." Yoda immediately scolds him for being wishy-washy. At first, this seemed horribly unfair to me. After all, Luke was willing to try so why was Yoda being so inflexible? What I see today is that Yoda was trying to teach the importance of unwavering intent. While this requires adaptability in situations beyond our control, if we don't stay aligned with what we are intending, it will never happen. In this way, we aren't trying, rather, we are actively doing until we accomplish what we set out to do.

Attitude, as it turns out, is everything. It can make or break an intent. If we dream something into our lives, it has a purpose. If it were impossible to accomplish a goal that we have for ourselves, we wouldn't have dreamed it to begin with. I learned that Spirit doesn't necessarily make the manifestation of our dreams easy. This is not done to punish us. Great Spirit is not an old man with a white beard lounging on a cloud in the sky poised to hurl lightning bolts in front of us as we journey through life. No. My experience of Great Spirit is that challenges are put before me so I can grow and learn.

Since I can remember, I've always felt more comfortable traveling in the spirit world than being here on earth. It was more natural for me to talk to God than another human when I was having a hard time in life and couldn't figure out how to solve a problem. When I was in elementary school, I stayed over at my paternal grandmother's house on weekends so I could go to church with her on Sunday mornings. Avó Maria was pretty keen on prayer and she encouraged all the grandkids to talk to God any time. One Saturday night after our ritual of watching my Avó's favourite show on TV, I went to bed. I lay in bed staring at the full moon outside my window. I prayed and listened for answers. It took me a while to figure out what to do with the answers I received. I implicitly trusted them, but now what?

The problem was that I had to learn the hard way that the physical world doesn't operate the same as the spirit world does. The spirit world is very fast and dreams unfold very quickly there. In order for those dreams to manifest on earth, it takes patience, perseverance, and time. The physical world is slow in comparison. To boot, we humans have created a reality that lays all sorts of obstacles in the way of Spirit. I learned that developing creative strategies for moving around obstacles was important if I wanted to see my dreams become a reality.

At first, I was like a toddler having a tantrum when I didn't get what I wanted RIGHT NOW! When the first thing I tried didn't work, I would get frustrated and discouraged, wanting to give up. I had all sorts of dialogue about how unfair this was and why couldn't things be easier anyway? I felt too stupid and unworthy of the dream half the time. This poor me attitude got me nowhere. Instead, it succeeded in draining my energy and my hope, making my stalking harder than it had to be. I was missing the point, which was that I had to learn how to manoeuver around the obstacles in order to gain mastery of the physical world so that I could be successful in creating my dreams here on earth.

Over time, I noticed more quickly when my attitude was going into the shitter. I won't lie: there were days where I felt bone weary and had to scrape myself up off the ground and get going anyway. Self-pity gets me nowhere so I learned not to stay in that energy for too long. When my strategies were not working, I developed a new strategy of calling on friends who I knew were good stalkers. I would present my problem to them and get advice on what my next step might be. Over the years, this has probably been the most enlightening piece for me because I realized that these folks think differently than I do and they've been able to teach me a lot about how to live in the physical world with less frustration.

My partner, Margaret, is a natural stalker. One day, she saw I was getting frustrated with a part of my dream I was trying to stalk out and I began going into my poor me attitude. She gave me that winning smile of hers and said in a playful way that broke me out of my pity party: "Honey, there's no guarantees in stalking. Part of the fun is to keep trying until you find something that works. Something that works in one situation won't necessarily work in another. Eventually, you get to your goal if you keep trying new things. And when you succeed, it's like YES! Total rush." She was energized just by thinking about it. Part of me wanted to kill her. I was thinking, "Fun? How on earth can this be conceived as of fun? It's total torture for me." But then I started laughing instead. It wasn't fun for me because my attitude was crappy. If I could find fun and creative ways to stalk, then my frustration would go down and my attitude would become positive.

Along with learning new strategies from talking to natural stalkers, I also started playing with one of my strengths: dreaming. I started stalking my dreams in the spirit world while I was awake as well as in my dreams and this added the playful element that I was missing. I'd take a problem into my dreamtime with me at night and then when I awoke in the morning, I set out to stalk the pieces that naturally fell in throughout the day from a dreaming perspective. For example, instead of going through pages and pages of stuff on the Internet looking for something I needed to find, I began using my intuition to choose the sites to look through in more detail. Not only did this save time and energy, it was also fun and I got to refine my intuition and make more clear intents as I went along practicing.

May 27, 2010

This is the first moontime I've had since beginning this process and I am noticing different cravings patterns happen (i.e. wanting to eat more often to "deal" with the discomfort, feeling tired and so wanting to grab for coffee or dark chocolate). I realize that this is what I would do before unconsciously. Victory: today, I did it differently. I did indeed feed myself when I was hungry but not to fill in during the uncomfortable times. During those times, I did some breathing and stretching. When I got home, I took some pain meds for cramps and had a nap instead of having a coffee and barreling through work like I wanted to do. I woke up feeling refreshed. So that was a victory. I know there have been lots of victories already and yet today I am struggling to keep a good attitude about it all.

Sep 28, 2010

Holy stalking, Batman! I got a lot accomplished today in terms of learning how transit works in the city of Calgary. Talked to bus drivers, transit folks, people on the street. I poured over maps and got clear on what I wanted. Thanks for the tip on holding my intent to find a place before I leave, Wolf Woman. I never thought of making an intent that is a "doing" intent during my dreamtime. I usually save those for my day intents. So that was an a-ha that I could do that. I saw yesterday how when things aren't going the way I want when I am stalking and I am running into snags, I can get into a negative mental space—especially if it is something that feels important or something that has to do with "survival." I woke up feeling anxious and realized that I was running a lot of self-doubt and

not trusting my stalker to do her work well. This created a lot of tension in my body. I want to learn a way to stalk in these situations where I do it with ease. I get there the way I am doing it currently but there is pretty high-energy cost and I often feel exhausted after.

Dec 7, 2010

A big weekend. Lots shifting in my inner landscape and it feels like my whole energy system is reorganizing itself. Have felt low energy for a few days now and wanting to sleep more than usual. So I am resting. Usually, I get really specific things to do to integrate things but this time, my totem animals just said to keep on doing what I have started in Calgary–especially singing and swimming. When I cut from the pattern of accommodating all those people, I didn't actually cut away from the pattern of accommodating in my journey. I still need to do that. Another thing I realized is how shitty my attitude has been since moving to Calgary when everything didn't work out the way I had imagined. I resolve to change that. A lot of challenge happened in November and a lot of gifts came along with that too. I see how my tendency towards resistance, drama, and making everything hard gets in my way. I have come home see that this is a real opportunity and I want to optimize it.

Chapter 4

THE SOUTH

South Introduction:
Sitting with Emotions

··

"With the help of your emotions, you can become self-aware and immensely resourceful in your relationships. If you can learn to focus and work honorably with the incredible information inside each of your feeling states, you can become intimately connected to the source of your intelligence, you can hear the deepest parts of yourself, and you can heal your most profound wounds."

-Karla McLaren from "The Language of Emotions:
What your Feelings are Trying to Tell You."

We humans spend so much time stuffing, denying, spewing, and avoiding our feelings that we never stop to ask them what they mean. In the book "The Language of Emotions: What Your Feelings are Trying to Tell You," social researcher Karla McLaren catalogues the emotions and tracks what they are actually trying to tell us on a deeper level. I used to find it helpful to put them into one of two categories: love and fear. I used to try to deny fear and focus only on love. This was a futile exercise. The problems with these ways of approaching emotions are: love is not an emotion, denial is not an honest reflection of what is so in the moment, and fear is not an enemy.

The so-called "dark" emotions are not our enemies either: fear, anger, shame, rage, and hatred. Fear connects us to our deepest instincts and points us towards actions that must be taken to ensure safety, for example. McLaren's book is filled with practices that support readers in mastering this empathic work. She also says: "When an emotion is healthy, it arises only when it's needed, it shifts and changes in response to its environment, and it recedes willingly once it has addressed an issue. When love is healthy, it does none of these things...Love does not increase or decrease in response to its environment, and it does not change with the changing winds." Love defies categorization.

In Hawaiian Traditional Medicine, love is the state of aloha that Great Spirit demonstrates to us unconditionally–no matter what we do, think, say, or feel. In truth, we are never disconnected from aloha; it is *we* who isolate from *it*. We do this by allowing fearful and worrisome thoughts to take over our mental landscape unresolved. When we do this consistently as a habit, we begin to believe we are unworthy or in need of fixing. Although we cannot really control which thoughts fall into our minds, we can learn to listen to what our emotions are telling us. In this way, we learn how we can reconnect with the Divine moment by moment when we find ourselves going off track.

This takes practice and rather constant awareness because many of us have the tendency to want to contract and protect ourselves when something challenging happens in life. In Hawaiian traditional medicine, the heart is the gateway in the human body that Spirit sends aloha through. Unless we practice living with open-heartedness, this portal becomes blocked and in some cases, closed, making life feel extremely painful. With willingness and effort, this vortex of light can be cleared wide open. One of my teachers says, "An open heart is the best defense." Through experience, I've found that to be true. When I am not trying to hide, protect, or defend anything, my heart can stay open to what is happening in the moment. The main way I've built resilience inside myself over time is by practicing taking the present moment as it is. Whether I like it or not is irrelevant.

When an addict is going through craving or withdrawal from a behaviour or a substance, the feelings–both physical and emotional–can be overwhelming. It's such a rush of uncomfortable sensation that it's easy to reach for anything that will make it stop. At some level, I believed that if I didn't make them stop, the feelings would annihilate me. So, soothing pain at all costs was the logical outcome of that thought. Except that if the thought itself is faulty, then there is a problem with following the so-called "natural" conclusions from that thought. When my teacher recommended that I just sit with the feeling without doing anything, I initially thought she was crazy. It never occurred to me that I could just sit with discomfort without trying to fix it.

What I learned by doing this is that there is a time limit to the craving energy wave. If I sit with discomfort long enough, it will start to dissipate on its own. I remember watching a film about a famous musician's life. I believe he had a heroin addiction. When he hit rock bottom, he decided to climb out of addiction. His strategy was that when he felt the craving wave coming on, he asked to be restrained. His wrists and ankles were tied down to a bed and he did major withdrawal without being able to move much. Everyone around him knew not to take him out of restraints, no matter how much he pleaded. I thought at the time that that was a horrible thing to do to himself. However, now I think: "Wow. That's a man fighting for his life." He knew he had to win over the cravings. It was hell. He recovered and so can anyone with determination and by tapping into the power of spirit that lives within.

When I work with kids who are scared of something, I explain fear as a hungry beast who needs to be fed all the time in order to survive. I have them imagine that rampant fear likes us to be scared but it can also turn into a friend if we look at the beast as a teacher. In nightmares, for instance, we can turn toward what is pursuing us and demand an answer to why it is plaguing us instead of continuing to run away. If you've never done that, try it. See what you discover about yourself. Fear has a lot to teach us if we have the courage to listen to what it is we are really scared of. Then, once we know what our fears are, we can ask ourselves if those thoughts are really true and what we can do in constructive ways to feel more secure on the inside. I've noticed that once I know the landscape of what my fears are, they automatically start to transform. I can then think straight again and get to work on resolving the issues causing the fear response. I discovered in many cases that my conscious and unconscious thoughts were creating the emotions in the first place!

> *"When you feel frustrated or upset by a person or a situation, remember that you are not reacting to the person or the situation but to your feelings about the person or situation. These are your feelings and your feelings are not someone else's fault. When you recognize and understand this completely, you are ready to take responsibility for how you feel and change it. And if you can accept things as they are, you are ready to take responsibility for your situation and for all the events you see as problems."*
> *- Deepak Chopra from "Seven Spiritual Laws of Success"*

We live in a time when it is acceptable to say: "so and so *made* me mad;" as if another person had control of our inner state of being! It can be hard to stay neutral when someone is laying into us, mocking us, blaming us, or shaming us. However, just because it's challenging doesn't mean it can't be done. I like to think of healing as a process of learning how to be your own inner cartographer. Every person on earth has a unique inner landscape they live within–whether they are conscious that they are constantly navigating that territory or not. It behooves us to know how we think, what we believe, what we do with our energy, and what patterns we run so that we can shift the ways we live that are not in our best interests. When we know our inner landscape by heart, we are much less likely to be at the effect of someone's unkind words or actions. We are more likely to see that in a neutral way as a reflection of her inner landscape rather than our own. This doesn't mean that we won't be triggered by someone else's actions or words sometimes but it does mean that we will have the tools to figure out why we were triggered and to set to work to shift what inside of *us* caused our reaction.

The emotions sit in the South of the medicine wheel with the waters of life and the plants who give away oxygen and sustenance without asking for anything in return. Like water, we can learn to allow our emotions to flow out of us instead of staying stuck or running out like raging rivers that destroy life. The South of the medicine wheel is paradoxically my strength and my weakness. I had to learn not to over-indulge in my emotions, to really hear them, let them go, and take action to change something in response to what they were telling me. This next chapter speaks to some of my challenges in this area and how I met and transcended them.

In order to consolidate your understanding of this direction from your personal, experiential and embodied perspective, I recommend doing the following ceremonies from "Shamanic Ceremonies for a Changing World" by Marilyn Keffer and Gael Carter. You can find more information on how to purchase a copy by looking at the Recommended Resources section of the Appendix of this book.

The 22-Day Emotional Workout Ceremony 1-8
The Monster of Anger Ceremony 1-10

Miscarriage

....

"Grief doesn't just bring waters of release to our psyches as sadness does, it drops us directly into the deepest rivers of the soul. In my experience, grief is so painful because [there was] no choice about releasing something, the loss or death has already occurred."

-Linda Kohanov from "The Way of the Horse"

In 2015, the book "Women's Power Stories: Honouring the Feminine Principle of Life" came out. It was edited by myself and Carell Mehl in order to support women in learning how to turn life's events into power stories. The introduction to the book states why this is so important for us to be able to do as humans: "While we cannot really control the external circumstances of our lives, we can always change the way we tell stories about our lives and ourselves. Far from being a semantic trip, these changes have a profound impact on our psyches. Our beliefs and what we tell ourselves shape the reality we live in. Our outer world reflects the inner world we create. To change the inner landscape is to change the outer." I wrote this piece called "Missed Carriage" that appears in the book:

Jewelled baby,
You came to me wanting to be mine.
Although I carried you only a short time,
I felt your brilliance shine.
Altered forever, the honour was sublime.

Even though I know I will be fine without your hand in mine,
I still miss the feeling of our energies combined.

I can't claim to be a woman who always knew she wanted to be a mom. I knew that this is what society expected of women but I didn't feel the pull towards this like some of my friends did. I watched friends have babies all throughout my adult years and I soul searched to see if being a parent was really mine to do in this lifetime. It wasn't until working with families and children for about a decade that I was sure that this was something that was right for me. However, finding the right person to have a child with without compromising my own life's journey and integrity was another matter.

It was with surprise, fear, and overwhelming joy that I found myself pregnant in my mid-thirties. I was in an unhealthy relationship with a man and I knew it. I also really wanted to be a parent and felt divided inside. Going through with the pregnancy was a no-brainer but what to do with a toxic relationship was not so easy considering this would be the father of my child. I told him I was pregnant after I'd arrived for my solo trip around Scotland. I reinforced that I didn't expect or want anything from him but he insisted on being part of the child's life. The thing was, I could not imagine co-parenting with him. He was twenty-six years older than me and had values that were vastly different from my own. Although it can be a blessing for a child to have parents with different views, I sensed it would be more of a struggle of wills than a mutually respectful acceptance of differences.

I traveled around Scotland in a dream-like state feeling my consciousness intermixing with that of the baby that grew inside me. It was unlike any feeling I'd ever had; I was awash in awe, love, humility, gratitude, and wonder. Life felt more magical than usual. I ended my four-week trip by doing an experience week at Findhorn in northern Scotland, which I'd been looking forward to for years. My cohort was an international one of thirty or so people. We were to work together in community for a week while exploring the spiritual energy and history of Findhorn. The day after I got there, I awoke to blood on my sheets. I was utterly heartbroken. All of the plans I'd been making for weeks shattered to the ground. I knew I had to find a way to get through the week while also grieving my loss. I decided to let the instructors know I needed the morning off and I went off into the woods to do a grieving ceremony. For two hours, I prayed and sobbed from the depths of myself. I'd never felt such grief before. I feared it would overtake me and I would never come out of it but I carried on.

When I rejoined the group, people were obviously put out by the fact that I was not participating in activities. Although I am usually a private person, I knew I needed to tell this group of people I hardly knew what had happened. So before our meditation time, I talked to them and reinforced that I wanted no pity from anyone. I simply wanted the space to grieve and participate, as I was able. Most of the people in the group respected my wishes and some did not. Some people took it personally that I didn't want to sit with them at dinner or chat idly with them. I simply could not do anything superficial. I was ruthless with giving myself what I needed and gave myself permission not to care about what others thought or wanted during this time. My intent was also to keep my commitments and demonstrate balanced leadership in my time there. I told no one of this pledge to myself.

Serendipitously, I ended up with the job of making sure the meditation rooms were filled with fresh flowers each day and that they were clean both physically and energetically. I went into the gardens every day with my basket to collect flowers. I would sit for long stretches singing chants to clear the energy each day and this practice brought me great comfort as I grieved my loss. It amazed me that I could feel such joy and such sorrow at the same time and then I remembered a saying in gospel music: "You can only sing as much joy as you can sorrow." They are two sides of the same coin.

I was grateful for my time at Findhorn. I met a great bunch of people and came full circle in that one week with each of them. Those with hurt feelings were able to step outside of themselves to imagine being in my shoes. They displayed considerable compassion by week's end. Another friend came to me at the end of the week and said something I will never forget: "I just wanted to let you know that I am leaving with such inspiration watching you this week. I've never seen such impeccable leadership from someone going through so much grief. It moved me."

I got home to the bittersweet event of meeting my one month old niece for the first time and cried tears of joy mixed with sadness. I did not tell my family I had been pregnant and I did not tell them I'd miscarried; I couldn't deal with their pity. I wanted to keep healing in private. Holding her was such a gift to me. I was joyful that the cycle of life continued in my family and that she was healthy.

Some people believe that the grief of the loss of a loved one never ends. That was not my experience. It took time and effort but I did heal. With the support of friends who did ceremony with me and held space for me to experience the whole range of emotions, I did recover. Now, I look back on that time as a gift hidden among tragedy. My relationship with the baby's dad ended and I felt free. It was not the right situation for this baby to be born into and I felt the spirit of my baby knew that and accepted that. She knew how much I loved her. She left me with the gift of knowing for sure that I was cut out to be a parent. She also showed me the importance of living in the present moment. This, after all, is where the power and the beauty in life can be accessed. And I know that even though I never got to hold her in my arms, it does not make our relationship any less real or treasured than those I've had with others. She is always with me.

The following journal entries go into more detail about the grieving process that continued in the months after my experiences in Scotland. As you can see, the grieving didn't just end right away.

In healing, there were layers of the onion that came off one by one, as I was ready to let go.

Aug 1, 2010

I am now back in Vancouver. I found out that the man I was seeing had not ended his relationship with his previous partner before we spent our weekend together in June. We have known for a while that his relationship with her was ending as she had decided a while back to move away to start a new life elsewhere. I had made it clear to him that I am monogamous and did not want to get involved with someone who was still in a relationship. So when I found out, I felt betrayed and I told him so. He knew where my integrity with myself was at all along and he chose to withhold information from me that would have affected my decision that weekend. I told him that if he ever put me in a position like that again while knowing where I stood, I would not be able to stay in relationship with him. Needless to say, lots of self-forgiveness work is being done on my end. Truth is that I had a feeling something was off and didn't follow it up. Now that I am no longer pregnant and it is just me to think about, I realized that I can't do anything about what happened and wouldn't want to; I learned a ton about myself and my bottom lines from that experience. What I know is that I have enough regard for myself that I can't keep hurting myself by staying in communication with him while he is in relationship with her. So when he calls today, I am going to tell him not to contact me until he has completed his relationship with her. And after all we've been through together, I also realize that I genuinely love him and told him so. I sure wish sometimes that things were black and white. This has all been a rollercoaster ride but I have learned that in the end, I WILL stand for myself so that is a victory. There is a phrase that keeps coming into my mind that you say: don't define yourself by the situations you find yourself in. I never thought I would find myself in this situation; it goes completely against my value system. And yet I know why I needed to experience this. I can't say I am fine, but I haven't collapsed either. I am sitting with all this and moving through it while doing my inner warrior thing and consciously staying in my heart to make decisions about how to proceed. I am not sure what to do about the desire I still feel for him and I am aware that some of it does not feel balanced or healthy. I've been dealing with it when it comes up by consulting my Dreamer. I toyed with not telling you any of this because I feel a lot of shame about it but my inner man told me that it was important to share it with you as someone who is supporting me in healing my relationship with food. That's all for today. I find myself in these moments of immense gratitude to you for everything you have taught me and all the tools I now have as a result. I am thankful to have you walking alongside me on this journey.

Aug 30, 2010

Had a dream last night that there was blood all over the sheets around me. I had a miscarriage in my dream. I woke up at 4:30 am this morning crying. I realized that I am still grieving. I've been putting a cap on the grieving and wanting to move on. And yet it seems to come in layers and waves. It's not self-pity. It's this deep thing that is just there after the loss. I just cried this morning for as long as it was there and sat with that feeling. Also in my dreams–uncontrollable eating and all the cunning to go with it. I could see the cunning but I didn't care. I woke up thinking: that's what I do. I just fill up that hole in the middle of my chest with other stuff instead of letting it be there and letting it teach me.

Create a small ceremony so not only you can grieve but that your body can heal and then make a conscious responsible decision about having children. You could say it is perfect timing in that your Dreamer sent all this to you in preparing your womb, mind, heart, body and spirit. Begin the readiness

to birth life in this world. Allow yourself to finish grieving and be joyful that your body is readying itself for you to conceive powerfully and consciously.
Wolf Woman

Sep 2, 2010

I did the ceremony for the miscarriage. Or rather, it did ME. I went to my massage therapist this morning for her to work on a problem I was having with my right foot. As she worked, I wailed. I realized that that was where I was storing all this grief. I felt all the stagnant energy come out of my womb. And that was the start of the ceremony. I was also guided to bury a little ceramic angel that a friend gave me to commemorate the loss of my baby. I thought I would keep it to remember her by but I realized while I was on the massage table that it held the memory of my pain and so I needed to put it to rest. When I got home, I dug a hole by the big cherry tree in my back yard where I had done a lot of ceremony over the years. I asked for any last trails of grief to be revealed to me and released them. Also did self-forgiveness that came up. The last part of the ceremony was to self-pleasure with the intention of healing my womb, body/heart/mind/spirit and preparing my body for a conscious birth. This was tremendously healing. I now know that it is okay to follow my intuition and to stand in what I know- even if it causes waves. I feel complete.

Dec 28, 2010

Went for a walk with Margaret today. Brought my drum. We sang together and she took me to her favourite tree. Was a really peaceful day. I set my dream intent last night to make peace with my decision to let the baby's spirit go. Just in a place of trust today. Had chickadees follow me along the trail and they kept landing on tree branches beside me as I walked.

Found out when I got home that they are about truthful and joyful expression. I am learning how to do that lately.

Jan 22, 2011

Fears of the future and the unknown coming up today. Went for a walk in nature and sat in the sun; it was above zero today. That helped me get perspective. I remembered what I learned this summer from the miscarriage: The future is uncertain. I remember thinking way far ahead and it never occurred to me that I might not carry her full term. I remembered how much pain that caused then.

Working with Anger

....

"The full healing of trauma is a process of coming back from near-death into life again. This process is not neat and orderly, and it is never emotionless. It follows the deep logic of the soul, where the remembrance of the original wound...reside. When we connect with this deep logic, we can understand the function of rage and fury in the lives of unhealed trauma survivors; we can see their fierce boundary energies surging forward to replace that which was lost in the trauma. We can also see that everyday levels of anger aren't called for, because traumatized boundaries have not simply been affronted or impaired. Boundaries broken in trauma (especially in childhood) are often completely destroyed. They often need to be rebuilt from scratch, and only rage and fury carry enough energy for the task. Rage and fury, then aren't always signs of dysfunction or instability; rather, they are specific healing responses to the instabilities created by trauma."

-Karla McLaren from "The Language of Emotions:
What Your Feelings are Trying to Tell You."

Out of all the emotions, anger was the hardest one for me personally to connect with. Anger was not an emotion that was welcomed in my family of origin–at least not from children. Although angry outbursts were common among adults, similar responses from children were generally assumed to be affronts to adult power and authority. I now know that this is quite common in authoritarian-style parenting stances where children are simply expected to obey adults without question or comment, but as a child, this was deeply confusing to me.

With no one to model for me how to deal with anger in a healthy way, I learned as a kid to suppress my anger. Occasionally, when there was no more room to stuff my anger inside me, it would all come hurling forth like a volcano exploding at full force in moments when I was pushed a bit too far. I had little command of myself in these moments and I usually paid dearly for the explosion in many ways: punishing myself on the inside, berating myself, feelings of shame and guilt as well as being punished by adults in the family for my "misbehaviour."

It was a vicious circle that lasted well into adulthood for me. I felt like I had no voice and no say in what happened to me. My boundaries were abysmal, if I had any at all. I was a walking victim. Through reading McLaren's work on emotions, I was able to accept feelings of anger as the messengers they are, teaching me that anger was a signal that my personal boundaries were being crossed either by myself or another. Once I had this piece of information, I was able to start identifying what my actual boundaries were. Before this point, I'd never even considered this because setting boundaries in my childhood usually led to being punished by adults in some way. Rather than being a liability, it was an epiphany to me that I had a right and responsibility to set and maintain personal boundaries in my interpersonal relationships. In fact, this was vitally necessary if I were to regain my physical, mental, emotional, sexual, and spiritual health.

At first, I learned what my boundaries were through paying attention to situations that triggered an anger response within me. Every time I felt angry, I learned to trace the feeling back to the boundary with the help of my south animal that is in charge of my emotions and my heart: the flicker. The flicker is a type of woodpecker common to Canada and parts of America that makes its living both in the air and on the ground. It is rare for woodpeckers to spend their time on the ground but this species does. Flicker medicine is aimed at digging for the truth. These birds have exceptional hearing. I watch them in the dead of

151

winter here in Calgary hanging off the sides of houses to hunt down bugs that are taking shelter from the swirling snow in the bricks and siding of houses. Flickers are survivors and they dig out nourishment wherever they can find it–even in scarce times. Because of their relentlessness, folks with flicker medicine can often trigger irritation in others because they will dig until they find the kernel of truth they are looking for, no matter what. Flicker helped me look past my own emotional reactivity to find the wisdom behind the emotion and what it was trying to teach me. And it still does today.

One of the most enlightening experiences that further helped me map out my personal boundaries was doing the "Monster of Anger Ceremony" from the book "Shamanic Ceremonies for a Changing World" by Marilyn Keffer and Gael Carter:

> *"[This] ceremony is designed to reduce the build-up of imploded anger...Anger is a naturally occurring emotion. However, a surge of anger causes your energy to rise strongly upwards in your body. When your energy rises upwards, you lose your center of gravity or 'centeredness.'"*

I had built up so much internalized anger throughout my lifetime that my container was full. I realized that I needed a healthy, safe way to discharge it. Centredness is important to a spiritual warrior because without it, we can't hope to make clear, good decisions for ourselves in alignment with minimizing impact of harm toward life. Martial artists know that staying in their centre of gravity (called the "tan tien" in qigong traditions) can mean the difference between life and death. The centre of gravity is found about two inches below the navel in the center of one's body. In shamanic practice, students learn to bring their energy down to that point at will during times where they feel triggered by something or someone or even themselves in order to gain mastery of their inner world and to understand their part in the conflict. This means resolving the inner conflict that caused the trigger response in the first place. It takes practice, but it can definitely be learned. Qigong master, Mantak Chia speaks a lot about the centre of gravity in his books, which are widely available.

The truth is, I had hints from my Dreamer that this was something that needed tending way before I even did the ceremony...

Jun 9, 2010

Forgave myself for the voices and for keeping all that anger inside me. Realized that that is what is held there in my abdomen–anger. Last night, I had a string of what I call "Fuck you" dreams. In one of them, a relative was telling me to help another clean up the dishes after dinner. I blew my top and threw the dishtowel at him, "Why don't *you* do it?" He was trying to calm me down and I yelled, "I am angry!" I don't know if I've ever said that out loud in waking hours. It felt really therapeutic in my dream. I've acknowledged to myself that I am angry or that I am feeling rage in certain moments (or periods) of my life but I don't think I've ever said it out loud. The anger is from years of being "good" to keep the approval of others at my own expense. I forgave myself for that. There were more "fuck you" dreams after but it's not really worth rehashing them all here. A victory is that I have a growing amount of strategies and I am not like that little girl in a white nightgown from my childhood nightmares who sat in the middle of an empty room holding her ears as a tornado of voices swirled around her giving her commands, yelling, and berating her. I have choices. And more than that, I am finally making choices now that are life-giving. Danced all that anger today. I called in my inner man and my warrior animal to help. Felt so good. Ended up dancing an improvised form with two guys. There are only two rules in this kind of dance, one of which is that you never hold onto someone's "landing gear" (i.e. hands or feet). Because each of us is responsible for our way to the ground, we need our limbs free. One of the guys kept grabbing my hand tight so that I was left in pretty precarious positions. I wrestled my hands free a few times and maneuvered myself into secure

positions. I never would have done that before. I would have just gone down. So my self-authority is returning.

I was terrified of what might be unleashed inside of me during the Monster of Anger Ceremony. I feared I would lose control of myself and harm others. This ceremony is an ancient way to heal dysfunctional anger patterns and so I placed my faith in the wisdom of the ancestors and the folks who had done this ceremony in the past in order to gain the courage to do it. The ceremony in its basic form entails gathering thick sticks from the forest floor, finding a dead tree, and hitting the tree with sticks, giving all the anger and the root causes of anger to the earth for recycling.

Once I started hitting the tree, all the pent up rage and fury started leaving my body. The force was so great that I was shaking. It was a primal experience through which I became aware of the various places in my past where my boundaries had been crossed. Far from being re-traumatizing, the knowledge was liberating to me. I was not crazy or unreasonable for feeling so much anger. More than that, I knew what boundaries I had to put in place from that day forward in order to stay in integrity with myself. I went through a huge pile of sticks in an hour and kept going until I felt spent. I slept for many hours, then, went out to do it again the next day.

Although it sounds like a simple ceremony, there really is no such thing; ceremonies are unpredictable by nature. It is important to make sure conditions and support systems are in place before attempting this ceremony yourself. It is for this reason that I highly recommend purchasing the book "Shamanic Ceremonies for a Changing World," which provides detailed instruction and support resources for this and many other personal ceremonies.

Shame of Addiction

....

"Shame derives its power from being unspeakable...If we cultivate enough awareness about shame to name it and speak to it, we've basically cut it off at the knees. Shame hates having words wrapped around it. If we speak shame, it begins to wither...[L]anguage and story bring light to shame and destroy it."

-Brené Brown from "Daring Greatly:
How the Courage to Be Vulnerable Transforms
the Way We Live, Love, Parent, and Lead"

Most addicts I've met carry deep shame around their inability to take command of their addictive patterns. They feel like they should know how to do this and they are ashamed of what they feel, what's happened to them, what they've done, and what they think. Shame is tricky. Shame told me that I must keep what I was feeling and thinking secret or else I would risk losing the approval of the ones I loved. Out of all the emotions I experienced at this time, shame was the most isolating, convincing me that I was unworthy, unintelligent, and unlovable. I believed that if I risked showing my true self, I would not find belonging anywhere. Of course, this really is just a big lie. Today, I know that shame is not my enemy; it was coming to the surface to give me a message: let go of that shit others heaped on you! I also was genuinely ashamed of certain decisions I'd made and that required me to find ways to forgive myself.

I was not aware of the full extent of how shame was impacting me during my addiction healing process. It wasn't until I read Dr.

Brené Brown's research years later after memories of sexual abuse came back that I began to crawl out of the pit of despair I felt inside on a daily basis. No matter how much personal work I did, that foreboding feeling that something was wrong with me just kept coming back. I had short reprieves but no lasting relief came. When I started to understand how shame is linked to sexual abuse, the puzzle pieces came together. I also saw that the cracks in my self-esteem and self-worth had already begun to appear before the sexual abuse happened.

Kids make the best decisions they can within the level of development they are in; sometimes, we come to funny conclusions about things as kids. Although keeping the abuse a secret seemed like a reasonable way to protect myself from the pain I imagined would happen if family members rejected or abandoned me if I told, it turned out to be a costly long-term strategy. I am not sure what would have changed had I not kept that secret. I don't know for sure if disclosing would have made my life easier or harder. What I *do* know is that taking my inner kid off the hook for making that choice was the key to letting go of the shame I felt inside. Today, I know that I am not responsible for what happened to me and that it says nothing about my true character.

In her book, "Daring Greatly," Dr. Brown talks about "shame spirals" feeling like building storms when something inside is triggered–an old memory, no matter how small or seemingly insignificant. I began to realize that those storms happened inside of me often and that they were, in fact, the root of that foreboding feeling I was experiencing. After reading her book, I started actively practicing speaking or writing about the shame spirals as I experienced them, sometimes in the form of power stories, and slowly, their grip on me started to fade. In fact, some of the impetus behind putting together the "Women's Power Stories" book came from this place of seeing that many women who shared their shame stories did not see the power in them because they were so caught up in the tragedy of what happened that they could not see the victory–and there is always personal power to be taken from any story.

This requires a deep trust in vulnerability, which Dr. Brown defines as: "uncertainty, risk, and emotional exposure." It took time for me to get used to the uncomfortable feelings that come with vulnerability and being honest with myself and others, yet in time, I learned that I could still rest in that space and trust its wisdom. Once I stopped treating my emotions as the enemy to be defeated at all costs and instead started listening to them as the messengers they truly are, life became easier. Brown also says: "It starts to make sense that we dismiss vulnerability as weakness only when we realize that we've confused *feeling* with *failing* and *emotions* with *liabilities*. If we want to reclaim the essential emotional part of our lives and reignite our passion and purpose, we have to learn how to own and engage with our vulnerability and how to feel the emotions that come with it." The only real failure is to give up on life and on ourselves.

During the course of an addiction, addicts don't always make decisions they are proud of. The impulse to soothe pain supersedes everything else. It's simply not a logical or measured state of mind. Healing requires us to move through the shame we feel around hurting people we love, stealing to feed our addictive impulses, and the financial and health messes we are left to deal with. There is no way forward but to clean up the disasters from our past day by day. This means taking full responsibility for all of our actions without inflicting further pain on ourselves. God knows that no addict needs to heap on more self-contempt–that is usually abundant!

In the course of my healing, I had to have vulnerable and tough conversations with people I love. For the first time, I had to be honest about how I was feeling and about the decisions I'd made. Sometimes, people didn't forgive me and I had to learn how to forgive myself anyway and move forward. Some people responded by attempting to shame me for my choices, the way I looked, and the way I lived. This was hard but it was also good practice at holding space for someone without taking on their baggage as if it had anything to do with me. And I also learned to live with the fact that my addiction cost other people precious life energy while they cared for me and cleaned up after my messes.

It was sobering to know I couldn't change the past but I could decide from that moment forward to take responsibility for myself in a way that was kind and compassionate. I learned to "be the person I needed when I was younger" (author unknown).

May 26, 2010

Last night I was so wracked with shame and guilt that I just lay there in bed overwhelmed. It occurred to me to put my hands on my heart and give myself some compassion. Slowly, the feelings eased. What came was that I had to repent. At first I thought it was to this friend that the conflict has been with. I asked for clarity from the dreamtime. When I awoke, I knew the repentance was for myself. It's not so much about the mistakes I make but how I treat myself on the inside. So I forgave myself for exiling myself. And for all the times I've turned into a puddle around something and instead of reaching my hands out to pick up and comfort that inner child, I've looked at her in disgust and given her one last kick before walking away. So food and body- just outer representations of what is really going on inside me. Crying as I ate breakfast this morning. I didn't know when I started how deep this all ran. I also realized that I am not sure I know where to begin. So some ideas that came were to put up a picture of myself in my room from when I was little to remind me to care for my inner kid. Another thing I realized is that I have spent a lot of my time developing compassion for others but have little for myself. That was my focus today. When I focused on compassion for myself, I had a lot more peace inside me–regardless of external situations.

Oct 10, 2010

Cunning was at work yesterday. The emptiness inside me just gets bigger the closer I get to moving to Calgary. With that comes increased cravings. I noticed last night at the theatre that I really wanted something sugary so I ended up eating popcorn for comfort but didn't curb that and I ended up eating lots and eating quick. Did some forgiveness. I feel ashamed of this drive inside me that I can't seem to control and how strong it is sometimes. It causes me to make choices that are not good for me. During some of the overwhelm yesterday, I e-mailed Ewan to ask if I could stay in his spare room the night I get to Calgary before my apartment becomes available. My rationale was: he is a few blocks away from my house and so it makes more sense to stay there than to take a 45 minute or more bus ride from my friend's. But this morning, I woke up from a dream that I had and knew that was a bad idea:

I was working in a bakery for the musician I went to watch last night at the theatre. He was impressed with my work and we got along well. I knew he was married but he seemed restless. He asked me at the end of a workday to have sex with him. He worked hard to convince me but I said no. So he went off to find someone else. I watched him seduce her in my dream. Later, I found him puking on the bathroom floor of the bakery after having too much to drink. I went to him and had an overwhelming urge to clean it up for him. Instead, I walked away knowing he had to clean up his own. Afterwards, I went back to the bakery and my family was in there baking Portuguese pastry. I sat at the table and ate bolas de Berlim and pastéis de nata and all the other sweet things I love. My family was happy but in my dream, I remember feeling disappointed in myself. There was no way to con myself out of it.

There are places inside me that are negotiable. I can feel them and I know some of them but not all of them yet. Those are places where I am likely not to choose my healing first. A part of me is scared to unpack those because I don't want to deal with what I find. I don't know what I am capable of or how much I can take; I guess I will find out, though. I keep connecting to the place inside of me that wants to heal, asking my healing animal and warrior animal to help.

159

Compassion

....

From the article "The Wondrous Path of Difficulties"

"Jack Kornfield: One of the great Buddhist teachings—it's a type of medicine, you might say—is to remind ourselves, and others, that we all have a great capacity of heart. We have within us Buddha nature, the capacity to hold all the sorrows and joys of the world. An aspect of our great openness is our ability to tolerate suffering... You have to include yourself in compassion, not just everybody else.

Pema Chödrön: Compassion toward yourself is something worth exploring more. In teaching Buddhism in the West, one of the first things that all of us as Western dharma teachers realized very early on was that most people we were teaching were really hard on themselves. Without self-compassion or some kind of loving-kindness toward oneself, nothing is ever going to happen on the spiritual path."

"If your compassion does not include yourself, it is incomplete."

-Buddha

I am still developing compassion for myself. Compassion for others has always been easy for me. In fact, as a teacher, compassion is a strength of mine and one of the reasons I can be effective with children. With children, I have no problem keeping my eye on the essence of their spirits even when they are acting in ways that are less than lovable. At the same time, my own inner kid was locked up in a jail inside of me with no light or nourishment. When this image first came to me upon seeking to form a relationship with my inner kid, I felt frozen, guilty, and shameful all at the same time: How could I be doing that to myself?

Because I had no idea how to have compassion for myself, I started seeking image-makers in the spirit world and in the human world to work with energetically. One goddess that I found immediate resonance with was Kwan Yin:

> *Kwan Yin is the East Asian bodhisattva of compassion. Although her origin is Sanskrit, she is now mostly associated with Buddhist practices. In the Buddhist tradition, a bodhisattva is a spirit who has gained enlightenment but chooses to devote him- or herself to service on earth rather than ascend into the spirit realms for eternity. Until all humans have become illumined, they will remain in this dimension. Kwan Yin tends to the suffering of the world with compassion and equanimity... As a motherly figure, Kwan Yin pays special attention to the suffering and pain of children. She is often seen flanked by two children who represent her earliest dharma students. Dharma is alignment with the divine laws of the universe; learning to work within these laws is the key to enlightenment. Kwan Yin supports all who call upon her to free themselves of their karma. Kwan Yin will teach the dharma to all who are sincere of heart but she is known to put people through challenges first to test their resolve... Kwan Yin is a shapeshifter who appears in any state necessary to free her students from ignorance.*
> *- Jennifer Engrácio and Carell Mehl from "Women's Power Stories: Honouring the Feminine Principle of Life"*

One of the patterns I started to notice when I monitored the self-talk of cruelty inside of me was that the voices were familiar. Many of them did not originate with me; they belonged to people in my past (family members, friends, mentors, and lovers). In some cases, I remembered the exact conversations where the words were spoken. I started to see how I was keeping the pain of those memories alive by continuing to speak to myself in that way. I had taken on the role of re-traumatizing myself daily, however unconsciously, even though the original trauma was in the past and many of those people were no longer in my life.

Dharma is really about making a conscious choice to step away from the effects of the past karma incurred in relationships. It's about awakening to our part in keeping alive the pains of the past and taking an active role in cutting away from these karmic attachments that keep us wrapped up in playing out past pain tapes in cycles. This is an area where shamanic medicine really shines because it is we who keep these very real energetic cords active and it is only we as individuals who have the power to break them and say, "No more."

The process of karmic tie cutting involves tracing back the voices and patterns to the original source and consciously identifying the unhealthy patterns we have chosen to continue with those people. I made a list of all the people I had unhealthy patterns with that included family members, friends, lovers, colleagues, and mentors and one by one evaluated my relationships with each. Some examples of patterns I went after include: seeking approval from others, allowing others to dictate the direction of my life, giving away my power to others, dominating others, and over-helping in order to feel useful at the expense of disempowering others. Of course, there are always light patterns based in unconditional love that I would never break with those people; I cherish those and always will. It was necessary to cut the negative energetic ties in order for me to regain the energy that is naturally lost to upholding these patterns. With this energy, I was able to rebuild my life in alignment with my own internal compass.

It should be said that this process took years. I had to clear with one person first completely and then move onto the next. This was emotionally draining and enlightening at the same time to see the responsibility I held in these relationships. In some, I was acting the part of the victim, giving away my power and then complaining that others were using me as a doormat. In others, I was acting as the rescuer so that my ego would get a boost while the people I was in relationship with became more disempowered. Yet in others, I was the persecutor punishing others for perceived or real transgressions. Sometimes, I played all these roles (described in the Karpman Triangle) in one relationship. I still encounter people that I have obvious karma with. Now, I hunt down the negative patterns and cut from them right away.

There is a period of rough seas once the patterns are cut where relationships go through challenges as both people learn to adjust to the new way of being. I didn't tell folks that I was doing this ceremony with them. I just did my part, knowing that is all I really have control over. Some of these relationships fell away naturally because there was no way to keep engaging in a healthy manner. Others deepened and strengthened as a result. Still others continued on in a neutral way with relationships morphing more into an "agree to disagree" sort of way of being with one another. For me, this latter one was especially true for blood family members where mutual respect was won mostly through honouring the very real differences between members.

Aug 26, 2010

Cravings are back strong. I guess it is not surprising considering the fact that I am now officially standing in the unknown after telling my family I am moving–no comfort here. And then there is this big hole that seems empty in my chest where I used to feel something, like a vacuum. I know it is just new space that has opened up and it feels awful. Been having conversations with the moon. She said, "If you want to fill it up so bad, fill it with love and compassion for yourself." So focusing on that keeps me out of panic and away from comfort food. And so here I am new and having to get to know myself all over again.

All of this left me with a sense of spaciousness where I was able to increasingly connect to who I really was at my core, what mattered to me, and where I wanted to go in my life. Today, I still don't make perfect choices. Depending on the day and the state I find myself in, some decisions are better than others. Connecting with Kwan Yin and the energy of self-compassion on hard days is ongoing work that I will keep doing until I draw my last breath. I've come to grips with the truth that as a child of Spirit living in a human body on a human plane, I am perfectly imperfect. And so are we all. Knowing we are all in the throes of this great struggle helps me to give myself some breathing room. I don't have to do everything well all the time in order to give myself loving kindness. In fact, when I fall short, it's when I need it the most.

Dr. Kristin Neff has made the study of self-compassion her life's work. Her site is filled with free exercises, resources, and practices that folks can learn to integrate into daily living that really make a difference. Some of my favourites are the meditations that bring us back to ourselves when we feel overwhelmed or lost. This quote from Neff's site says it all:

> *"Instead of mercilessly judging and criticizing yourself for various inadequacies or shortcomings, self-compassion means you are kind and understanding when confronted with personal failings – after all, who ever said you were supposed to be perfect? You may try to change in ways that allow you to be more healthy and happy, but this is done because you care about yourself, not because you are worthless or unacceptable as you are. Perhaps most importantly, having compassion for yourself means that you honor and accept your humanness. Things will not always go the way you want them to. You will encounter frustrations, losses will occur, you will make mistakes, bump up against your limitations, fall short of your ideals. This is the human condition, a reality shared by all of us. The more you open your heart to this reality instead of constantly fighting against it, the more you will be able to feel compassion for yourself and all your fellow humans in the experience of life."*

Cultivating Joy

....

"To let ourselves sink into the joyful moments of our lives even though we know they are fleeting, even though the world tells us not to be too happy lest we invite disaster–that's an intense form of vulnerability."

-Brené Brown from "Daring Greatly:
How the Courage to Be Vulnerable Transforms
the Way We Live, Love, Parent, and Lead"

As someone who grew up amongst folks who survived a Portuguese dictatorship under António de Oliveira Salazar, living in the state of waiting for the other shoe to drop was commonplace. Salazar controlled the people the way most dictators do: using secret police, taking people away from their communities, and encouraging neighbours to "out" each other for being disloyal to the state. The economy was tightly controlled and the people lived in poverty off government rations in constant states of scarcity and fear. In the 1960s, he led Portuguese citizens into brutal wars in the African colonies in an effort to hold onto them politically. Many people came back from those wars in varied states of Post Traumatic Stress Disorder with entrenched addictions to substances that numbed pain. Understandably, joy was not something I saw modeled growing up too much. I had to learn it–or rather, allow it to unfold in my life.

I remember naturally feeling joy as a kid whenever I was up in the cedar tree outside my house, colouring in books, making art, or when I was singing in choirs. Engaging in activities that are meditative and creative by their very nature always worked to take me out of the anxiety of living in the future and the horrible things that might befall me. On my addiction healing journey, my healing animal (the elephant), showed me all of the times it had been with me in my childhood to remind me to stay present in the flow of life. When I was ten, my art teacher gave us the assignment to make something out of papier mâché. I remember looking up at the ceiling and seeing an elephant in my mind's eye. I can still feel how absorbed in the present moment I was making that elephant. Today that piece of art is in my bedroom to remind me that joy is available to me in the moment when I choose to enter into the creative flow of the universe.

> *"Joy is different from happiness in that it is deeper and larger somehow. It is closer in its essence to contentment, but instead of coming forth after an achievement, joy seems to come forth during moments of communion with nature, love, and beauty–when you feel as if you're one with everything."*
> *-Karla McLaren from "The Language of Emotions: What your Feelings are Trying to Tell You"*

I used to think that joy was a state that I could and should maintain at all times if I were to live a truly happy life. Today, I know that this is a persistent illusion and I am naturally skeptical of anyone who claims to be able to blow rainbows out of their asses continuously. That may sound jaded or harsh, however, I feel that we do ourselves a disservice when we hold this up as the ultimate goal in life. Chasing one emotion at the exclusion of the rest is a dangerous, lonely, and isolating venture because it prevents us from being with our emotions as they naturally occur.

This inability to be intimate and present with ourselves is at the root of all addictions. This robs us of our humanity and the ability to experience the range of what it means to be human. Gaining mastery in life requires us to know how to navigate and understand what our emotions are telling us. We can only do that if we get to know all the emotions and if we are willing to let all of them go when we've learned the lessons they bring. Emotions are meant to flow, not stay stuck or suspended inside of us. Eventually, all dams break if the force of water is great enough. Holding on to joy, sadness, or any other emotion is not a wise way to live.

One day, Wolf Woman asked me what got me up out of bed every morning. "What do you live for?" she asked. I got teary and I said simply, "Beauty. I live for the beauty I create but also to experience the beauty that's all around me when I pay attention to it." Years ago, I watched a film called "Scared Sacred" made by director Velcrow Ripper. Ripper visited several "ground zeros" around the world that were still reeling from devastating human-created destruction. He interviewed people who had lived through these events and juxtaposed their pain against the absolute natural beauty they lived in. What struck me the most were the vivid colours and textures of the cinematography. If beauty is all around us, why do we as humans choose to put our attention on everything we feel is "wrong" with life, trying to control its natural flow? We are so scared of truly living that we forget that life is inherently sacred as it is.

> *"[J]oy...arises naturally when you've done honest and strenuous work to arrive at a place of communion with all parts of yourself and the world."*
> *-Karla McLaren from "The Language of Emotions: What your Feelings are Trying to Tell You"*

After years of engaging in ceremony and healing work, I started to feel joy more regularly. This was not something I could manufacture or create at will, but something that arose in moments when I was truly present to beauty. Going after all the places within myself where I was at war with life on a regular basis started to change my inner landscape. I regained the connection with myself that I'd lost in childhood and I started to feel more unity with other humans. Joy started to arise when I was truly able to be present with another person–even in moments of suffering. This was perplexing at first until I realized that being present with suffering eventually leads to the truth: that we are always connected to all of life. Remembering that is the key to joy.

As much as I pray that the human species will evolve past suffering one day, for today, it's part of our reality. So is joy. I cultivate joy in my life by regularly and consciously engaging in things that put me in creative flow: nature walks, playing with children, dancing, singing, drumming, physical affection, writing, reading, learning new things, heart to heart communication with others, ceremony, teaching what I've learned, prayer, meditation, and experiencing the creative works of others. Recognizing beauty is a practice and a choice each of us can make a commitment to. We can do this most easily when we do not deny or stuff the suffering but rather allow it to move out of us wherever we find it. In this way, we keep our connection to Spirit clear and strong. Of course, the things that bring out joy in you may be different. I ask you these questions: What gets you up out of bed every morning? What do you live for?

Chapter 5

THE SOUTH WEST

South West Introduction:
Listening to the Dreamer

··

"Dreaming requires courage. You need to admit to any self-fulfilling prophecies of victimhood that you've created or bought into, let go of them and write something better."
- Alberto Villoldo from "Courageous Dreaming:
How Shamans Dream the World into Being"

I wrote this short story that follows. It is called "Mother Mary Comes to Me" and originally appeared in the book "Women's Power Stories: Honouring the Feminine Principle of Life" edited by Carell Mehl and myself.

Since I was really little, I remember feeling an attraction to the spiritual aspect of life. The first song I learned was the "Avé Maria" in Portuguese. Although my parents were somewhat lapsed Catholics, they supported my desire to go to church on Sundays by allowing me to go with my grandmother (Avó Maria)–a devout Catholic. I loved the ritual of mass, the prayer, and the songs. I remember sleeping in my dad's old bedroom at my Avó's house and praying to Santa Maria and Jesus when I needed direction in my life. From a very young age, I always received an answer and I always felt better after a praying and listening session. Mary was not the self-sacrificing, pitiful, weak woman that the church made her out to be. Rather, I experienced her as a powerful, compassionate, and balanced spirit who knew the wisdom of following God and surrendering...

In my twenties, I began exploring other spiritual systems. After searching, I finally found a path with heart that I could follow. Shamanism was natural to me. I'd always prayed, connected to nature spirits, listened to my dream... guidance from the spirit world, and found peace in solitude. There was no dogma to follow and I could pray directly to Great Spirit without an intermediary. My way of being with God and the value I placed on the spiritual aspect of myself were validated at long last.

I have no interest in converting anyone to anything. When I look back, I see how personal the spiritual journey is for each person I've met. And I am so thankful to my parents and Avó for supporting me when I was young in finding my own way... When I go on shamanic journeys, Mary and Jesus still come to me speaking their words of wisdom and letting me know they are always with me to guide and protect me. They remind me that being authentically who I am is enough.

It was by practicing and studying shamanism that I learned to hear and identify the true voice of my own spirit, also called "Dreamer" or "Higher Self." Through journeys, I met this luminous being and got to know her more intimately throughout the years. At first, I found it hard to believe that there was a part of me that could never be broken, hurt, screwed up, or depressed. I had the tendency to see her at first as something other than me–the way I saw Jesus or Mary as enlightened prophets. Her benevolence, beauty, and compassion bowled me over time and time again. You see, shamanic cultures have always known that there is a part of our beings that is pure spirit and they trained people to tap into the wisdom of the dreamer within. Our Dreamers know what our life purpose is in this lifetime and are the only ones who can guide us perfectly on our journey in order to accomplish our purpose.

At first, I had a lot of resistance to the idea that there is a part of me who absolutely knows what I am meant to be doing, how to do it, and how to accomplish it. I would follow my ego's idea of what I should be doing and totally neglect to consult with my

Dreamer to see if this plan of mine was even worthwhile. I learned the hard way that refusing to go in the direction that my Dreamer was sending me in was counterproductive and often painful. When I didn't listen, I had a lot of messes to clean up in my life that took energy away from living my dreams.

The following chapter is all about the energy of the South West of the medicine wheel, which is the place of our personal and collective dreaming. Shamanic cultures have always known that we are intimately and spiritually connected to the dreaming of the planet and to life's creations on earth. Nothing can break that connection and so it is to our benefit to learn to align with that stream of energy in order to create the lives we want for ourselves instead of giving our power away to others' ideas of what we should be doing with our time here on Earth. In the following pages, I describe how I worked with my Dreamer and how I learned to interpret her messages in order to heal myself.

In order to consolidate your understanding of this direction from your personal, experiential and embodied perspective, I recommend doing the following ceremonies from "Shamanic Ceremonies for a Changing World" by Marilyn Keffer and Gael Carter. You can find more information on how to purchase a copy by looking at the Recommended Resources section of the Appendix of this book.

Meeting your Dreamer Ceremony 2-1
The Warrior's Act of Dreaming Ritual 1-1

Moving to Calgary

....

"To understand that life is a wise teacher willing to show us our higher self, revolutionizes how we live...We see life as trustworthy, here to usher us into a deeper self-connection. We also know it's inherently good, a mirror of our own internal state of goodness. This approach recognizes that we are fundamentally interconnected to all that happens in our life, so that we are co-creators of the reality in which we live. Life doesn't happen to us, but happens with us."
-Shefali Tsabary from "The Conscious Parent"

The truth is that I didn't set out to make Calgary my new home. If I am honest, I knew in 2000 after living in Scotland to finish my undergrad degree that my time in Vancouver was coming to an end. But how does one leave one's family, friends, and the place one grew up in? It was the classic dilemma between ego and Dreamer. I knew eventually that my Dreamer would have to win in order for me to truly live my life's purpose. This could simply not happen if I stayed in the place I was most comfortable in.

I was visiting friends in Calgary at the end of June 2010 when I found myself dreaming into the landscape of the prairies. I clearly remember standing outside a restaurant by an evergreen tree waiting for my friends to come out when the tree started speaking to me. This might sound like a strange thing for folks who are not accustomed to listening to the natural world this deeply, but to a shamanic practitioner, it is a regular part of life that we choose to engage with in order to hear the truth of who we are and to meet life more fully. Everything in nature has its own consciousness that we can learn to tap into. The tree said, "You belong here. You are needed here. The nature spirits welcome you." Immediately, my gut instinct knew she was right. I felt frozen and excited all at the same time.

Jun 28, 2010

Wolf Woman, I thought it pertinent to let you know that I have decided to move to Calgary as of Oct 31, 2010. I have been feeling a pull away from here for many years now and Spirit has told me that my time in Vancouver is over. After talking to friends in Calgary, it seems that my leadership is welcomed and needed there and I am happy to serve in that way.

When I got back to Vancouver, I started plotting my plan of action. I came up with a date to move, and I followed my Dreamer's lead in how to execute this dream. Indeed, I did move to Calgary four months later. I purged a lot of my belongings, hired movers, and left my old life behind me. Telling my family was probably one of the hardest things I've ever done.

You see, Portuguese families are generally a tightly woven group that extend membership even to folks who are not blood relatives. Along with all my blood relatives, Vancouver was home to lifelong friends and extended family members. I was the first person in a long time to move away from that fabric; this scared me and it is safe to say that it was super hard for them too. My relatives went through the range of emotions and so I practiced holding space for that while remaining firm in following my journey where it was leading me. Not all the interactions were smooth so I had to stay on my surfboard during rough seas for a while. Family is everything in Portuguese culture and I felt like I was betraying them by leaving. One thing about me is that I have a loyal heart so this decision tore me up inside. Still, it was the right decision to make. The right decision is rarely comfy on all levels.

I learned that sometimes, life gives us choices like that where neither of the options is easy, but we still have to choose. If I stayed, I would have been betraying myself and because I have to be able to look at myself in the mirror everyday for the rest of my life, I had to make the choice to do the thing that would be most life-giving for *me*. Far from being a selfish act, I realized that if I stayed, I would also be betraying the gifts that Spirit gave me. I saw the bigger picture connected to these gifts and knew that I had to start taking them out into the wider world.

Co-creating with Spirit

....

"Intuition is not a single way of knowing–it's our ability to hold space for uncertainty and our willingness to trust the many ways we've developed knowledge and insight, including instinct, experience, faith, and reason."
-Dr. Brené Brown from "The Gifts of Imperfection"

Shamanic practitioners the world over know that there is a matrix of creation that infuses all of life. We humans can tap into it for guidance and wisdom if we choose. When I connect with it, it looks to me like a spider web weaving all of creation together in an energetic fabric that forms a tapestry. I remember the first time I saw this with my own eyes. Near the beginning of my shamanic studies, I participated in an ayahuasca ceremony with an ayahuascero (ayahuasca shaman ceremonialist).

Ayahuasca is a sacred plant of the Amazon that ayahuasceros call "the vine of death." It is called this because it supports the transformation of all that is untrue inside of ourselves in the particular ways we have each created our inner worlds. For centuries, this plant has been used in ceremony by the tribes of the Amazon rainforest to support people in connecting with their Dreamer and with this fabric of creation often referred to in aboriginal traditions of North America as Great Spirit. Other faiths call the matrix by other names: God, Allah, the Divine, Yahweh, the Source, the Goddess, and so on.

I've sensed this web with my intuition my whole life but my mind had done a good job of creating serious doubts around what

I was experiencing. I have never experienced such fear before a ceremony before–or since. I now know the fear was simply my ego's grip tightening because it knew some lies were going to be revealed, thereby lessening its power over me. The ceremony itself was beautiful and powerful. The icaros (medicine songs) that are sung during the ceremony sent me to a place deep inside that I'd forgotten. The ayahuasca spirit sent me on a journey of seeing what was really real and helped me to peel away layers of falsehood I had bought into and built up around myself as forms of protection in a world that largely believes that Spirit does not exist.

Part way through the ceremony, I began seeing bright lines of light appearing all around the room. They were strangely familiar to me though I couldn't place where I had seen them before. I noticed that the lines were connected to every living thing in the space –including the plants and the crystals. Everything with consciousness in the room was infused with the energy of the matrix. I traced those lines back to myself and I was shocked to see my luminous egg stretch in front of me. I put out my hands and watched this energy expand outwards. The auric field was a real thing! I don't know how long I watched all of this in awe, but when I came out of that ceremony, I was never the same in the best way possible.

Many years later, I was holding a swath of fabric made by Peruvian artisans and I recognized the matrix pattern I saw in their designs! I won't say that it was an easy ceremony for me. It was probably the hardest one I've ever done and I wouldn't recommend it to anyone who is simply "curious" about plant medicine. I learned the power of going into ceremony with a strong healing intention for myself. Though I got exactly what I needed, that might not have been the case if I hadn't been in such a strong circle of support with honourable and experienced people leading the ceremony. This really was an initiation into living a life committed to being in the stream of Spirit instead of separated from it.

As I went back into my everyday life, I began seeing how often I slip out of that stream and go back into "Muggledom." "Muggle" is a term from the book series "Harry Potter" that refers to those who don't believe in magic. My journey with shamanism has been all about learning how to co-create with Spirit from the magic and connection I feel with every fiber of my being. In a world that does not respect the spiritual aspects of life, this is a daily challenge in some ways. As someone living in an urban setting, I stay connected by getting out into nature every day. I pray. I attend group ceremonies. I work my medicine tools and practices. I ask for guidance. I listen to what I hear deep inside myself. Then, I put this wisdom into action in my everyday life.

Not listening has cost me a lot of heartache and pain in life. On the contrary, deep listening has opened up worlds of limitless possibility that have forced me to dance along the edges of who I think I am and what I think I can do. Though listening has its own challenges, in my view, it is definitely the easier way to go with the potential of fewer messes to clean up along the way. Since I began listening, I am able to support myself through mistakes more easily. I am more willing to let go of lies about who I am and what I am capable of. I am able to be neutral with other peoples' energy and just be in the moment as it is. I can see more clearly what my role is in events and can shift into more positive ways of interacting with others, the Earth, and the world. I can more clearly see the lies in a culture that tries to suck the power of Spirit out of us daily.

Sep 18, 2010

The other day when I was on the massage table I realized there was a lot of energetic "stuff" I was carrying for others. Didn't know what to do with that so I just left it. I had a dream last night where I was traveling but always late because I had to pack up this massive amount of shit. A cat came to play with me at one point (something I normally welcome and engage with) and I shooed it away because I had to pack. So when I woke up, I looked at my nightstand and saw my ceremonial knife and my rose quartz crystal from my altar this summer. I was guided to use these to cut away that excess baggage that was not mine and send it up to Spirit so it would be taken care

of in a good way. I am discovering ways I have been/am naïve around certain things. For example, trusting that other people will treat me the way I treat them. That naïveté is partly what has gotten me in trouble this past year. It is almost like a way that I want so much to believe in the goodness of folks that I dismiss my intuition and don't always see the shadow aspects that are working in that person. So yeah–learning to trust that niggly bit of my intuition is a big lesson lately.

Dec 20, 2010

My intent for today was to co-create with Spirit. I ended up having a pretty magical day–pulled another song and found some crystals I'd been looking for at a good price. Nothing went as I "thought" it should go and yet I found myself navigating around obstacles to accomplish my goals. So learning that it is okay if things are not working the way I think they should go–there is often a better way is what Spirit seems to be telling me. I had so much resistance to the financial learning thinking it would take away from my creativity and things I like to do. Now I see how it can actually bring more freedom. That is a new way of seeing for me. Also finding it interesting how the healing work I am doing on my body, food and with myself is leaking into these other tonal (physical life) areas and shining a spotlight on what needs to be worked at.

Healing in the Dreamtime

"Dreaming is an action that harnesses the powers of imagination, love, interconnection, intuition, and Spirit in order to literally re-order the inner reality needed to manifest the outer reality we want to live in. We are always dreaming, whether awake or asleep."

- Jennifer Engrácio

An essential part of my journey was very much about acquiring new strategies for working with pain, discomfort, hurt, anger, and anxiety. These were all the feelings I was trying to self-medicate. I did not want to acknowledge them and the thought of asking these feelings what they were trying to teach me was unfathomable. I simply wanted them to go away–magically. What I learned was that, ultimately, the only way to release the pain was to face it and treat it as a teacher. I also discovered that there are a variety of indigenous technologies which I refer to as "shamanic tools" that are brilliant at supporting the process of personal transformation and release of pain and trauma. I learned these tools with the support of my teachers and applied them in order to heal myself. I honestly thought at the beginning that it would be people from the outside healing me. Instead, my support team witnessed, asked questions, made suggestions, and taught me strategies so I could learn to heal myself.

One of the pieces of wisdom I discovered is that aboriginal people the world over consider the dreamtime the "real" time. When we are asleep, we are not necessarily unconscious. It is a time when our egos cannot interfere with the information we get from the spirit world and our own Dreamers. The information, though cryptic at times, is more reliable in some ways than information we receive in our waking dreams. Daydreaming with a purpose in waking hours is considered a wise use of time and attention in many aboriginal cultures. It is a direct way of connecting with the fabric of the universe to glean knowledge and wisdom contained there. We can train ourselves to dream in waking hours via meditation, thereby learning to neutralize the ego through regular practice.

My teachers taught me the power of dreaming and using it intentionally. During a drum journey, I set up a medicine wheel in the nagual. This is now a safe space I can go to at any time to do healing work and speak to my Dreamer. In addition, I began making dream intents before bed and upon waking that gave me direction from my Dreamer and brought more cohesiveness to my life as a whole.

The following journal entries offer a window into how I used the tool of creating a dream intent each night before sleeping to mine information about what needed to heal and how to go about it in waking hours. As you can see, the waking hours also reflected part of my dreaming from the night before in a type of infinity loop of information I used to track my healing path and follow it.

May 21, 2010

I had a dream last night that an ex-boyfriend knocked on my door after a few years of not seeing each other. When he saw me, he was pleased that I was bigger (he always said he liked more "voluptuous" women). I told him that I was working on food addiction and he scoffed at that. He went in and out of wanting to be around me in the dream. Although I was saddened by his response, I was pretty committed and resolute in my dream about healing this piece. I woke up feeling pretty hopeful. In the past, what a lover thought of my body would derail me. I've never had boyfriends that had issue with my body; they all loved it. However, that would also keep me in a cycle of addiction so I would not lose their love and affection. Forgave myself for that. I now know that my commitment to myself is the most important thing. Working on the self-love.

May 23, 1010

Had dreams of my inner man last night. Unlike other times I've dreamed of him, we were cohabitating in a harmonious way in my dream. When I woke, I decided to bring him into my nagual medicine wheel and ask for his help on this journey with food addiction. Here's what he said, "Clean up your nagual space. No more bringing other people here for conversations with their spirits. I will be ruthless with your cunning. You need to 'dance' me for the next two weeks to really know me and to get me into your body. Call on me for help with nagual discipline." So that's a piece I didn't have before. Called on my inner man during mirror exercise. He told me to forgive myself for not being a warrior on the inside. So I did. There was a distinctive shift in how I felt in my body when I did that. Like strength and vitality returned.

Sep 8, 2010

I dreamed I was in a cathedral that I was once in long ago. My family members left the church after taking all their potatoes and onions from their fields back home. It felt like a reclaiming of some fruits that were lost to us somehow. I, on the other hand, took stone effigies of angels, children, and Mother Mary. There was a feeling like I knew what to do with the objects–that they had some magical purpose. It felt like a confirmation of my move to Calgary and that everything was going to be okay. Also been seeing how I have linked sex with men with my self-worth or worthiness; this has been a pattern in previous relationships too. During a meditation, I got an image of a small me in a cave shivering and flinching.

I had a conversation with her and told her that I couldn't pull her out of there; she had to come of her own accord. That she was not a victim–she consented to being in there. So she came out. During dance tonight, I recommitted to my healing. Been floundering lately.

Dec 30, 2010

Woke up suddenly from an uncomfortable dream last night. I've never had a dream about a sweatlodge ceremony before and this one seemed real in a way. You were there but you weren't leading the sweat; you were congratulating me on all the changes I'd made. I hesitated to go into the lodge. The energy felt off in there. I went in, started a song and then ended up coming out. While outside, you said, "Well done with healing the family piece." In my dream, I called back those entities that weren't serving me in that past situation. I pulled a woman's body off the top of the lodge that I realized was the former me and I started fighting with her. I forced myself awake because I didn't like where the dream was going. I called my energy back from that dream and realized that it was just my fears of transforming. Talked to Spirit and pledged to keep transforming anyway.

Feb 8, 2011

I dreamed last night that I was covered in shit. I was walking in it and it was in my mouth. I've had similar dreams before in relation to family members. A First Nations' elder I worked with in Vancouver told me that to coastal peoples, when people have dreams like that, it means someone is dumping their anger on them. Last night, I danced my feminine again and I remembered that part of me. What a relief! The theme was welcoming the Chinese New Year of the Golden Rabbit and what comes with it: beauty, feminine energy, and the moon. On my walk home, I saw a white rabbit sitting in the snow. It did not move. It was looking straight at me. I've never seen these in the city before and in the last week when I've gone out for walks at night, I've seen 4 of them, perfectly white. You and Tiger's Breath were both in my dream. Tiger's Breath told me to "Call out the bullshit–don't put up with it." I will take that advice.

Practicing Gratitude

"We notice that joyful people are grateful and suppose that they are grateful for their joy. But the reverse is true: their joy springs from gratefulness. If one has all the good luck in the world, but takes it for granted, it will not give one joy. Yet even bad luck will give joy to those who manage to be grateful for it. We hold the key to lasting happiness in our own hands. For it is not joy that makes us grateful; it is gratitude that makes us joyful."

-Brother David Steindl-Rast
from "Gratefulness, The Heart of Prayer"

If you had told me at the beginning of my healing journey that I would be grateful for the challenges on my path, I would have either rolled my eyes at you or attempted to kill you with a glare. I had gone through most of my life just trying to survive the day. Perhaps gratitude comes naturally for some people, but for me, it was a daily practice. I was brought up to look for danger around every corner and it took a while for me to learn to relax into life.

We all go through traumas in life, however great or small. Even the rites of passage we all must go through have their little or big deaths inherent in them: birth, puberty, and elderhood, to name a few. It's not the traumas we go through that define us but how we work with pain as a life teacher. The truth for me was that I was so caught up in cycling around in past trauma that I had no time for seeing the positive spiritual aspects that were being forged within me. I have compassion for that person I was because I didn't know another way to deal with that pattern back then. It wasn't until a certain amount of baseline healing had been done all the way through to completion that I began to see life more clearly.

As the storms inside me began to pass, I started giving gratitude for things I'd taken for granted would always be there: the rising sun, clean water, the earth, food on my table, a warm place to sleep, my body, and clothing. Without these things, I simply could not survive at all and yet they had been there when I was going through my darkest times; I just didn't have my attention on the positive that was all around me. I was scared that if I relaxed my guard, I would be harmed. Being grateful for blessings seemed like a liability when I was in this frame of mind.

Don't get me wrong: I wouldn't wish some of the traumatic experiences I've had on anyone. Gratitude is not about painting a rosy picture that covers up the real injustices in the world. Rather, it is a practice of being thankful down to our bones for all of the experiences in life and the way they have of supporting the building of our characters and shaping our journeys–knowing there is a part of us strong enough to survive and thrive through it all. This requires trust in life's wisdom. Being real with the issues at hand while still seeing the beauty in life is what hope means to me. Without hope, we really are doomed! Hope and gratitude keep us going in rough times. They gently point our inner compasses to true north so we don't lose our purpose in life.

As I did my spiritual healing work, natural gratitude began to spring up inside of me. I still had to be mindful of practicing gratitude but it also began to solidify as a way of being inside of me over time. Even today when I find myself slipping into a negative frame of mind, I can redirect my mental obsessions by focusing on all the things I am grateful for in that moment. Dr. Brené Brown says that this is an inherent quality of what she calls "wholehearted" people. It's not that wholehearted people don't face adversity. We all do. They just have a very different take on how to move through it than someone who focuses on the doom and gloom of it all.

I share these following passages from my journal at the time to illustrate how I was able to find gratitude in some of the most challenging situations. Trusting my Dreamer and the flow of life to guide me were integral portals to gratitude, and therefore greater joy.

Dec 29, 2010

Felt really powerful in myself today as if I have stepped into integrity with myself in a new way. I feel now that I am just who I am. Somehow, being away from Vancouver has helped me to blossom into and stand in that. The funny thing too is that a lot of the energetics and relationship dynamics between my friends and I here in Calgary closely mimic those I have with my extended family. It has been really neat to re-write how I work with those energetics without the attachments I have with family–a whole new world of just being straightforward. And it is also changing the way I relate and talk to my family on the phone too. I'm glad I moved here and I am starting to see the wisdom of my Dreamer.

Jan 4, 2011

Also noticing feelings of loneliness diminishing. Maybe it is because now that I am settled, I re-aligned with why I moved here. I like that things drop in during the day and I can tend to them on Spirit's timing. I am grateful I dreamed in this flexible job all those years ago! Don't know if I could have done all the healing in such a short time if I hadn't.

Jan 15 and 16, 2011

I am still a little stunned at how much stuff I seem to be doing without hesitation. After I get the okay from Spirit, off I go. Needless to say, when I completed my reiki course, my Dreamer was bouncing up and down happy. Maybe she was surprised I actually did it! I just felt a tremendous amount of gratitude and humility thorough that process. I am grateful for that tool and for the shamanic ones. I never thought I'd be living a life like this. It fits so well with my heart and spirit. Joyful and humble today.

Jan 18, 2011

Had an overwhelming feeling today to just give up on lots of fronts. So I knew something was up because I love all the things I was going to give up on. I sat with that feeling throughout the day as I did other things. As I sat in the bath tonight, I realized that I asked Spirit to keep me humble a while back and that is what is happening. I notice my tendency to go into self-importance in some instances where I feel my own knowing being called into question. Spirit is teaching me the places where I do not have enough experience or knowledge to proceed on my own. So humility. And it is hard to be brought down to earth when a part of me is already in the dream of it. Giving gratitude for that gift from Spirit while also doing mucho forgiveness. God it is not pretty to look at myself this close up!

Jan 28, 2011

Bumping up against self-importance lately. There have been lots of victories in the last while and I can't believe I've accomplished some of the things I have. I never imagined I would ever have the courage to move away from my family, write a book, date someone so much older than me, or pursue my sacred dream. And I am reminded to remain humble and grateful because I know I didn't do it alone. I've had lots of help along the way.

Feb 11, 2011

I was pretty exhausted today and yet called my warrior animal to help me through the day. Went for a walk in between appointments and working and that helped. The smell of the ocean and the cedars brought tears to my eyes- never realized how much I missed it. Sending up big gratitude for the shifts as of late with my family. I don't really know what to make of this whole thing. Just grateful.

Chapter 6

THE SOUTH EAST

South East Introduction: Righting Self Concepts

"Shadow work means actively working with and embracing all parts of ourselves that are not pretty, not acceptable, and not liked by others...[A] huge amount of life force is locked away in those parts of ourselves we deny and divorce, as it were...And we don't lock away only the so-called bad things, usually we also hide talents...we are not ready to own for some reason."
- Imelda Almqvist from "Natural Born Shamans"

I want to preface the beginning of this chapter by saying that although the environment we grow up in shapes our first beliefs about ourselves, this does not mean that those are carved in stone forever and ever amen. If it were true that we could not change the way we see ourselves as human beings, then no one who had ever gone through any kind of trauma would ever heal. There are enough examples of inspiring people who have done just that in the world for us to know transformation is possible. One such person that comes to mind is Oprah Winfrey. I remember watching her show in 1986 one day when I came home from school when Winfrey told the world that she'd been abused as a child. I was eleven at the time and I remember thinking: "Wow. What courage this woman has!" I watched the show for years afterward and noticed how she had a gift for identifying and shifting her own inner beliefs to connect to her own values. Today, it is evident to me that she has also found a way to support others through this process by bringing attention to the inner workings of being human in her magazine and in her shows.

For most of my life, I actually had no ability to focus on what might be good and right inside of myself. I walked through my life taking on whatever judgments and ideas other people had about me as if they had something to do with me. I was so enmeshed in my relationship with others that I didn't even know I was a separate person with my own needs, thoughts, feelings, and life trajectory to follow; this epiphany didn't occur to me until I was twenty-seven years old. This codependent pattern started with good intentions, albeit unconsciously, when I was young in order to help me survive the world and particular family structure I was born into. I've since talked to other addicts who also developed this pattern in order to keep volatile adults in their lives at bay; the thinking goes that if we anticipate their moods and make sure angry caretakers get what they want, we won't suffer as much at their hands. Although effective in some ways, this strategy carried into adulthood has some pretty hefty consequences.

When I first started learning to tune into what I needed and giving myself that, my family and friends were pretty upset and angry that I was disturbing the status quo. Some people insisted I was being selfish and uncaring; it took courage for me to stay the course knowing that if I didn't take care of myself, I'd be no good to anyone. This, I learned when I studied family therapist Virginia Satir's work, is normal. Systems Theory says that when one element in any system changes, the rest of the elements must also shift–even if they want to stay the same, they cannot. So although this dissonance between loved ones and myself was uncomfortable at first, I learned to interpret it as a sign that what I was doing was actually working to help me differentiate myself from others. Just because we have folks in our lives that we love does not mean that we will share the same values they do. It turns out that this is a natural and healthy thing for our psyches. We don't need to see the world in the same way in order to love and respect one another. This type of identity work happens naturally in our development when we are teenagers. It did not feel safe for me to do this work at that time in my life. Therefore, it was an area of arrested development for me that I had to work on in my late

20s and throughout my 30s. I am living proof that it can be done at any age!

> *"Shamanic work is about psycho-spiritual development and about achieving the highest possible integration of all aspects of the self in alliance with what spirit tries to express through us. In general terms, shamanism talks about dark and light 'arrows' we can aim at 'targets.' The dark arrows are attachment, dependency, judgment, comparison, expectation, neediness and ego self-importance. They keep us stuck. Light arrows are illumination, introspection, trust, wisdom, seeking balance, open-hearted communication, will, intent, and focus. They move us on."*
>
> *- Christa Mackinnon from "Shamanism and Spirituality in Therapeutic Practice: An Introduction"*

The following chapter speaks of the energy of the South East of the inner medicine wheel. This is the place of our self-concepts. I had to learn how to develop appreciation for myself without inflating my ego. I had to become aware of my patterns in order to break them and consciously choose new ones. I had to accept myself for who I was at any given moment so that I could clearly see where I was at in my evolution in order to choose where I wanted to go next instead of being at the effect of my behaviour. I learned to love my quirks and to follow my passions as an expression of my spirit. In the process, my own values were uncovered and I was able to come into alignment with them. All of these contributed greatly to my ability to more fully identify and live my life's purpose. They were the keys that helped me heal my addiction to being filled up from the outside. They continuously turned me inside myself to find fulfillment, happiness, and meaning in my life.

In order to consolidate your understanding of this direction from your personal, experiential and embodied perspective, I recommend doing the following ceremonies from "Shamanic Ceremonies for a Changing World" by Marilyn Keffer and Gael

Carter. You can find more information on how to purchase a copy by looking at the Recommended Resources section of the Appendix of this book.

The Shield of Physical Mastery Ceremony 1-12
The Dismemberment Ceremony 2-0

Relationship with Ewan

"A mirror reflects the images it encounters as they are; it does not attempt to judge or change them. As you refrain from judging or attempting to change things, you may find you will have no need to speak. The better you are able to hear, the better you are able to see. Listen from the heart and you will be able to see clearly."
-Catherine Kalama Becker and Doya Nardin from
"Mana Cards: The Power of Hawaiian Wisdom"

To add more challenge into the mix, I decided to enter into a relationship with a man at the beginning of the addiction healing process. Ewan was the father of the baby I speak of in a previous chapter that I miscarried. At first, I thought this was such a cruel cosmic joke, sending this tumultuous relationship to me in the middle of an already hard journey with addiction. However, I'd been asking Spirit for a relationship with a soul mate for years. I thought Ewan was "the one" at first. My Dreamer insisted I follow through with the relationship even though I had serious red flags right from the beginning. It was only in retrospect that I understood the brilliance of her dreaming.

In shamanism, all relationships provide mirrors for us to gaze into that help us see ourselves more clearly–the good, the bad, and the ugly. Although there were some beautiful things in our relationship and we clearly had affection for one another, most of the reflections I was getting back were all around my shaky self-concepts as a woman. The thing was: I had very low self-worth. It makes sense to me that on a spiritual level, my Dreamer needed me to see that in order to heal it. When I wasn't paying attention to the other signs, she sent me a relationship within which I could no longer avoid seeing the truth about myself.

At first, Ewan appealed to my neediness, albeit unconsciously. He loved my body, he desired me, and there was a lot of passion. This felt really good at first. It gave me an external feeling of worthiness. But after a while, this started to wear off and I began to notice how I was allowing my boundaries to be crossed by him just to get that "enough" feeling. When I write this now I see how sex was really just another way to distract myself from the truth of my low self-concepts.

Through the course of this relationship, I learned what my bottom lines were in relationship, what I truly needed, where my values were, and what my boundaries were. In previous relationships, these were always a bit of a mystery to me because I was so focused on feeling loved from the outside. But this time was different because I'd already committed to loving myself first when I asked Wolf Woman to guide me in healing myself. As I recovered healthy boundaries, inner love, acceptance, and continued to live in increasingly sober life, the ways I'd been giving away my power in relationship became really clear.

Ignoring my intuition caused me to dismiss my values, emotions, and my integrity. Avoiding hard conversations so I didn't have to enter conflict left me in a state of inner turmoil, sometimes for years. Not setting personal boundaries had made me a doormat for others. Lack of communication with my Dreamer kept me blind to what needed to heal inside me. These were all the things my relationship with Ewan put right in my face. I could no longer ignore these things. I had to face them. And I did.

As you know already, our relationship didn't work out. In the fall of 2011, we called it quits. It was sad for both of us. However, I do believe it played out the way it was meant to for both our healing journeys. And it was definitely not a waste of time; so much learning and personal growth came out of this for me. Although I would not wish to go through another relationship like that one,

I am glad I did this one. In the entries below, you will see some of the more specific pieces I worked with and how I went about recovering self-respect and self-esteem within the context of relationship with Ewan.

Jun 16, 2010

I am in a new relationship with a man who is really lovely. He LOVES my body. You know where this is headed, right? Well, looking in the mirror this morning, I was overcome with a sense of panic. If my body keeps changing, will he still be physically attracted to me? What does he think of this part, etc. So I put a stop to that nonsense. I put my hands on my heart and did my forgiveness. I don't know what will happen as I lose weight and my body changes. I just know I am committed to myself first.

Nov 16, 2010

As you know, we are working with an altar for raising funds for the book. A part of what has come out is me working with Ewan in order to learn financial pieces. He has been doing this for years and has a lot of knowledge. Woke up feeling crappy and nauseous with huge resistance to going over there and seeing him again. But what kept coming up was: the dream of the book is bigger than you. You need to get that book out there to the people. I ran myself a hot bath and sat there. I had no idea where the resources were going to come from inside me. I felt tapped. So I went to my nagual medicine wheel and my horse said to stay in my nagual medicine wheel the whole time I was with Ewan. The horse would guide me. Just had to be really ruthless with him at times. I was proud of myself. This isn't easy and if it were up to my ego, I would have just walked away from it a long time ago. I am learning this part of warriorship: How to do the hard things that make a difference for the greater. Still working on not collapsing afterwards but

it seems to take a lot of my energy to keep facing him and our relationship.

Dec 1, 2010

Been in my nagual medicine wheel today. I let go of the attachment to the outcome of how things go with Ewan. It is clear now that whatever it will be will not be what I had in my imagination. I left that up to Spirit.

Feb 6, 2011

I hear it is difficult. Remember the kind of relationship you want. He may or may not be able to give to you the way you desire. Wolf Woman

Not quite sure what to do with your words. Been thinking about them all day. I don't know that I want to be in a relationship with someone who doesn't communicate with me.

Body Image

....

> *"Addiction is always a poor substitute for love."*
> *-Dr. Gabor Maté from "In the Realm of Hungry Ghosts:*
> *Close Encounters with Addiction"*

I dreaded my second assignment from my teacher. I had to look at myself in a full-length mirror naked each day and notice my inner dialogue. I was horrified at the way I spoke to myself in my head. I came to realize that it was incessant and I could not get away from myself by sinking into the comforts of food. I could barely stand it the first day:

May 3, 2010

I started today by looking at myself in the mirror naked. Realized I was picking at the things I didn't like (my abdomen, my stance, hair on my body). Also realized that the person I feel like I am on the inside doesn't match the picture I have of myself on the outside. I thanked my body for all she does for me and accepted where I was at today.

All these years later, I wish I could say that these voices have gone away completely but they haven't. I am not sure that they can in the misogynistic culture we live in here in North America where girls and women of all ages receive a barrage of "not enough" messages every day that they are not: good enough, pretty enough, skinny enough, shapely enough, tall enough, short enough, young enough, happy enough, accommodating enough, strong enough, smart enough, fit enough, fashionable enough, and capable enough. I could go on with this list, but what's the point? Women–and increasingly more men–live with these unrealistic, meaningless, and demoralizing expectations every day. It's all over social media, on TV, at the movie theatre, in magazine advertising, and at the mall. Unless you are hermit living in the woods, it's impossible to avoid these subtle and not-so-subtle messages we all receive every day.

Luckily, they don't have to go away in order for us to take command of what we "do" with the voices. Although there are promising new signs in media of a backlash against these continuous messages (i.e. the Dove ads), I don't think that focusing our attention solely on changing the media is going to cut it. We need to change ourselves and what we believe about the information we are consuming. We need to ask ourselves questions and think critically about these messages instead of digesting them as truth. For example, who is really benefitting from spewing these messages? What is the cost to you when you believe them? How can you begin to change your body image if it's in the shitter?

The most impactful way I find to continue to counter these messages is through physical exercise–not because it keeps me fit or helps me shed fat. It shows me what is really true about my body and its inherent beauty, functionality, wisdom, and meaningfulness. After a dance class, one woman came up to me in what I suppose was a well meaning statement to exclaim how surprised she was at the agility and flexibility of my body. She had assumed that because I carry some extra weight, that my body is not capable of dexterous feats. I simply agreed with her: "Yes. My body is agile and flexible." Not to mention the fact that I can carry a 250-pound man on my back with ease! I can't really blame her: as a culture, we jump to all sorts of unreasonable conclusions based on what we hear, see, and read in the media. In this example, it is clear that this assumption was simply not true. Bigger bodies are not necessarily less capable or functional than smaller bodies.

Smaller bodies are not necessarily stronger or more agile than bigger ones.

I devised a practice to stop my contribution of adding unconsciously to that damaging field of energy that is created by these "not enough" thoughts. Whenever I caught myself picking on my own or another person's body in my mind, I'd stop and send forgiveness into the matrix of life. Then, I would consciously find three things I found beautiful about the person I was looking at. Over time, I began to gain command of the way these voices infected my thinking and the way I was adding to the negativity out there.

My obsession of looking a certain way was really my attempt to get the love and acceptance I refused to give myself from the outside. I learned with time to accept my body as it was even though the voices were still present. I keep using my body and challenging it with new, interesting tasks. I keep connecting with, learning about, and moving with it to understand its needs and purpose better. My body doesn't exist to be a sexual object for another's pleasure. It is here to carry my spirit on my life's journey and to allow me to experience living in a pleasure-filled, physical way. I cannot accomplish my life purpose without it. My body will never give up on me. It will be with me until I die. How I interact with it matters.

> *"Our minds and spirits can be just about anywhere, while our emotions are often ignored or trapped in the amber of unexamined issues, but our bodies can only be here now. Our bodies cannot move backward into the past, and they cannot run into the future; our bodies can only live in the present moment. Therefore, if we can center our attention in our bodies, we'll be here now. It's as simple as that."*
> -*Karla McLaren from "The Language of Emotions"*

In the following journal entries, the struggles I had with body image and the discoveries I made are brought to the fore.

May 6, 2010

Mirror Exercise: Still with the "picking" voices. However, able to sit in acceptance while also bringing perspective: I danced my ass off last night and it felt so good with *this* body!!

May 7, 2010

Mirror Exercise: Voices continue. Today I asked myself some questions: Where do these voices come from? Are they cultural? Or did they originate with me? Memory of my grandmas on both sides–looking at them as a kid and seeing strong, sturdy, unflappable women. Both had bodies like mine. Discovered that I hold a belief that I am strong, sturdy, and unflappable when I look like them. Somehow, I wired in that belief like that. Of course, my grandmas were strong because of life circumstances, not necessarily because their bodies were bigger.

May 16, 2010

It seems like the relationship with my body is the most challenging thing for me right now. I look in the mirror and cannot find anything of beauty (unless I think of how others would see me). It's really hard for me to accept that this is where I am at after all the work I've done with my body in the last 6 years. I feel like I should be at a more accepting place with my body. And now I wonder how I could've gone all these years not knowing that I had such low regard for my body in these ways. I'm angry at myself for living with this illusion for so long.

May 22, 2010

While doing the mirror exercise, I focused on things I like about my body: hands, feet, skin, face, hair, and calves. Voices were still there in the background and there was also a gentleness that came with focusing on something different.

May 24, 2010

Mirror exercise was different today. Was more able to accept where I was at and even felt good in my body despite the murmurs being there. I am glad those voices are getting quieter. Noticed strong legs–something that was pointed out to me in Contact Improv yesterday with an exercise where we had to lift our partner.

Sep 14, 2010

Woke up sobbing this morning. Realized that a part of me that I'd cut off when I was just a baby was integrated back. My Dreamer told me how its absence had affected me–namely why I have the tendency to be really hard on myself. The phrase that came and filled me was: I have affinity for myself.

AFFINITY-a spontaneous or natural liking or sympathy for someone or something

Sep 15, 2010

Did the mirror exercise this morning. I was sort of bracing because it's been a while and I didn't know how I'd respond and didn't want to go into the berating thing. People have been telling me that I look fantastic and because I have been making so many big changes and working the energy, I've not allowed myself to really own those changes that have taken place. So this morning in front of the mirror, I looked at my body first and the berating voices came back, "Well, that's better. That still doesn't look right, etc." But then I got the idea to start from my face and that's when I saw it: the joy, excitement, and the space. And when I looked at my body again, I saw the areas that have been sculpted since I started this process in the spring: my face, my legs, and my arms. These seem like the places where the extra weight has come off first. It's strange because I really love being in my body, dancing, and moving. But when I go to look at my body it is a whole different deal.

Sep 23, 2010

Did the mirror exercise today. It is still hard to look at myself without critique. But today my hands just naturally went over my body to soothe those mean comments in my mind and reminded me what is true about this body: that it has done me good and that it is a good body.

May 12, 2011

Went for massage therapy today with the intent to relax some sore muscles. I noticed I've gotten better at receiving. I also noticed that I was not self-conscious about my body–even though it was a man massaging me–like I likely would have been a while ago.

The Trap of Seeking Outside Approval

"When we can let go of what other people think and own our story, we gain access to our worthiness–the feeling that we are enough just as we are and that we are worthy of love and belonging. When we spend a lifetime trying to distance ourselves from the parts of our lives that don't fit with who we think we're supposed to be, we stand outside our story and hustle for our worthiness by constantly performing, perfecting, pleasing and proving. Our sense of worthiness–that critically important piece that gives us access to love and belonging– lives inside of our story."

-Dr. Brené Brown from "The Gifts of Imperfection"

It took me a while to understand that I had no control over other peoples' perception of me. If I had, then all those years of people pleasing and doing everything others wanted me to do would have worked. I would have grown up feeling "approved" of. The thing I came to understand was that folks who don't approve of themselves cannot and will not be able to fully approve of others. In the world of perfectionism, there are no winners because there is no such thing as perfect. Perfection is a very subjective thing. I can watch a piece of theatre and think it is the most beautiful performance ever and the person beside me could think the exact opposite. Who is really right? Can anyone be right in such a situation?

Seeking outside approval, while it makes sense to the survivalist in us, is really simply a waste of energy because no one will ever approve of us one hundred percent of the time. Family and friends may have the best of intentions, but they are human too and prone to judgment. We all have a preferred aesthetic. We all have different values that form our own truth. But my truth is not the same as your truth and so approval is really an inside job. The question for me became: can you accept yourself and all of your mistakes, learning to hold yourself through them with kindness without shirking responsibility for your bad choices? Can I remain in integrity with what is true for me knowing it won't necessarily be so for someone else?

May 15, 2010

Today, the voices told me as I looked in the mirror: "You take up too much space." So we're back to this again. I know this has something to do with allowing my shining to come through. My spirit guides told me that they see me singing in front of thousands of people. Last night, I was at a concert. The opening act asked the audience to sing a part and so I sang right off the bat–being comfortable with singing and all. I got an immediate reaction from the people around me. The voice in my head, "Jen, tone yourself down." I kept singing with less gusto. Not quite sure what to do with that. It's like I know it shakes people up sometimes and I am not always sure I want to be the one "disturbing" their inner worlds. I also know that I can't just keep avoiding situations where I may irritate or disturb others. It's going to happen sometimes. A friend showed me how I dim down my shining. I am happy to do my thing in a quiet way but quite frankly, the idea of taking up more energetic space than I already do is a bit daunting. I know this has something to do with my food issue and the relationship I have with my body. I am not sure I am connecting the dots yet though.

I realized that I make myself small to avoid criticism and to blend in but as a friend of mine so aptly put it: You could not blend in if you tried! And I suppose she's right. Who am I kidding? Although I am fairly empathic, I don't always perceive the correct information.

I misread things. I make mistakes. I jump to conclusions. It can be hard to be completely accurate about what someone's motives are. More to the point: who cares? As someone who has to live with myself all day, every day, until I die, my opinion counts the most.

The more I began to identify my own values, my own definition of beauty, and source my knowing from inside myself, the more I was able to stay neutral with the judgments and preferences of others. When I found myself judging others according to my "truth," I would remind myself: "Jen, they have their own truth. You would not wear that outfit or listen to that music, but that speaks to something in their truth or aesthetic that you simply don't understand or relate to." In this way, my curiosity began to be peaked and my judgments began to fall more to the background. I am no saint–they are still there–but I can put them into perspective now in a way that I simply couldn't before.

May 28, 2010

As I stood in front of the mirror, I was reminded of a contemporary dance I went to see at the local theatre on the theme of "home" yesterday. It was all about our ideas of what and where "home" is. This is resonant for me because I have been living kind of like a gypsy all year moving from house to house. I know that a physical building does not a home make. One of the dancers described home as being an internal place during the Q and A. I had thought about this as an idea and written a poem on it a year ago. However, this morning, it came back to me that it might be good for me to locate where my home is inside of me. I realize in this process of healing food addiction how much of my sense of stability comes from the outside and when that crumbles (as it inevitably does when all things change), so do I. I wanted to find a more enduring sense of home and stability that is not dependent on others or inanimate objects and so it only made sense to find that within. So "home," it came to me, is not only wherever my body is (as I wrote in my poem) but is a location in my body. When I

touch that place or focus my attention there, I am immediately soothed. This was a revelation this morning.

Honouring myself and my truth in this way did not make me selfish, inconsiderate, or prone to tunnel vision. Instead, it helped me broaden my definition of what truth really is and that it can take multiple forms. There are a lot of different ways of being "right" that don't result in someone else having to be "wrong." This is an unnecessary dichotomy we humans we've created.

I see this a lot working with families. Parents have an idea of what their kids "should" be doing and what careers teens "should" be pursuing. Usually, this is based on the parents own life experiences and interests. Because of the generation gap, parents assume that what worked for them will also work for their children, forgetting that their children are unique individuals living in a different time than the ones they grew up in. How do we honour other pathways, even if we don't understand them?

I follow one pretty basic rule of thumb: if what the person is planning is not harming themselves, others, or the Earth, I butt out. It's simply none of my business how other people live their lives. Just as I have a Dreamer, so does every other person alive–whether they are aware of this aspect of themselves or not. That Dreamer has all the information about the person's pathway and it might look starkly different from my own, but it doesn't mean the person's on the wrong track.

This makes a lot of sense to my logical mind. If someone's life purpose is to shine the light on social justice issues, the way they go about walking their path may look really different than someone studying to become a chef. Is the chef doing the wrong thing just because his path is not the same as the lawyer's or the activist's?

No. It may simply be necessary. The other thing I realized is that life is not a competition. There is room for all of us to live in our full shining. As pioneering dancer, Martha Graham stated, we don't have to shrink and give up parts of ourselves to make sure others fit in:

"There is a vitality, a life force, a quickening that is translated through you into action, and there is only one of you in all time. This expression is unique, and if you block it, it will never exist through any other medium; and be lost. The world will not have it. It is not your business to determine how good it is, not how it compares with other expression. It is your business to keep it yours clearly and directly, to keep the channel open. You have to keep open and aware directly to the urges that motivate you. Keep the channel open. No artist is pleased. There is no satisfaction whatever at any time. There is only a queer, divine dissatisfaction, a blessed unrest that keeps us marching and makes us more alive than the others."

Self Awareness

....

"Most of us are not raised to actively encounter our destiny. We may not know we have one. As children, we are seldom told we have a place in life that is uniquely ours alone. Instead, we are encouraged to believe that our life should somehow fulfill the expectations of others, that we will (or should) find our satisfactions as they have found theirs. Rather than being taught to ask ourselves who we are, we are schooled to ask others. We are, in effect, trained to listen to others' versions of ourselves...The trick...is to separate out our version of our story, our version of ourself. The pilgrimage we are making is to our own core, our own reality, our own sense of self and self-expression."

- Julia Cameron from "Vein of Gold:
A Journey to your Creative Heart"

More than anything, the healing journey is one of self-awareness. Once we become aware of the patterns, beliefs, ways of being, energy that we run, and the ways these are not giving life, we are in a better position of healing them. When we know ourselves really well–our light and our dark–we can make more sober choices in how to proceed in life. Seeking ways to heal that work for each of us is a lifelong process.

My 8-year-old relative recently asked me a good question: "You know that thought we have before we do something bad? Where does that thought come from?" I asked him what he thought and he said, "I really don't know. I just know that it gets me sometimes."

I could only answer this question from my own experience: "I know that 'bad' voice you speak of and it can sometimes be really hard to resist it. All of us humans have good and evil in us; it's our choice to feed the beast or to feed the light. Every time we choose to feed that 'bad' voice, we give that dark power strength. Every time we choose to feed the light, we strengthen the good in us and in the universe. We humans have been around for 200,000 years and as a species, we have made a lot of bad choices. We have also made a lot of good choices in that time. I feel that 'bad' voice comes from that cloud of 'bad' choices throughout time that hangs over us. We can stop feeding it by making more good choices and maybe one day, the cloud will disappear and we will all be free of that darkness forever." Then we both sat in silence for a while considering all that.

I should say that I am entirely comfortable with being wrong about what I sense in terms of our light and dark natures. In shamanic terms, we all have different perceptions of reality and if my sense turns out to be wrong, at least I can say that I consciously lived in a way that reduced harm to our species and the earth. From a shamanic perspective, we are all swimming in that collective dark cloud as well as the light cloud every moment of our existence; what we do within that collective consciousness of our species matters. The fact is, we are human and prone to making mistakes.

On my healing journey with addiction, I learned that I didn't know myself and my patterns as well as I thought I did. I learned to go deeper into the shadow aspects of myself with the help of my shadow animal, the skunk. At first, I was scared to go into the shadowy aspects of myself because I didn't know what I'd find there. I sent my skunk into the dark mass and I was genuinely surprised when it started bringing out aspects of my light that I'd thrown in there as well as the dark ones. This included dark acts from previous lifetimes. Far from being a depressing and defeating, these drum journeys with my skunk gave me hope and restored pieces that had been lost in some cases for lifetimes. I also learned that deeper levels of forgiveness are possible for all of us–no matter what we've done. This was deeply sobering and it helped me commit to not feeding the "beast" in the future now that I could clearly see the harmful far-reaching effects my actions had had on others.

Some of the pieces my skunk helped me pull out of my shadow were my self-concepts. I'd spent much of my life seeing myself through other peoples' lenses and this distorted my ability to see myself as I really am at the core of my being. To fix this, I had to keep going inside and asking myself questions like: Who are you? What do you stand for? Why do you get up every morning? What feeds your spirit? What are your contributions going to be to the world while you are here? One of the biggest delusions I was living under was that I was not powerful and had no ability to impact change in my reality when the truth is that I am the only one that can!

We've all done horrible things throughout our lifetimes. None of us is squeaky clean. I learned to use this piece of knowledge to improve my relationship with myself and Life.

Nov 29, 2010

I went for a walk along the river for a couple of hours this afternoon. I went out with the intention of asking the nature spirits to help me heal on all levels as I walked and I got some reflections back from nature that were really helpful. First, I noticed it was fall. All the leaves are now off the trees and shrubs and I remembered: Jen, this is the season of letting the old die away getting ready to incubate the new. My transition to life in Calgary has been more like demolition of the old and I've been fighting that. But of course, it is hard to build a new life on old foundations so it is apt. Another thing I was excited about was learning more about my medicine name: Snow Hawk. Specifically, the snow part of it because I have never lived anywhere where I can observe snow for long periods of time. What I got from my conversations with snow this afternoon is that snow is a form of water that is always changing–it is malleable and adapts to the environment. I held snow in my hand and watched it melt and I molded it into all the shapes I wanted. I noticed that I could not keep it in

one form and it did not resist my molding of it. I saw that I am like that too. I have always seen this need for variety and consistent need to grow as a kind of flakiness. A flaw in my character somehow. Today I let go of the inner conflict I had with this and accepted this as part of my nature. And there *is* consistency in snow and in me–the constant is that it will always change. And I embraced my snow-like nature. I sense that this will help me to focus more on living in my naturalness instead of how others perceive me.

Chapter 7

THE EAST

East Introduction: Feeding the Spirit

"To be truly healthy, you need to carefully and courageously assess your approach to the universe. The universe is wide open, and full of forces willing to work with us two-leggeds. Yet, most people go through life as if they were ignorant of these forces. They act like they are not really sure where they are going, where they have been, what they are doing, or why. They are taught to experience only through the brain and not through the senses. To walk a true spiritual path one must 'feel.' The greatest tools for opening up to the universe are a sense of awareness, intuition, and the ability to feel life and the universe as it happens, all around you and through you."
-Sun Bear from "Walk in Balance: The Path to Healthy, Happy, Harmonious Living"

It's not surprising to me that addictions seem to arise more in cultures that have lost connection with their spiritual nature and the spiritual energy in all of life. The hunger, franticness, and pain felt by addicts is often linked to a spiritual disconnect inside of them. There is a horrible void that nothing seems to fill: no relationship, no substance, no behaviour can take the place of Spirit in one's life. Many of us carry this deep knowing within us. The courageous and tenacious never give up seeking re-connection. Teachers from many spiritual traditions have taught that we are here to find our purpose and then to give it away to the world so that it feeds life. This giving away of what we are good at and what we know, in turn, feeds our souls deeply–the ultimate win-win. This has certainly been true in my own personal journey. I challenge you not to believe anything I say outright; try this out for yourself and see what your experiences teach you!

Sadly, in the fairly recent secularization of the Western world, people may have gained an element of freedom from fanatic religious dogma, but they also lost the importance of finding some way to connect to the spiritual essence of life. I've never been much for the theory that we live, we do stuff, and we die as if life has no meaning. I don't believe that we are alive to just go through the motions, pay bills, and waste away. This programming starts very young. In the name of "education," our school systems tend to suck the life and spirit out of children in order to "civilize" them. As an educator myself, I've seen so many excited, passionate, and spunky kids enter kindergarten only to see them completely disillusioned and bored by the end of the year. My calling since 2004 has been to work alongside kids to develop a way of educating that honours the talents, spirit, and quirks of each learner. I've seen what kids can do when they are respected and treated as the conscious beings they are. Thankfully, the number of educators and parents who do this kind of work in the world are on the rise.

Traditionally, many cultures worldwide wove spiritual practices into their daily lives. Many farmers had a practice of thanking the nature spirits and often held festivals and ceremonies to celebrate good harvests and ask for healthy crops. People prayed before eating their food to give thanks for sustenance. There were rites of passage ceremonies that marked all of the different transitions, accomplishments, and stages in a human's life from birth to death. These practices were not superfluous; they helped feed life and supported the many changes that happen in the course of a lifetime. Returning to some sort of regular meaningful spiritual ritual can be like an anchor for addicts who are struggling.

Storytelling is a ritual that can be helpful, as many Alcoholics and Narcotics Anonymous groups can attest. I could have hidden the spiritual aspects of myself while writing this book, yet I really would not be describing how I was able to heal my addiction. It wouldn't have been an honest rendering of the process because recovering my connection with Spirit *was* the missing link. Seeing my own spirit as a perfect reflection of the Great Spirit helped me to see that I was not a horrible, broken person. On the spirit level, I was whole and radiant. This gave me motivation to heal the parts of myself that were not in alignment with that truth. Once I began participating in ceremony, reaching out to similarly minded folks, and doing my personal healing work by utilizing shamanic tools, I started on the road to recovery. Before I made this commitment, my life was painful, without meaning, and felt like drudgery day after day.

In the earth-based tradition I study, the direction of East on the medicine wheel is the place of spirit, fire, and illumination. This place on the wheel says that enlightenment is possible for anyone in any given lifetime. Our relationship with the spirit world sits here. In the following section, I describe ways that I began feeding my spirit and recovering wholeness in the East of my inner medicine wheel.

In order to consolidate your understanding of this direction from your personal, experiential and embodied perspective, I recommend doing the following ceremonies from "Shamanic Ceremonies for a Changing World" by Marilyn Keffer and Gael Carter. You can find more information on how to purchase a copy by looking at the Recommended Resources section of the Appendix of this book.

Medicine Totem Ceremony 0-14
Self-Growth Forgiveness 0-19, 0-20

New Beginnings: Calgary

*"Where is the line between pleasure or comfort and numbing?...
Are my choices comforting and nourishing my spirit or are
they temporary reprieves from vulnerability and difficult
emotions ultimately diminishing my spirit? Are my choices
leading to my Wholeheartedness, or do they leave me feeling
empty and searching?"*

*-Dr. Brené Brown from "Daring Greatly:
How the Courage to Be Vulnerable Transforms
the Way We Live, Love, Parent, and Lead"*

Although I had great friends in Calgary and an already-made community there, life was still challenging when I moved. I found myself wandering the streets downtown where I lived wondering what it must have been like for my relatives to move from Portugal to Canada all those years ago. They didn't know the language, they didn't understand the culture, and they had no work. How lost and scared must they have felt! Somehow, knowing what my ancestors had survived gave me strength. I could feel the ancestors in spirit backing me too. I knew I was on the right track.

Initially, I thought I'd stay in Calgary for two years while I was deciding where I really wanted to live. I've noticed life has a funny way of changing my plans. I met my life partner and deepened my roots in the community, ultimately deciding to stay and make Calgary my home. I still miss the ocean and the rainforest dreadfully, yet I have learned to love the magic of the prairies. I am not the first person in history to write about the freeing effects that the open sky and unending horizon of the prairies brings to the psyche. There was so much literal and figurative space I felt here in my dreaming that was so new and endless.

The following entries from my journal give a flavour of what life was like those first few weeks in Calgary as I adjusted to a very different environment, physically and culturally.

Nov 1, 2010

Today was my first full day in Calgary. It felt so good to walk into my new place and to walk around my neighbourhood today. It is a new start and I am relieved. Went out for Halloween with friends and the little girls last night. It was a lot of fun and although part of me would have loved a candy, it was really not a big deal to be around all of it. So progress. I am feeling an overflowing sense of gratitude today...Life is pretty magic if I listen to Spirit.

Nov 3, 2010

Was a challenging day. My head is pounding, my heart feels raw and I am going to bed. It feels stormy inside me and I am weepy and have been struggling all day to keep it together. Tomorrow, I paint my place. Friday my stuff arrives. I am staying here with Ewan two more nights while my apartment airs out. I wanted to find somewhere else to stay but Spirit said stay so...I have been praying for help. Not in a good space right now. Talk to you tomorrow.

Nov 4, 2010

Today was a good day. Woke up feeling good. More clear. Asked for guidance in my dreamtime. Painted my apartment and my pacing was good. Noticed myself integrating a lot of the things my body taught me a few weeks ago. I wasn't sore and I didn't burn through my energy fast like I usually

do barreling through a task. Looking forward to moving in tomorrow officially.

Nov 5, 2010

Now in my new place. Stuff has all arrived. This is where I am at today: lots of sorrow and grief. Tears amidst unpacking, which I am grateful for; keeps my body moving and my mind more still. Processing as I look through boxes.

Nov 6, 2010

Last night was tough. Deep crying. After my stuff came and I had set up, it all just came pouring out of me–all the stuff I was keeping at bay just to make it through the tonal stuff I had to do. I was heading for a pretty big collapse and called on all sorts of help to keep me out of that pit. In the end, I went there but I felt the support of the universe. Sometimes, I get flashbacks to the grief I felt when I lost the baby in the summer. Just that deep, deep loss where there feels like someone blew a hole right through my chest. Night times are hard though alone in my apartment without my usual support systems. Spent the afternoon out in nature again by the river and that helps the most. I thought of calling friends in Vancouver but it didn't feel like the right thing to do. They'd only worry and what good is that? I know I am not alone in it. I feel alone right now though. Victory was going into the grocery store. I just did my usual thing. I saw chocolate and looked at it thinking, " That's weird. I don't even desire that. It wouldn't help my situation right now any way." A few months ago, I would've been looking for an escape hatch.

Nov 11, 2010

Strange getting used to so much time alone and so much space after living with roommates for so long and having family living near by. So there is a lot of time at my disposal right now, which I am getting used to. Been working with Spirit to figure out how best to use that time.

Nov 13, 2010

Today was about making peace with my decision to move to Calgary. I spent a lot of the day just sitting with this huge emptiness inside of me. Although there are tough moments, I am enjoying having this time to cultivate my inner garden and manifest creative projects I have been working on for a while. So although a part of me craves companionship and a rich fabric of friends like I had in Vancouver, I know that will come in time. I have a feeling I won't always have this much time at my disposal so I have resolved to really enjoy it.

Nov 15, 2010

Another tough day. Walked a ton all around the city instead of taking buses and that helped. Spent more time out in nature. Then on the way home, I found myself at the cathedral. A mass was just starting when I went in and I just sat, cried, and prayed. Was sitting by the Virgin Mary icon (the unofficial patron saint of Portugal). This was immensely comforting to me as when I was a kid, my grandma encouraged us to pray to her when we were lost. I feel lost. And I can't say that I have any answers at the moment but it was healing to sit in there. The priest talked about "patient endurance" and that resonated with me. I am good at the endurance. Not so great at the patience with myself so that was my day intent this morning. I know I will be okay and can feel my ancestors support. It's just those moments where I feel like I am falling into a deep pit where I wonder... Good thing I've got all this time because I am not able to focus on any one thing for too long lately. So my work is happening in chunks and spurts instead of a continuous line of engagement.

I am learning to trust that. To deal with what is up and let the rest of the stuff come in where it needs to.

Nov 20, 2010

Had a dream last night that is re-occurring of a strange man who follows me. I walked into a school and suggested to the principal that he close the access through the back stairwell because that's how he came in. So the principal did but then he showed up in the cafeteria and came and sat at my table. I was not scared of him like I have been all the other times. I was pissed off that he had the gall to sit at my table. I dumped my food on his head and walked away. This is progress. For most of my life I have felt like a slave or a victim. I am fighting back now. It feels like a turning point in my addiction to food- I dumped my food on his head. And Calgary is the start of the rest of an unbound life.

Role of Ceremony and Prayer

"Ceremonies are the most ancient form of spiritual technology on Earth. Ceremonies are simple or complex rituals that can be done indoors or outdoors. They take you out of non-ordinary time so you can hear the voice of your Higher Self (your soul). When you need direction in life, a ceremony can help you make decisions from the highest part of your being...Your Higher Self...is a direct line to Spirit and it is always trying to get your attention. It tries to alert you to important moments of opportunity, even though they may be camouflaged by loss and sadness. It knows who you really are–beyond your ego's protests and beyond your fears."

- Marilyn Keffer and Gael Carter from: "Shamanic Ceremonies for a Changing World"

Ceremonies place us directly into the stream of what is unknown to us. We do ceremonies in order to get clarity in our lives amidst all the clamour and confusion of mainstream living. Some traditional ceremonies have changed in order to suit the needs of people living in today's modern world, however, their main function remains the same over thousands of years of human existence: maintaining and regaining inner balance. Entering ceremony regularly is a vital tool in today's world of distractions because ritual keeps us in alignment with our individual life purpose. For me, ceremony is an arrow that points me back to myself so I don't become lost on my journey.

"You can discover magic yourself when you do ceremonies. If you are already aware of the magic in the world, ceremony will help you discover even more magic! Ceremonies can teach us how to use magical tools (altars, medicine wheels, wands) to call something we want or need into our lives, for protection, for working with life's challenges and for calling forth our gifts, so that we can live the best life we can while we are here on Earth. Ceremonies can help change our inner worlds so that our lives work better and we are happier people. I don't know about you, but in my life, it can be so hard to hear my own voice among people telling me what I should do, what I should think and how I should act. So many 'shoulds' can drive a person crazy! As Grandmother Ann states, spending time doing ceremony can help people to hear their own voice so that they can follow their own inner wise magician in their lives."

- A. Dickie, J. Engracio, and K. Inksetter from: "The Magic Circle: Shamanic Ceremonies for the Child and the Child Within"

Ceremony and prayer go hand in hand. Prayer is what we do in ceremony to ask for what we need; ceremony is the container that allows us to listen to the messages from the spirit world after we've asked for help. Many of us have been taught to pray but few of us link the answers to the process of listening deeply in the many ways that Spirit can speak to us. Ceremony trains us to listen to omens from nature, to the ways our Higher Selves whisper in our ears when we are quiet, and to ancestors who might come to remind us who we are and where we come from.

It wasn't until I started hearing people praying in a sweatlodge in 2005 that I felt I really learned how to pray–even though I'd been praying since I was a little girl. The prayers were heart-full and sent up to Spirit without attachment. I can't presume to know what someone needs, but I can send them my heart prayers and then let go. I can always pray for myself and let go of how those prayers are answered.

"I've also been grateful for the abundance the Earth shares with me each and every day–the giveaway of all the plants and animals that make my life possible. I received a confirmation from the Earth the other day at the gas pump of all places! I was praying and thanking the Earth for her giveaway of gas so that I can get around and do my work in the world. I was deep into it when I smelled gas and felt my feet wet. I looked down and the gas pump was overflowing gas onto my shoes! I wasn't even pulling the 'trigger' anymore. It was just flowing. I laughed and told her I got the message. It stopped. In all the years I've had my license and filled up with gas, this has never happened. I love the mystery of living and of Spirit. And I wonder what would happen if more of us prayed without attachment for an end to violence, for more peace on the planet, for alignment with the Earth."

-From blog: Living from the Inside Out (Oct 25, 2013)

In the following entries, I talk more about how I utilized ceremony to gain direction, align with my Higher Self, and heal myself.

Aug 6, 2010

When I went walking around the lake today, I was invited by an old willow to go sit against her trunk and she started talking to me. I grew up around this area and this lake is where I spent my summers. The willow told me that she remembered me from when I was little. I asked her what I was like and she said free and sad at the same time. I knew what she meant. She proceeded to tell me that there was never anything wrong with me and that the confusion came from taking on other peoples' stuff. I feel this is an important key to the addiction: learning what is my stuff and what isn't and either way, dealing with it in other ways rather than grabbing for food to soothe that feeling that there is something wrong or bad about me.

Aug 10, 2010

Did the Water Self-Forgiveness Ceremony today and I feel much lighter. I was still holding onto this idea that I was somehow bad at my core and so making mistakes was not acceptable. I've been punishing myself for my mistakes as of late. The good news was that cleaning up my past was relatively recent; I didn't have to dig into the distant past and so it showed me how far I'd come. I celebrated that victory and it made it easier to forgive myself.

Dec 2, 2010

Went down to the beach today and did a ceremony. It was a day of cleaning up the past. So I threw a rock in for each thing I wanted to release and embraced a piece for my new life.

Mar 24, 2011

When I woke up this morning, my body was still super sore. I realized after getting in touch with my mesa that there was some energetic stuff going on that didn't have to do with the fall on the ice. Realized that despite dearmouring and knowing how to run my energy, I've been defaulting to suppressing my life force in certain situations that are stressful for me; one of these is being myself even in the face of judgment from others. I worked on this pattern tonight at Reiki. This new way of being with my lifeforce feels expansive and the pain in my body dissipated quite quickly.

May 7/8, 2011

Went to a sweatlodge ceremony in honour of Mother's Day yesterday. It had never occurred to me to give gratitude and pray for my female lineage going back in time but that's what came during the ceremony. It was really powerful to see all the life-giving things those women made possible in my life as well as releasing patterns that are not serving me. Today, I visited with a colleague who was visiting Calgary. Sometimes I don't realize how much my life has changed for the better until I have conversations like these. She said, "Did you ever imagine your life would be like this?" I emphatically said "No! That's the great part about living is the unfolding. One decision can lead us in a whole different direction we never imagined." And I saw that I am more comfortable with living my life one day at a time. I don't mind the not knowing as much as I did a year ago.

Utilizing Animal Totems

"The true shaman, the true naturalist, works to reconnect conscious human life with Nature and Spirit through totems and ritual...What we consider imagination is a reality in some form on levels beyond the normal sensory world."
-Ted Andrews from "Animal Speak: The Spiritual & Magical Powers of Creatures Great and Small"

Throughout this book, I've already spoken a lot about how I've utilized my animal totems to show me where I needed to heal and how to do it. I realize this may seem strange to someone who has never experienced a drum journey into the spirit world and I don't expect to convince anyone of anything. It's really something one has to experience to believe. I was skeptical when I first started journeying and I wondered if what I was experiencing was real; my mind was in overdrive. At first, it was hard to stay present because I didn't expect to sense or see anything. When images and sensations started coming, I didn't know what to make of them or how to interpret them. It took a while for me to figure out my own dreaming symbols and what they meant to me. It took time to learn to quiet my mind before a journey.

Interestingly, I began seeking out shamanism because I started having dreams that I couldn't figure out on my own. In one dream, four dogs came to me in different colours: yellow, black, red, and blue. They were passing off a baton to one another the way folks in track and field do. In the next scene, they turned into horses of the same colours. It wasn't until I was talking to a local elder one day when I discovered to my shock that there was a story about dogsoldiers. He told me that dogs were used in North America to carry items from camp to camp before the re-introduction of horses by Europeans. These dogs were called dogsoldiers by some aboriginal people at the time. When horses were introduced, they took the place of dogs in the tribes and also inherited the name of dogsoldiers.

This is not the only time Spirit validated for me in a dream that the spirit world is real and alive. In another dream, I was running alongside five great horses all of different colours. I was breathless as I watched them galloping by. The scene then changed and I was walking with my dad along a familiar path in the forest by his house. I looked up and saw five owls: one snowy owl and the rest great horned. I tried to show my dad but he couldn't see them. I was perplexed as to why these particular animals came in fives when I awoke, so I spoke to Tiger's Breath about it. She informed me that the number five in the Mayan tradition sits in the center of the medicine wheel with a person's power. I felt a strong connection to both the owl and the horse. She had me choose which animal was most like my essence at the spirit level: the horse.

However, I always had ties to the owl and didn't understand why. When I began studying lomilomi, I was sitting on a lanai in Hawaii when I felt the presence of a spirit owl sit on the railing beside me. The owl told me that it was the animal that would work with me to develop my Traditional Hawaiian Medicine skills. Later, I found out that one of my lomilomi teachers' totem animals was an owl that had started coming to him when he was just a child growing up in Hawaii. This was years before I actually met this teacher in person and now I know that his totem was calling me to service!

In another dream, I was sitting in a tattoo parlor beside a guy on a bench. I looked down and saw that he had a red bird tattooed on his calf. When I asked him what kind of bird it was, he responded that it is a "red eagle." I had never heard of a red eagle before so when I woke, I went to my copy of "Animal Speak" to look it up. To my surprise, it turns out the Hopi people call the red-tailed hawk the "red eagle." Because my medicine name is Snow Hawk, this definitely caught my attention.

Another time, I went to meet another totem during a drum journey and she showed me the most unusual thing: this black jaguar was playing with her prey. She taunted them endlessly before attacking. When I went to research this on the Internet later, it turned out to be a true fact about jaguar's hunting behaviour. I had no idea about this before jaguar showed it to me!

What I know over the last decade of working with my animals is that they are real and ready to support me on my spiritual journey. They know things that I don't know consciously and they can help me find missing pieces that I need in order to live my Sacred Dream here on earth. Since I began working with them, life is easier. They show me how to bring the reality I am experiencing in the spirit world down to earth in ways that I can't always figure out on my own without their assistance.

In addition, they speak in the language of symbols and metaphor. The ego has a harder time interfering with messages that come in these forms. I've discovered that messages from my totems have a different "feel" to them than the ones coming from my ego. Time is suspended and I enter into a different space when my totems enter the scene. I am no longer operating in ordinary reality; all my senses are flamed on. They don't have to come only in the dreamtime; they also come when I am awake to give me messages.

Oct 4, 2010

Went today to find my Past Life animal. It is a phoenix and I learned that the reason it is my animal is because it teaches me not to fear looking at the past lives and healing them. That doing this will bring more energy and pleasure into my life. I kept seeing it rising and then falling in ashes and then rising again and it felt in my body like an orgasm that was increasing with each lifetime that healed. What it comes down to is self-love. I learned what I needed to do to empower myself.

Jan 23, 2011

I saw two of the hugest ravens I have ever seen today after telling a friend the other day how weird it was to not see many crows here in Calgary. They landed pretty much at my feet and watched me. Raven medicine has been around me a lot lately. I have been trying to figure things out a lot with logic and the message seems to be: magic is afoot. Don't try to figure it out mentally. Another thing I found in "Animal Speak" said that ravens teach how to go into the dark and bring forth the light. With each trip in, we develop the ability to bring more light out. This is definitely how I feel lately. I go to those really dark places sometimes where I wonder how long I am going to be there and then when I come out. Now I have a nugget I didn't have before: the animals always know their way out. I can trust that.

Forgiveness

....

"Forgiveness is the end result of a deeply emotive process of coming back from the devastation of trauma and betrayal and into strength once again. You'll understand anger's profound connection to real forgiveness and you'll understand the true definition of mercy: mercy can only arise from a position of strength that gives you the ability to harm, tempered by the ability to control your impulses and choose not to."
-Karla McLaren from "The Language of Emotions"

Harry Uhane Jim is a Kahuna, healer, and teacher. He is the author of the book, "Wise Secrets of Aloha." He was born and raised on the island of Kauai in Hawaii. In 2015, I traveled to the Big Island in Hawaii to take a Group Ho'oponopono workshop with him and I interviewed him on the "Going Shamanic" radio show. He says, "there is only one type of forgiveness: now or later."

The course description from his website reads as follows: "The Hawaiian Culture has concepts and skill sets that co-create balance and abundance; this is called Ho'oponopono. It's about forgotten ways of thinking and feeling. At its root, Ho'oponopono is a technology of forgiveness and allows us to release that which keeps us feeling stuck in negative thoughts and patterning. The Hawaiian time-evolved practice of managing trauma and transforming chaotic patterns into shapes and vistas of order and profound peace is presented in an interactive and trance breaking experience. This workshop is dedicated to setting aside focus skills based on pain, shame, and guilt, while embracing a skill set to bring focus skills of joy and presence. The human experience can take negative energy and turn it into positive forms. We can embrace the paradox and change the current of chaotic patterns. Stop negotiating life and start navigating!"

One thing that Uncle Harry says is that we practice ho'oponopono to maintain our sovereignty. If we are full of attachments and resentments to others based in the past, we are not really free. We think we are punishing the "offenders" but really, we are punishing ourselves indefinitely by not forgiving and letting go. Forgiveness frees us from the ties that bind us and keep us from moving forward. This goes back to self-concepts based in how others see us. These unforgivenesses keep us from seeing ourselves the way we really are. Uncle Harry says in the interview: "the way to get to grace is to eliminate shame in the space." In Hawaii, hands-on healing via appropriate touch is called lomilomi and it is designed to support the process of ho'oponopono body, mind, heart, and spirit.

Most of us have experienced trauma in some form or another. This is the legacy we are born into, in part. We are also born into the light of our ancestors. So again, we have a choice which one we feed. In my experience, the original trauma itself is not what causes the most harm in the long run. What causes the harm is really the way we "hold" and "feed" the trauma within us. Righteous anger gets me nowhere. This doesn't mean I ignore the injustice that occurred. Anger channeled into actions that give life is one of my reoccurring routes to forgiveness.

An example of this happened in my journey toward forgiving the person that sexually abused me when I was a kid. After this memory emerged, it took me about a year's worth of steady ho'oponopono work until I felt that I had forgiven myself, him, and the circumstances around the events. I cycled through anger, rage, shock, denial, depression, acceptance, sadness and pretty much any other hue of emotion you can imagine in that year. One day I felt good and the next day I didn't. I was angry at myself for doing so much work and not being able to get to true forgiveness. After about six months, I realized that it was just going to take some time because there were so many layers of healing throughout generations that needed to be done. I saw that as I was doing the work for myself, I was also doing it for the people in my lineage who had been through and perpetuated sexual abuse.

I experienced this work peeling off layers of crap that had stuck to me and the people in my lineage for generations. In shamanic terms, it makes sense to me that the energy of sexual abuse found me in this lifetime; because it was already present in the legacy my ancestors left behind. To be clear, I don't believe that people call abuse into their lives. What happened to me wasn't my fault or my responsibility. It did point out unhealthy patterns that I was buying into handed down from generations that put me at greater risk of abuse: extreme passivity and submission expected of me culturally as someone born female, giving away my power, keeping secrets that were harmful, and not standing up to harm. As I realized that the person who abused me was likely also abused as a child, more compassion began to settle inside of me. Vengeance would not save me or him from further pain; it only perpetuates it.

I knew I was alternating between all the points on the Karpman Drama Triangle conceived by Stephen Karpman in the late 1960's and used often in psychotherapy as a way to create healthier communication strategies between people. The three roles that people play in unhealthy interactions are: victim, rescuer, and persecutor. I did not know how to be assertive, create boundaries, and stay out of other peoples' business. Instead of being the victim and playing the "poor me, I never get anything I want" part, I learned to get better at problem-solving in order to get my needs met. Instead of being the persecutor and blaming my feelings and impressions on another person, I learned to speak assertively and state the problem clearly without trying to find fault in others. Instead of rescuing people from their self-created drama, I learned to be more of a coach when people asked for help and otherwise staying out of their business unless a situation was life threatening in the moment.

Jun 19, 2010

Relief that I am on this path to healing and regret that it took me so long despite numerous nudges from the universe. Forgave myself for that. Also curiously needed to forgive myself for my growth and the ripples that sends out into all my relationships. Forgave myself for being strong. Strange what comes out of this forgiveness work.

April 10, 2011

What really is backlash? It is someone who can't handle confrontation and has a need to throw energy back when they can't handle it. Leaders must be willing to be unpopular and hold their space regardless of what is happening.
Wolf Woman

I realized that the processing is not helpful because the learning happens in the moment. All I need to do is engage and tweak as I go along. I process because I think the answer is "back there" somewhere; it's not. I am learning to tap into that and make peace with interactions that maybe didn't go exactly as I wanted. The Anger Ceremony helped me to see that speaking my truth does not mean there will be harmony outside of me immediately (an expectation I uncovered); it *does* give me more harmony inside of me which is helping me to hear where people are coming from without taking it personally. I learn by doing. I am wading through the interactions with friends and community members with the intent of holding that mantle of a leader now. The self-forgiveness is helping in this process.

Growing a Sense of Humour

"There's a certain sense of humor that is absolutely necessary for our human condition. When we have that sense of humor, things become workable. It's the part that we put on top of our ordinary human experience—and we all put something on top of it when we started our spiritual search—that creates the problem. You then not only have your own suffering, you have all these ideals and images that you hold up for yourself. That puts a layer of spiritual suffering on top of the basic suffering."

- Jack Kornfield
from the article "The Wondrous Path of Difficulties"

Let's face it: humans are a weird, illogical, complex, neurotic, and crazy bunch. There are no exceptions to this rule. We make things a lot harder and complicated than they need to be. We worry about things we can't change from the past and things that have not even happened yet but might! We look everywhere outside of us for answers to life's questions and rarely ever ask our inner wise ones to uncover the secrets of our own inner universes. We keep ourselves in states of misery just because they are known and comfortable in some way.

When I started this journey, I was overweight by society's standards, but losing weight was not my goal. I simply wanted to learn to love myself. I wanted to feel good in my own skin. I wanted to find joy in life. I was 220 pounds when I began my journey and 5'4" tall. In fact, I am still 5'4" tall. That never changed. You see, I found humour somewhere in this process too! And I became much lighter in spirit. Thank goodness because it makes a huge difference.

Hawaiian Kahuna, Uncle Harry Uhane Jim, says, "When you laugh, you cannot think. And that's good for healing. Negative energy doesn't like laughter." It's tough to lift heavy energy from one's inner medicine wheel with more heaviness, as it turns out. It's a lot easier if we learn to keep it light and laugh at ourselves on our healing journey. I discovered I could be light and still do the inner digging work needed to heal. The lightness helped me to release the pain with more ease and grace.

Many spiritual traditions hold sacred those who have a special gift of using humour to shed light on human foibles. Think of jesters in courts in Europe, clowns, tricksters, or heyokas in the Lakota tradition. When this individual does his or her job well, the object of the humour does not feel targeted as much as enlightened. These folks are not there to simply make jokes so people will laugh; their humour comes with a spiritual message that lightens as it enlightens.

The Hanged Heyoka
Is a contrary
Who challenges
By reversing convention.
She is irreverent,
Spontaneous
And creative.
She transcends reason
And paradox.
She sees the holy
Through the whole.
Never intimidated by
Limited thinking–
She simply goes beyond it!

-M. Keffer and G. Carter from
"Shamanic Ceremonies for a Changing World"

In Alberta where I live, the traditional trickster figure is the coyote. I know when I encounter the coyote when I am out in nature, that it is an omen that I need to see things in a new way. A few years ago, I did an overnight ceremony to face and overcome my greatest fears in life. I had just set up camp and got myself comfortable in my chair enjoying the sunset when I heard something rustle in the bushes. When the coyote and I saw each other, we both jumped up with a start. After he ran off as fast as he could, I burst out laughing. Right then, I knew this was going to be an interesting ceremony.

As day turned to night, my fears intensified. I had chosen to do this ceremony at the end of September in Calgary thinking that the evening might still be warm and tolerable. I hadn't brought anything to make a fire. In the early hours of the morning, the temperature dipped below zero and I was freezing cold. Again, all my fears started up again and I thought I might not make it through the night. I realized how many times I'd just given up in my life instead of trying to find solutions.

I decided to pray to the coyote to show me how to look at this situation with some humour. All of the sudden, I felt my body stand up on its own and I started dancing and laughing. I must have danced for two hours in my ceremonial space in a trance-like state. And when I stopped, it was dawn. I felt the sun on my skin and I laughed as I thanked coyote for reminding me how resourceful I could be if I thought outside the box.

> *"Through puns and clever jokes, shamans distract their clients, opening them up to participating in the hard work of admitting some responsibility for their problems. If a patient recognizes her part in creating an illness, for example, she can empower herself to relieve it. In shamanism as in other aspects of life, humor heals."*
> *-Barbara Tedlock from "The Woman in the Shaman's Body: Reclaiming the Feminine in Religion and Medicine"*

When our lives aren't working, the trickster helps us to see things from a polar opposite view. There are limits to what the mind can accomplish with its tendency to want to pigeonhole and set beliefs in stone. The trickster shakes things up and jiggles the mind's normal way of operating so that the person who is healing can see the illusions they've been living under clearly for what they are: mental tricks.

I knew I was finally beginning to heal these deep, heavy pieces when humour started to return to me without my having to do anything new. Instead of getting overly serious about my situation, I was able to laugh at the tangled webs I can sometimes weave while finding ways to untangle myself. These journal entries show how I used the situations I found myself in to bring some lightness to my journey the year of the addiction healing.

May 6, 2010

This afternoon, I found myself trying to "push through" my work when I felt tired. Then I had a coffee and sat at my computer. I had only gotten through half my coffee when I knocked the cup over and it crashed onto the floor. I am taking that as a sign. Definitely no distractions from presence by eating and drinking at the computer.

May 30, 2010

Was on the bus pondering whether or not I am having some kind of mild nervous breakdown as my mind is racing, it occurs to me, "Dude, you're crashing like all those other addicts you hear about." I had an internal chuckle and felt some relief at understanding a bit about what is going on inside of me.

May 31, 2010.

Yesterday, I was unconsciously watching this woman in a restaurant eat bread with butter. When I realized that I was

staring in a kind of envious way, I diverted my glance and had an inside laugh. So this is how it is...all insidious-like.

Sep 24, 2010

It's okay to be lighthearted you know with all that's happening!!
Wolf Woman

Yeah. I know I am being hard on myself. And definitely too serious lately. And although I've wanted to plenty of times, I haven't gone out and eaten a whole bakery so really, I am doing pretty good! I live on a street that might as well be named "Baked Goods Heaven" too so that's saying a lot! And that I am doing good on that rollercoaster even if half the time it is not screaming in excitement but fear.

Dec 19, 2010

Dreamed last night I was eating lots of muffins. So I now know when I have those dreams that I am going through big transformation. I used to panic that it meant I was sliding backwards on my healing journey. I actually thought it was funny when I woke up, but in my dream I felt bad for being sneaky about the muffin eating.

Jan 5, 2011

During our meeting in October, you recommended I just cut anything from my life that isn't working. This has been a lot easier for me in Calgary away from old attachments and I am seeing the wisdom of just allowing the transformation. I was in the shower this morning thinking about a past life piece I am going to work with a friend this afternoon and I thought: "Yeah, you know, why all the serious?" It just weighs me down. I do one piece and another one comes up right after that. Like that Whack-A-Mole game. That's just the way it is going to be until I die so might as well make peace with that and start being lots lighter.

Jan 21, 2011

My relationship with Ewan has been frustrating for me the last two months. Today I noticed that he is trying things in small ways. Duh. This stuff is obviously way outside his comfort zone. So remembering to keep inviting without expectation. How can it be that I am so good with this stuff when it comes to kids and I forget as soon as I am in an adult relationship?! Attachment...Ha!

Jan 22, 2011

Ewan and I get closer, fears come up: What if we're too different? What if he starts trying to control me? Blah blah blah. I know I am at a point right now where I can create anything I want. The blank canvas is a little intimidating sometimes and I am afraid to commit even though I know what I want in my heart. What if I screw it all up? *Sigh*

Fuck it! I am going dancing.

April 6, 2011

Went for a walk today and saw flickers everywhere. I've been thinking more about the places I am strong in leadership and the ones that need more work. Found myself worrying about the things I don't know how to do yet. Consulted with flicker about being a leader and it said that I am a digger; I know when I don't know something and I dig to find the information when I need it. This relaxed me to receive this information. The flicker showed me digging inside myself as well as digging outside myself. I see that I dig outside and inside for this information about how to be an effective leader. Then a magpie dropped a poo bomb in my hair from a tree above so I figured I was on the right track.

April 28, 2011

Sense of humour has returned today along with simplicity. I had a laugh at how I can make things super complicated sometimes! As I was fretting about the leadership stuff, my Dreamer reminded me to just take a walk already!

Chapter 8

THE NORTH

North Introduction:
Catching Faulty Beliefs

"An error does not become truth by reason of multiplied propagation, nor does truth become error because nobody sees it."

-Mahatma Gandhi

It is a misunderstood idea, this "real world." Folks accept that it is true that such a thing even exists because this is what we've been conditioned to believe. People speak about the world as if it is something static and as if there is only one reality that we all agree upon. This is simply not so in shamanic terms. Every decision each of us makes is continuously changing the fabric of the universe–this is something that is being studied by some modern scientists and something that shamans have known for a long time. Shamanism says that each person creates his or her own reality and therefore experiences the world in very unique ways. For example, five people can witness an event and relay five very different stories about what happened. Does this mean they are lying? No. Not necessarily. It means that each person noticed different things and experienced the event based on their own worldview and way of being in the world. There is nothing wrong with this. This is actually a part of our humanness. We are not all the same and we do not all want the same things in life.

As children, our parents enculturate us so that we can survive in the world. It is meant as an act of love, I believe, and starts off with good intentions. However, depending on the beliefs, values, and customs of the countries we find ourselves growing up in, these cultural "norms" can cause serious rifts in our psyches and in our self-concepts. Although following these customs as children can be a good survival strategy–especially if we are growing up in oppressive environments– these beliefs and values do not necessarily serve us as adults. Many of these beliefs are not even said explicitly in families; they are simply understood and followed without question.

As an educator since 2000, I have noticed that the reason why many adults want quiet, obedient kids is because they do not want their view of the world challenged. They fear change; many learned this way of parenting from their parents and it's all they know. Bold and empowered kids question the status quo–not because they are rude or bad–but because they are being true to themselves and following their impulses, wonderings, and curiosity about the world. Children are not yet adults and it is unfair of us to expect that from them even on the basic scientific level; humans go through natural stages of development where certain behaviours are just not possible to expect. For instance, expecting a toddler to talk things out instead of hit when s/he is angry is not within the toddler's ability yet. This does not mean we can't teach this skill as the child grows, but it's unfair to punish a toddler for it. I highly recommend learning more about human developmental stages if you are a parent, as this information can start to support your parenting journey.

The values of fairness and equality matter to most children. Parents who learn to operate out of love instead of fear can develop respectful relationships with their children that are not rooted in relational power struggles. Whether parents put their energy into fear- or love based parenting, the amount of energy is the same. The only difference is that fear is a bottomless pit with little reward and love results in genuine connection between parent and child that lasts a lifetime. Some of the best books on building up this healthy relationship when kids are young appear in the Bibliography of this book. Two of my favourites are "Hold onto your Kids: Why Parents Need to Matter more than Peers" by Doctors Gordon Neufeld and

Gabor Maté as well as "Conversations with a Rattlesnake: Raw and Honest Reflections on Healing and Trauma" by Theo Fleury and Kim Barthel.

So what kinds of beliefs and thoughts need to be shifted in order for us to thrive instead of just survive as humans? There are a few common ones that I've seen in my work, though each person will have different belief structures that are unique to them. If we were taught to be seen and not heard as children, for instance, we may hold onto the beliefs that no one cares what we have to say and that it is never appropriate to speak our minds. You can perhaps see how this thinking may lead to victim-type thinking. These children tend to develop into adults who truly believe they have no personal power. On the opposite side of this spectrum, a child who grows up with no boundaries or with parents who did not know how to parent in a balanced way may grow into an adult who feels entitled to bulldoze her or his way through relationships and situations to get what s/he wants without care for the needs and safety of others. As Yehuda Berg said, "Hurt people hurt people. That's how pain patterns gets passed on, generation after generation after generation."

Whether we were neglected, over-controlled, ignored, abused, or not seen for who we were as children, all of these imbalances can be corrected by us as adults through practices of mindfulness, recapitulation, and active self-compassion explored in this chapter. Only the individual can do this work for him- or herself; we can learn to parent ourselves in good ways as grown adults. There are no shortcuts.

The North is the place of the mind, of the winds, of wisdom, and knowledge. This is also the direction the animals sit in. The animals can teach us relaxed presence, naturalness, and vigilance, so we can be flexible in our thinking and adapt to changing circumstances. This chapter illuminates some of the faulty beliefs and thinking patterns I needed to change in order to heal the North of my inner medicine wheel.

In order to consolidate your understanding of this direction from your personal, experiential and embodied perspective, I recommend doing the following ceremonies from "Shamanic Ceremonies for a Changing World" by Marilyn Keffer and Gael Carter. You can find more information on how to purchase a copy by looking at the Recommended Resources section of the Appendix of this book.

The Journey from Ignorance to Wisdom 2-12
The 22-Day Mental Workout Ceremony 1-9

Recapitulation

"We talk to ourselves incessantly about our world. In fact we maintain our world with our internal talk. And whenever we finish talking to ourselves about ourselves and our world, the world is always as it should be. We renew it, we rekindle it with life, we uphold it with our internal talk. Not only that, but we also choose our paths as we talk to ourselves. Thus we repeat the same choices over and over until the day we die, because we keep on repeating the same internal talk over and over until the day we die. A warrior is aware of this and strives to stop his internal talk."

-Carlos Castaneda

The recapitulation practice of "stop[ping] one's internal talk" is ancient and originated with the Toltec people. What they discovered through this extensive inner detective work was that every memory from the past and every relationship we've ever had take up space within us in the form of energetic attachments. Some of these are healthy and feed us energy but some of them are not. Humans have the tendency to focus on the negative and stay stuck in past energy loops through their compulsive thoughts, habits, and patterns that suck up valuable life force energy. Some of these include toxic thoughts and beliefs, re-living trauma and abuse, going over past events ad nauseam to think of what they could- or should have done differently, and negative self-talk. Ancient Yaqui sorcerers developed shamanic technologies to support the process of silencing the mind that are still used by skilled shamans today.

I began putting the recapitulation skills I learned into motion in my life before undergoing a rigorous, seven-day intensive ceremonial week. The process involves first identifying a pattern that is not working in your life. Then, using a specific breathing and moving pattern, a shamanic coach cues you to recapitulate all the times the pattern has ever appeared in your life; this is done in a very specific way. The breathing and moving makes sure we don't stay stuck in re-living or indulging the experiences and it also has the effect of starting to break up those well-worn neural pathways in the brain so that we can't go back to that pattern as easily afterwards in our everyday lives. When the thread that's being worked on is complete, all we are left with is a void-like feeling where we are able to access what quality was there before we started that pattern.

Among those of us who have done the intensive ceremony, there is a joke that we lost our minds in the very best way possible. Some of my friends even made a humourous theatrical video about it! If I hadn't been so desperate to stop the never-ending stream of thoughts, I might have had a fear of losing my ability to think through things in a logical, rational way. I know some folks I talked to that prided themselves on their logical intelligence felt this way beforehand. However, what I experienced after the ceremony was absolute silence that allowed me to heighten my presence in the moment. After so many years of being lost in thought, it felt weird to be so in tune with what was happening in the now.

However, I also learned that this is the only place where true power exists; trying to find it in the past or in the future was a futile waste of my precious energy. From this place of awareness, I was able to discern what the best course of action was in any given moment, not based on my past experiences, but based on what was *actually* happening now in the moment. I realized my tendency to defer to past events and the fact that they were often not relevant to the task at hand. I became much more efficient in running mental energy and no longer felt exhausted right from the moment of waking up. I noticed that my capacity for innovation also increased the more my energy returned.

The journal entries below may give readers a flavour for the kinds of patterns I recapitulated and what I learned about myself through the process. I still use a mini-version of this technique today when I find myself stuck in a memory or line of thinking that is compulsive. This is a way of making sure my mind stays quiet and it helps me to act out of clarity instead of reactivity in my life. It's also helped me to see reality for what it is instead of what I'd like it to be. Even in the most challenging moments, I am mostly able to hold my neutrality and discern the proper course of action that is being asked of me. If I can't hold neutrality, I see what is triggering me and I disarm it by recapitulating. I now know that I can only truly take command of what happens inside of me and I consciously put all my energy into doing that instead of trying to control external events.

Jan 26 and 27, 2011

The victory is that something has shifted around my tendency to beat myself up; I am not so hard on myself anymore and I've noticed more ease–even when I make mistakes (perceived or otherwise).

Feb 25, 2011

I did the recapitulation you suggested the other day. Got down to the before the self-hatred started. Lots of self-forgiveness for taking on responsibility for others in my family. And the fact that in this lifetime, I made a choice to do that when I was young and felt I couldn't go back. What I now know is that I am only responsible for me and that's okay. I knew that as a concept before. Now, I know it in my body/spirit/heart.

Feb 26, 2011

Now who am I? The question I've been sitting with since yesterday. Feels similar to how I felt after dearmouring in some

ways: a fresh start. I feel old patterns coming in and yet I don't act them out the same way. I am letting them pass through.

Mar 14, 2011

Because my mind was driving me nuts, I decided to start recapitulating by myself now. The pattern I worked with today was: wanting others to take care of me. I did this with the help of my animals. What was there in the before surprised me: deep peace. A lot around taking responsibility for my own actions then. Lots of apologies and self-forgiveness.

Mar 22, 2011

You're being thorough which is great but also remember to be efficient - like the animals - when they make a change it is pretty quick, then the rest is walking it out.

Tiger's Breath

So I took this to my mesa this morning to see why I wasn't quickly moving the patterns out. Realized it was a pattern I needed to recapitulate: being stuck in the past. What was there in the before: knowing I had everything I needed in this lifetime to complete what I came here to do. I had a belief that I needed to comb the past to find something I'd lost. There was also a belief that things don't change, which, of course, is not true. Lots of pieces to restore to myself and others. Also self-forgiveness. Noticed in a conversation with a family member tonight that the stickiness of connections was not there. My relationships are improving.

Mar 23, 2011

Did another recapitulation today: pattern of projecting into the future. What was there in the before was a sense of possibility at any moment. I had this idea that the future was more or less fixed. What I now know is that it is always changing. Self-forgiveness and restorations to some folks: mostly around thinking they would never change.

April 18, 2011

I recapitulated the pattern of working hard today. Been noticing this tendency is draining my energy and is unnecessary. It is also tied to the alopecia (hair loss). What was there in the before was lightness and listening to Spirit. When I asked why I started this pattern, the answer was that I believed people around me when they said I wasn't working hard enough and I needed to put in more effort. Did forgiveness. Being strong is another one I recapitulated. What was there in the before was saying yes to life and a feeling of openness. I started this pattern in order to cope with all the challenges that being open brings. Forgave myself for not seeing my vulnerability as a strength.

Beliefs

....

"We do not see things as they are.
We see them as we are."

- The Talmud

This article, "Going Mental" originally appeared on my blog on October 12, 2012:

> *Lately, my mind is driving me mental. Seriously, the inner dialogue has been unreal! Old stuff floating back that I thought I'd healed has been taking up space in my mind. I finally got fed up with it and decided to make a dream intent to heal my mind in my dreamtime. Last night, I woke up from a dream at 4 am (a time I affectionately call "happy hour" for spiritual healing in my life). In my dream, there was a furious, big man coming after me with a weapon. I started running until I could see some people coming down the hill in a park. I yelled at a woman holding a cell phone to call the police. She started dialing and the man stopped his pursuit. Usually, I wake up in the middle of the chase when my legs won't run anymore and he's about to seize me so this was interesting to me.*
>
> *I decided to use my shamanic tools to tell me what it meant and what to do about it. In my mind's eye, I drew a circle of protection around me and called my totem animals in to support me. I knew this had something to do with my ego and the thought occurred to me to call my ego outside my circle so we could have a chat. At first, all I saw was a white swirl that*

was chaotic energy: angry and furious. I witnessed it until it slowed down to a stop but I couldn't see anything. So when the energy was calm, I asked, "What do you look like?" Then, he appeared: the spitting image of Lord Farquaad, the evil character with "short man's complex" in the animated movie, Shrek. Of course my ego would come in this form! It made me laugh. We proceeded to have a conversation.

"Okay," I started, "why are you so angry?"

He started going on with a list of decisions I'd made recently that he thought was irresponsible. He was furious I hadn't listened to the orders he'd been barking at me.

So I calmly replied, "I know you think you know what's best for me and you are trying to survive. Telling me what to do and how to live my life is not your job. That job belongs to my Higher Self."

He looked at me puzzled and a little irritated, "Then what is my job?!"

I checked in with my inner wisdom and knowing that the ego does best when it has a job to do, I said, "To keep an open mind."

He looked at me in disgust. "What? How will I protect you from harm?"

"That's not your job. I have a warrior animal and my own instincts for that. In fact, when you go into panic and you are so loud in my head, you put me at more risk because I can't hear what Spirit and my Higher Self are directing me to do. I will not tolerate your cruelty and abusive behaviour any longer. I want to live in peace with you."

"No," he retorted. "You want to annihilate me."

"Yeah, " I responded, "That might have been true in the past when I thought you were an enemy that needed to be conquered but I don't feel that way any more. I've hung up my boxing gloves and I'm no longer going to war with pieces of myself I don't particularly like. Now you, lay off and stay in your role. I actually want you to stay. Do we have an agreement?"

> *He agreed and we sat there looking at each other for a long time in silence. I felt tremendous compassion for him and then my butterfly, my totem that helps with my mind, came and landed on my heart in the center of my chest and when I listened, I knew it was right to now invite Lord Farquaad, my ego, into my circle. He seemed relieved and perhaps a little bit touched to be out of exile. And everything became really calm in my space for the first time in months. I forgave myself for allowing my ego to harass me and run my life unchecked as well as forgetting to use my tools. I also forgave myself for banishing the pieces of myself I didn't like and vowed to accept them and live in peace with them.*

The journal entries below show how this lack of connection with my ego wreaked havoc in my life. Releasing harmful beliefs is, for me, a deeply healing process that is becoming increasingly compassion-filled the more I practice. I feel the access to my inner wise one has also expanded as a result.

Sep 14, 2010

My dreamer showed me that I wasn't inherently bad because I made mistakes. That I have a high level of integrity and the times when I do harm are because I am trying to get my needs met in the way I know how. When I know better, I do better kind of thing. And that my intent is not harmful 99% of the time. And even in times when I respond spitefully, etc. I don't stay there. I do own it and move through it. A part of me still feels like I've got to punish myself or else I will not get better. It is not totally gone but I feel like I have some perspective today that I didn't have in the same way before.

Sep 20, 2010

A friend sent me a video today about a gentleman who has no arms and legs that was totally inspiring to me (see resources

page for the video link). In 4 minutes, this gentleman amazed me with what he could do with his body as well as his attitude. It was such a good example of no pity. So when I walked out to the lake today, I had an inspiration to go up to my nagual medicine wheel and talk to my horse (my center power animal) about how to utilize the energy this man displayed for my healing. The thing I noticed about this energy was that it was a no matter what the conditions, there is a way to do it and it is your job to find it. My horse told me three things:

1. I learned to take in peoples' energy in order to understand it and survive in my childhood. It gets stuck when I try to "solve" stuff for others. To let folks solve their own stuff even if I have a sense of what it might be. I don't have to waste my energy trying to figure it out for them. That is enmeshment and co-dependence.
2. No pity with standing for my bottom lines. Doesn't matter how other people will take it. What matters is that I stay true to myself, even if it means "betraying" another.
3. The world is not going to create an environment that is sensitive to my needs. It is up to me to create that environment–to choose that environment from moment to moment–within me. And to act on what my insides are telling me I need for my health and wellbeing in that moment.

Dec 23, 2010

My day intent for today was to let go. I am seeing that a lot of the logic and old thinking patterns of my mind are getting in my way. It is like I can't think of a way something is going to possibly work out and so I block out other possibilities. I am learning from working with mesas that there is always a way to bring something to form and it often doesn't look the way I thought it would.

Don't do too much processing!!! Enjoy your life!
Wolf Woman

I took this with me into the bathtub today. Message: send all of it up to Spirit. I don't have to process it for it to shift and transform.

Jan 14, 2011

That feeling of being bad grew throughout the day again and so I asked my shadow animal for clarity. It was a restoration piece around allowing myself to transform and giving myself comfort and soothing instead of expecting it from the outside. My skunk brought me back a baby soother. Forgave myself for not finding a good way to soothe myself after my soother was taken away as a toddler. Eating dinner after that restoration felt different so I know that piece of seeking food for comfort is shifted. Sending up big gratitude to Spirit.

Jan 31, 2011

My relatives are not happy that I am not staying with them when I come to Vancouver. They pulled the guilt card and I took it on. This surprised me! Not that they pulled it but that I fell for it! Ended up going up to my nagual medicine wheel to work with my shadow animal around it. Discovered and gave away beliefs I had about what families "should" be. For one thing, that they "should" be one particular thing. Others: "We should always be nice to each other." Or "We should tell each other everything." Also restored my ability to put my attention where I wanted it to go rather than having that dictated by my family members. Lots of forgiveness. Prayed to Spirit that I do what's best for me when I go visit–even if it is not the popular thing to do.

Mar 3, 2011

Did the recapitulation on myself last night and it had to do with deservement. Growing up, food was used as punishment and reward and as a control tool so that made sense to me. I had it linked to being a bad kid. I made a dream intent to reconnect with the earth and the pleasure that food brings and I noticed that I was more grounded as I ate today. Self-forgiveness too for allowing the abuse and not standing up for myself. Was interesting to do the recapitulation on myself. That was the first time and I felt those places where I wanted to give up and my totem animals helping me to pull through.

Relationship Myths

"sacred cow: someone or something that has been accepted or respected for a long time and that people are afraid or unwilling to criticize or question."
-Merriam-Webster Dictionary online

Although my inner idealist can go after altruistic goals, this aspect of me in the dark can turn into a zealot who has strong opinions about how the world should be and how people should behave. I once did a ceremony called Ignorance to Wisdom where I had to examine my beliefs. I was shocked at what it was costing me in my relationships to hold some of these stances. Some of the blind spots I had were actually making me vulnerable to danger. I've already established that I have no control over the choices of others and so how I think they should act is also irrelevant. Forcing others to do what I think is right is also, as it turns out, a violent act because we each have free will.

To impose my own values on someone else–altruistic or otherwise–is disrespectful of their sovereignty. Of course this doesn't mean that we shouldn't have laws or that violent folks should be allowed to roam the streets hurting others, because it would also not be responsible of a society to allow harm to come to its citizens. On a personal level, however, I became increasingly conscious of how the way I treated folks who were in relationship with me was more dictatorial than mutually respectful at times. It was harming my relationships at deep levels. I did this because of my need to feel safe; attempting to control the outside world was a default I went to in times of uncertainty.

In fact, I realized that I did not have a good relationship with the unknown. I began to see that there is more mystery in life than things I know for sure. After recapitulation week, I realized that even the things I thought I knew I didn't really know. All I had was my perspective and experience. I came to see that others had their own that were just as valid as mine. One night, I had a dream that I relayed in an e-mail to Wolf Woman:

I was standing in a wheat field watching a scene in front of me. A woman who had Indian Goddess Kali–like energy was making love to two men. After she was done making love with the one behind her, she literally slashed him to ribbons with her fingernails and he died. She continued making love to the other man unfazed. I was disturbed by the scene but fascinated at the same time. I noticed new life growing where the dead man's body was–his blood feeding the earth.

To me, Kali represents the insidious ways the ego can work to try to prevent change. Kali finds those beliefs and chops them away unceremoniously. I came to the sobering realization that there are no guarantees in relationships. This includes the illusion that they should or will last forever. And I also saw that just because a relationship doesn't work long term doesn't mean it was a failure. Sometimes the most loving thing we can do is to respect differences that are too big to bridge and let each other go. I thought back to all the folks I'd dated and I was so grateful to each of them for helping me to figure out another piece of the relationship puzzle. What did I want in a relationship? What did I need? What were my bottom lines that I would not budge from? I didn't know the answers to many of these in earlier times in my life. Relationships are serious growth edges if we are willing to see ourselves mirrored in the other person and to take responsibility for our own actions, thoughts, and feelings.

As you will see from these journal entries, some of the sacred cows I'd bought into came from my culture, some came from the society I grew up in, and some came from my own experiences. Ultimately, however, all of them morphed inside me as my own creations. I saw life through my own unique filters. I feel it is worth asking ourselves if our beliefs are really true. Just because we believe something doesn't make it helpful to us. Just because our egos are telling us something is true doesn't make it so. We humans like certainty because it is comfortable but as we grow, our values will also change as we learn more about ourselves and the world. This is as it should be if we don't want to stay in ignorance.

Not knowing can cause more harm to ourselves, others, and the planet. Now, I get curious about another person's worldview and value system–especially if it is way off the track I am familiar with. I consider where their point of view might be valid in my own life. Although sometimes what is required is to agree to disagree, I can still be kind to folks I don't agree with and find places where we can meet on common ground. By shutting people down, I was missing valuable chances to learn more about life.

Sep 3, 2010

I know I need to clean up my relationship myths this year. Two have been revealed:

1. **I must give up part of my own authority in relationship with men so that their egos are kept happy–otherwise the relationship won't work or I will never find a mate.**
2. **I must take care of men–that there are some things they simply cannot do for themselves.**

Of course, these myths come from my culture. These are the myths I have been struggling with in my relationship with Ewan and I now see how they were operating and what they were costing me (and him because that is so disempowering

to think that men are not capable in some ways). These myths are not my truth and so I let go of them.

Sep 12, 2010

I realized upon waking this morning that what Ewan and I have had running is lust. It can be exciting and fun but after a while, it just exhausts me. I make love for connection, play, to exchange heart and soul energy, to transcend with another. That's what I want. I want the sensitivity, the tenderness and the yum in sex. I want the juicy and not so much the aching. I want to feel that something life-giving happened between myself and the other. And lust feels like another addiction; another something that just fills me up from the outside. So I made a decision to just be friends with Ewan. I need some time to figure out how to fill myself up.

Sep 16, 2010

Woke up again from a dream crying. It was a big one. Basically, an ex-boyfriend proposed to me. He is often in my dreams and seems to represent my heart's yearning and how I am interacting with it. In all these years, he's never proposed to me before in a dream. He had all these rings for me to choose from–all metal ones that were too small. He'd sized them according to my finger size in high school. None of those were as interesting as a plastic "jellybean" ring I had in elementary school that was also among the choices. I smiled when I saw it and it reminded me of playfulness and joy in relationship. I initially said yes to marrying him but I realized that I had made a mistake when I went to the washroom and Ewan appeared and said, "Is that what you really want?" And the answer was no. I realized that I've been operating out of these old pictures of what a committed relationship is. When I woke up, I went to my nagual medicine wheel because I was so confused. My raccoon (dream animal) told me I was wearing two masks that needed to come off in order for me to really move towards the kind of relationship with another that I really wanted in my heart. I heard a while back that every seven years our bodies are completely new; that our cells are always dying and regenerating and this is the cycle of time it takes them to completely regenerate all over our bodies. So I am in my 5th cycle of being new. I just turned 35. And I decided this morning after waking up from that dream that I am going to walk with my new self toward a field of possibility for my life that I know I never imagined for myself.

Dec 2, 2010

Since the talk I attended on relationships a couple of weeks ago, the piece that has been rocking around my old paradigm of living is the bit where she said: Trust no one. Only yourself and God. I hated that statement and a part of me has been reeling against that for two weeks not sure I wanted to live in a world where I could not trust anyone. I see today the wisdom in that statement too and places where I didn't assert myself with Ewan for fear of losing the relationship. In the end, here I am–just me again. And so why not go through life just trusting myself and God? I want reliable; well, that is constant. Me and God. And I also have started to really shift my sacred cows about trust. I now know what they are: That a relationship isn't worthwhile unless I can trust the person and if that trust is broken, my happiness goes along with it. I am willing to accept now that it is myself I need to trust. I see how that is a big burden to put on someone, responsibility for my happiness. I forgave myself for all the ways I caused myself pain with that sacred cow.

Trust Versus Faith

Trust is based on your life experiences of what trust is. No one except for you know what that level of trust is. Even through communication. Therefore trust is an unreasonable expectation because everyone has their own personal life experiences of trust and while it may change over time no one is the same. Faith on the other hand is knowing a person is doing the best they can and sometimes their best works and sometimes it doesn't. Base faith on agreements and a person's ability to keep their agreements through actions, words and deeds. They are walking their talk and see if what you need as a faith bond and what another needs meet up. Have faith people will change as they grow and hopefully you grow together. Love is not a binding agreement, it is possibility. Faith creates the possibility of deeper love. We only have our words and actions.

Just some thoughts,
Wolf Woman

Dec 12, 2010

Woke up in the middle of the night frozen in fear. I lay there for a while and when I noticed I was barely breathing, got up to do qigong and get my energy running well again. I felt a weight on my chest for a while now and that spot ended up being where I stored my life disappointments. So now that I know about sacred cows, they are mooing all over the place. Turned out that my skunk (shadow animal) told me I had a belief that life was supposed to go smoothly. When I let go of that belief I saw how much pain it caused because every time I had a disappointment, I would beat myself up thinking I was doing something wrong or had made a mistake when really, it is just a natural part of life. I also realized that I had a belief that I would get to a place in my evolution where I would just be coasting. But if I've committed to personal growth, I will never be coasting. There is still a part of me that wants to stay in the boring routine just because it is safe and it is warring with the other part of me that knows that it is not my nature to stay stagnant. I like beauty, surprise, adventure, learning new things, and variety. My power animal is a horse, for goodness sake!

Dec 13 and 14, 2010

My idealist sacred cows are getting a run for their money. Holy shit. Uncovered some not so pretty ones after one of these people snapped at me for what I thought was an unjust reason. Ready? Yuck. I hate to admit them out loud.

1. People should always be nice to me
2. People should be nice to each other

Saw how these beliefs kept me in an unresourceful, dependent, needy state. Can see why some folks are snappy in the face of this sticky energy. So it is good because it teaches me the places where I lean on people and the places where I drop the ball on my dream. Struggling with people not following through. Being able to depend on someone's word is important to me. I hate having to scramble last minute to pull up the slack or make other arrangements. Some of the people have said they would do something and then not come through and not communicated. I have talked to them about it; they seemed to justify their actions though. Not too happy about that. Will work with my shadow animal about how to deal with it.

Mindfulness

....

From a chapter called "Learning To Sit With Your Shit:"

> *"Lightbulb moments, through mindfulness, rewire my brain...*
> *Now, what I've learned is that I have to feel uncomfortable...*
> *to change...I have to stay mindful to that power of addiction,*
> *every single day...This mindfulness stuff is new to me. I was*
> *wired and trained to react; slowing down and thinking are*
> *things I am still working on."*
> *-Theo Fleury from "Conversations with a Rattlesnake"*

Initially, a part of me thought that my addiction would be healed when I no longer had the compulsive thoughts and cravings in response to stressful moments. The reality is that I spent a lifetime paving well-worn neural pathways in my brain and traveling those highways for years. Although I broke those pathways up and weakened them through recapitulation, some of them are still there five years after my healing process ended for addiction. From talking to other addicts, I've come to realize that mindfulness is an unending process in life. Any one of us can be caught up in some weird trigger that comes out of the blue at any moment. Although I can't control the thoughts that come into my mind but I can certainly question them and get curious about them. Every time I do that, I get a nugget of wisdom about myself as well as an opportunity to change my response. This practice alone starts to build new neural highways in my brain that give me novel options for responding to stimuli that are triggering for me. I am able to be at peace with the fact that those thoughts are there and they no longer have the hold on me that they once did.

Sitting through cravings, I got the chance to really see how they worked and what happened at every point in the "wave," as I like to call it. I noticed that the wave was not creative; it did the same thing every time with more or less intensity depending on circumstance. Einstein once said that the definition of insanity is: "Doing the same thing over and over again and expecting different results." I learned to track the thoughts that led up to the wave in order to catch it at the beginning the more and more I practiced. When I was conscious of what was happening, I had a much better chance of working through a situation rather than just reaching for food. It was not comfortable or easy. It took me a while before I was successful at sitting with it. Early attempts were challenging. In fact, meditating for even a few minutes was so painful I'd end up in tears and would not be able to continue.

After practicing for a long time with determination and strategy, I learned that I would not die if I didn't follow that train of thought with an action. I could sit with discomfort and listen to what it was teaching me. A Buddhist monk I worked with for a while taught me to imagine in my mind that I am cutting the thought with scissors and throwing it away when I find myself following a thought thread that will lead to self-harm. The mantra was: cut and cancel. That worked really well for me; I still use it today. Then, I simply get back to being an observer of thoughts. How often I went off track didn't matter; what I focused on was the act of catching that moment when I followed the thought. I don't do sitting meditations much anymore. I find that I am able to get into that mindful state in the act of doing whatever it is I am doing now. However, that did take years of practice. I know that for some people moving meditations are more effective than sitting ones.

In shamanism it is common to work with our inner masculine and inner feminine to bring them into balance. Shamans notice that each person has these aspects within them regardless of their gender. Our inner feminine is represented by the left side of our bodies; she is our intuitive, dreaming aspect who is very closely linked to our Dreamer. She knows our sacred purpose and knows how to lead the way if we tune into her. Our inner masculine is represented by the right side of our bodies; he is our active element who knows how to stalk out parts of the dream to bring it into form in the physical world.

The Toltecs knew that our inner Dreamer and Stalker work together in a perfect marriage inside of us. The Dreamer gives direction to the Stalker based on our life purpose; our Dreamer knows what our purpose is and shows us what we need to do every step of the way and she will show us if we ask and listen. The Stalker is not supposed to call the shots. His role is to seek out ways to manifest the dream; he is persistent and does not give up, trying many new things until something finally works. When he is stuck, he has conversations with his Dreamer half to gain inspiration and new ideas for how to proceed. My inner man acted as my personal bullshit detector. I have a cunning mind and so I had to watch that my actions were not coming from my ego, instead that they were coming from my Dreamer. Before the smallest act, I learned to check in with her so that my addict aspect did not take over.

Aug 6, 2010

Was feeling restless and uneasy today as well as tired. I got the familiar feeling of wanting comfort from food. But I was also hungry so it was a bit confusing. When I talked to my inner man about it, he said to eat the blueberries and hydrate myself but to leave the carbs out for now. With my blood sugar up a bit, I felt better but the feeling was still there so he directed me to figure out what it was about. It turned out that it was not really my stuff at all. I've come back from my trip really changed and my family has been a bit anxious about the new me. So I am riding the waves of that. I was laying on my stomach on the grass to help me figure this all out and so I just sent that energy into the earth. I immediately felt better and my inner man told me that now I could eat the carbs. Before

I left for Scotland, I was warrioring through but it was like something on my "To Do List" like I've got to get this done. Now, that urgency is not there. I am still doing my work but it is based in present time and in the process of it rather than the end result and when I am going to get there and wanting to get it over with already. It is just another way I used to try to skip all those uncomfortable feelings...to get it over with. And I feel more grounded with knowing that everything that needs to get done will get done. My trip taught me a healthy respect for my Dreamer and my Stalker and the way they work together. I really got to see them in action and get to know the dynamic in a clearer way.

Dec 31, 2010

Went to the post office to pick up a package from a relative that came for Christmas. Inside, she lovingly wrapped up a variety of traditional Portuguese sweets that we make for Christmas. Of course, I can't eat most of them. At first because I was so touched by what she packed in there and what she said, I thought: "But she went through all this care." Then my integrity with myself kicked in and said: take them to a friend's house; he and his boys will eat them. In her card, she wrote in Portuguese: "It was a hard Christmas for me without you but I want you to know that I support your decision to move and I am proud of you." So all the healing and transformation seems to be working. I am totally stunned, personally. Who knew?

Jan 19, 2011

Last night as my dream intent, I chose to re-commit to my healing. I never imagined at the beginning of this healing process that I would have to re-commit so many times! I guess life is like that though. It seems like the more things I master, the more challenges appear and I am learning to be more comfortable with uncertainty. I have moments, like yesterday, where I don't know if I can pull all this stuff off in a good way and my fear of not getting the approval from those around me gets at me. The victory here is that these times of collapsing are getting fewer and I can pick myself up a lot faster than I used to be able to.

Self-pity and Self-importance

> *"Sorcerers had unmasked self-importance and found that it is self-pity masquerading as something else...Self-pity is the real enemy and source of man's misery."*
> *-Carlos Castaneda from "The Power of Silence"*

This pull between self-responsibility as warriorship and falling into self-importance and self-pity is ever present in a spiritual journey. One of the challenges a spiritual warrior has is to be aware of these energies when they are present and transform them by doing the inner battle of taking responsibility for one's part in the situation our self-pity and self-importance is attached to. This is also the essence of ho'oponopono: if we are caught up in reactivity to something, we have a part in the situation and when we forgive our part in it, we gain more inner peace and balance. This is not a forced or surface act; ho'oponopono and spiritual warriorship require us to dig deep inside of ourselves to take ultimate responsibility for all our reactions and responses to the situations life throws at us in order to help us grow and evolve.

I want to talk about the difference between a spiritual warrior and a warrior in the way mainstream society knows this term. Modern day warriors come in the form of soldiers who fight in armies supposedly for an altruistic cause. They are not taught to question whether war is really needed; they are trained to obey orders. Over thousands of years, we humans have well trained in the belief that the only way to deal with interpersonal conflict is to go to war. In this way, taking lives is justified. As a history minor,

I studied wars throughout history to see how many conflicts were actually resolved by going to war and I did not find any. War and violence usually breeds more war and violence. The exiled leader of Tibet, the Dalai Lama, understood this when he refused to go to war with China after the Chinese invaded his country:

> *"War is obsolete, you know. Of course the mind can rationalize fighting back but the heart...would never understand. Then you would be divided in yourself, the heart and the mind, and the war would be inside you. The very purpose of religion is to control yourself, not to criticize others. Rather, we must criticize ourselves. How much am I doing about my anger? About my attachment, about my hatred, about my pride, my jealousy? These are the things which we must check in daily life."*

I personally feel that in the modern world, having warriors in place that will defend life if needed is important. We are living in a time when technological "advances" have created weapons that can wipe out life by pressing a button. After thousands of years of intergenerational trauma, there are a lot of unstable people in our world. I honour the men and women who are willing to go to war in order to defend the lives of others. I believe many modern-day soldiers feel they are doing the right thing when they serve their countries. I personally cannot stand behind going to war in the supposed name of God, to secure resources, prove a point, or further divide groups of humans as if we didn't all belong to the same species.

In my experience, what the Dalai Lama is getting at in this quote is the element of spiritual warriorship that is necessary if we are ever to evolve beyond warring with ourselves and others. First, we look inside to see how we are contributing to the conflict. Then, once we've done our own healing work on those internal issues, we see what actions need to be taken in the outside world, if any. This might involve standing for the wellbeing of the environment, of children, of reproductive rights, of the elderly, and so on. Many spiritual warriors in history have shown how tremendous gains can be made through non-violent resistance including Martin Luther

King Jr., Mahatma Gandhi, and Nelson Mandela. These men all looked inside to change their inner states before leading people in non-violent acts that revealed truth to the public. They insisted on freedom and equality without going to war with weapons. Instead, they utilized all aspects of their medicine wheel intelligences (heart, mind, body, spirit, life force) to spark change in the world.

I am sure all these spiritual warriors faced down their own self-pity, wanting to quit many times. They had to talk down their "poor me" and "why me" voices. They faced down their self-importance and arrogance in order to remain focused on the main issues, using their influence to ripple out transformation to the masses. In my smaller way, I did the same in order to heal my addiction to food, sending ripples into my lineage. The inner warriorship continues on my spiritual journey today–a challenge I happily undertake each day because it's the only thing I really have full control over in life. What I do inside myself matters.

Jun 14, 2010

The horse is my power totem–the animal most like my spirit's essence. Been thinking more about what you said in terms of horses standing for no pity and relating it to the spin I went through while assisting and helping with the sweat. I took this up to my nagual medicine wheel and talked to my horse. Well, she basically gave me a non-stop tongue-lashing. The gist: "Everything you have been praying for is manifesting in your life. This is what you do with a gift from Spirit. Yeah it's hard. Stop your complaining and do your fucking work." So then I got it. I am wasting energy on harping on the "this is hard" thing. My energy needs to go into the work, self-forgiveness, and walking this path that I chose.

Aug 10, 2010

I realized is that I have developed some good stalking strategies this summer that are working for me: mindfully holding a heart

space for myself and my process, utilizing ruthlessness (which has been surprisingly healing), and learning to recognize self-pity and self-importance when they are present and to shift out of those states. I don't need to inflate myself (self-importance) in order to pump up my ego and reinforce how "right" I am. I also don't need to sink into self-pity when things get hard. I can just be with what is so in the moment and figure out where to go from there.

Chapter 9

THE CENTRE

Centre Introduction:
Transforming Addiction Spirals

....

"How might I counsel my young self differently, given the neural insights I've collected since then?...Learn to say no in a way that can catch and take hold, and support it with a different view of yourself, so that ego fatigue doesn't leach away all your resolve. Fill your life with meanings rich enough at least to compete with, if not defeat, the well-worn synapses of imagined value. Remind yourself that the imagined value is deceptive–that's the way it works. Your brain echoes with messages that can inspire victory or defeat...Those messages can't be eradicated, but you can add other, gentler voices into the mix. And don't give up. The brain loses a great deal of flexibility with addiction, but it doesn't lose it all... There are only a few things that can be done to beat addiction, and addicts have to change many parts of themselves in order to carry them out."

- Mark Lewis PhD from "Memoirs of an Addicted Brain: A Neuroscientist Examines his Former Life on Drugs"

I like this hopeful message from Dr. Lewis because it shows that no matter what our choices have been in the past or what we've experienced, change is possible. One of the hardest things was to keep coming back to a place of choice and to keep re-committing to my healing. There were times when I was dwelling on all of the harm that others had caused me in my life and I refused to take ownership of what I'd done to myself to extend that harm. There is a big piece of responsibility we each must take for what we do inside of us (consciously or unconsciously) with the input we receive from others. And this does not mean that the people who harmed us are not without responsibility for their own actions–of course they are! However, healing does not come from being stuck in blaming or shaming others or ourselves for past mistakes; healing comes from forgiveness and taking action in the present to create different results in the future.

As much as we may not like to hear this information, Dr. Lewis' book also shows how our brains are in some ways vulnerable to addiction by virtue of how they are designed. There is a physiological and chemical reality to our make-up as humans that we can't ignore. We can stack the deck in our children's favour, for instance, by learning all we can about how the brain develops so we can change our parenting practices to support healthy development in our children. Many of the child-rearing skills we inherited from our ancestors are unwittingly contributing to the epidemic of addiction in North American today. In fact, instead of "skills" we can call them "dysfunctions" because many of our ancestors were traumatized people themselves who never developed good parenting skills because they simply had no healthy models from which to learn. I began to see on my journey how much of an energy waste it was to blame and shame my ancestors for simply doing the best they knew how to do with the knowledge they had. It is incumbent on us today as a society to begin to learn all we can about how addiction really works so that we can teach future generations of humans better strategies for living based on a "thrive" model of living instead of a "survive" one.

As descendants of traumatized people, we can do nothing to change the past. However, we can transform ourselves into healthier, well-balanced humans so that we can begin to be image-makers for our children. Even through the dysfunction, I can see how my relatives were able to do better in their parenting than their parents did. There are patterns my grandparents ran, for instance, that my parents were able to overcome. Decisions my grandparents made to come to Canada increased the possibility for me to break the patterns that had plagued my ancestors by raising me in a more politically and economically stable nation. I received the benefit of being part of the first generation in my family to not have to struggle to get an education or live at poverty level. I believe that this took me out of basic survival so that I could begin working on refining my character.

The centre of the medicine wheel turns all the other directions or spokes of the wheel. The centre is the place of life force and sexual energy where anything is possible. It's the void we are all birthed out of and the place we go back to when we die. The centre is catalyst, transformative, and chaotic; it shakes up our inner norms so we have a shot at reorganizing our inner worlds in a way that works.

Transformation happens by working all aspects of the inner medicine wheel in order to see what patterns are working and which are not. I had to change on every level of being in order to heal my addiction. This was my work to do and I did it. It took effort on my part, a community of support, a willingness to look at what was causing my pain and constant mindfulness. This next chapter goes into these themes in more detail.

In order to consolidate your understanding of this direction from your personal, experiential and embodied perspective, I recommend doing the following ceremonies from "Shamanic Ceremonies for a Changing World" by Marilyn Keffer and Gael Carter. You can find more information on how to purchase a copy by looking at the Recommended Resources section of the Appendix of this book.

Determining your Principles Ceremony 2-15
The Battle Katchinas Ceremony 2-17

Abuse and Trauma: Connections with Addiction

....

"Addictions always originate in pain, whether felt openly or hidden in the unconscious. They are emotional anesthetics... they ease psychological discomfort...The research literature is unequivocal: most hard-core substance abusers come from abusive homes."

-Dr. Gabor Maté from "In the Realm of Hungry Ghosts: Close Encounters with Addiction"

I have physical and sexual abuse in my personal history. Going into the details of what happened and who did it really would not serve the purpose of this book: it's irrelevant, in fact. It is likely, based on current research, that the perpetrators had physical and sexual abuse in their histories too. This does not excuse the harm this did in my life but it does shine a light on the cyclical nature of abuse. Kids do not have the reasoning ability to see that adults are, in fact, responsible for their own actions. Many tend to think they brought on the violence themselves.

It wasn't until I read Theo Fleury and Kim Barthel's book "Conversations with a Rattlesnake" that I realized years after healing my addiction that the abuse was not my fault. Like a lot of kids, I grew up thinking I was bad. If an adult hit me in a moment of their own frustration or impatience, I thought that was my fault. In the book, Kim reinforces over and over with Theo that the abuse was not his fault. It was not until half way through reading that book that I realized I was still holding on to the belief that I had instigated the abuse in some way. Really, I was just being a kid and it was incumbent on the adults to guide me in healthy ways instead of violent ones.

I want to present some dire and perhaps daunting information but before I do, I also want to underscore that it is absolutely possible to heal from these experiences; the past does not have to define the rest of your life. Part of the reason for this book is so addicts know that they are not doomed to live a life of pain and despair. I kept seeking support until I found it. I surrounded myself with people who believed in me and had the experience and expertise to help me. Most importantly, I didn't give up on myself.

According to a *National Post* article by Sarah Boesveld dated April 22, 2014, "More than a third of Canadians have suffered some kind of child abuse in their lives." These statistics include physical abuse (including corporal punishment by caregivers) and sexual abuse. While this article goes on to hum and haw around how serious the prevalence of this is in our society, the fact is that it is not the severity of the event itself that necessarily determines the impact it has on someone's life but how the person internalizes what happened. The spanking of a toddler, though still legal in Canada as a parental discipline strategy, can have serious effects on the psyche and self-esteem of a growing child.

We know today that the first three years of a child's life set lifelong patterns in motion–for better or for worse. How we treat children matters. Many countries in the world have chosen to take this data seriously and have banned corporal punishment in the home and in schools. Many are also creating public policies that extend useful and meaningful support to addicts. There are also many programs available to parents today who want to learn better parenting skills. Sadly, in North America the "War on Drugs" has really turned into a war on abused people who are addicted to numbing out pain.

I say this not to shame parents or to excuse the addict's behavior, but rather to really shed light on the harm that's being done to one in three people in Canadian society. In your mind's eye, picture all of the people you know–including friends, family, and colleagues–and put them in a football stadium or out on a field. Divide that mental image into thirds and then isolate one of them. That is how many people you know that have endured some sort of abuse in their lifetime. Just because they've never admitted it to you, doesn't mean it didn't happen or isn't happening.

In fact, these statistics are problematic because people who have been abused often don't report it so the numbers may actually be higher than we think. It goes without saying that many of these are children who do not know their rights or may be afraid of the consequences of telling. It is also a fact that many of the folks abusing children are family members and close friends of the family so that further causes a conflict inside of the child around disclosure. Many people do speak out and those in authority positions do not believe them or further shame them for what happened. Others are so ashamed by what happened and feel so powerless that they never even tell the people they love and trust the most. Many more develop the coping strategy early on of blocking these memories out so they can function in every day life; they may not even be consciously aware that they were abused. Many of these people wander around feeling depressed and suicidal without knowing why.

> *"It's pretty important to teach kids that their bodies belong to them and that they can decide who touches them. To walk over this boundary in young children makes them more easy targets for sexual and physical abuse. I feel pretty strongly about this. When we force kids to hug or kiss people–relatives or even their parents–we send the message to them that they are not in control of their bodies and what happens to them... Not only was I forced to hug my rapist in front of people on a regular basis...but one of the reasons I never told anybody about the sexual violence was because I assumed behaviors such as the forced hugging meant that the violence was also acceptable for him to do."*
>
> *-James St. James*

I have also met addicts who say they did not experience abuse but still found the everyday stressors of living in our society unbearable. Some of these folks turn to substances to numb out the pain of pressurized living. The following is a story called "Beauty in Disguise" written by Brooke from the book "Women's Power Stories: Honouring the Feminine Principle of Life:"

> *I was addicted to cocaine. None of my friends knew. Nobody knew. Although now in hindsight, some of them admit to having a feeling about it but to mostly being in denial. I was good at hiding it. I'll never forget driving in a car with another friend when I admitted that I wanted to die... It was a blessing in disguise because they all rallied behind me. The hospital was going to release me and they advocated for me to be admitted. My living situation was unsafe, I was indeed suicidal, and I'd simply use again if I left. They knew I needed treatment. It worked. This new [treatment] center had room for fourteen women. I was looking around at all these women and I thought: 'I don't belong here. I wasn't physically, mentally, or sexually abused in my past.' A lot of these women had been in the cycle of addiction for ten to twenty years. I was only two years into my addiction. I found myself comparing my situation to theirs. I felt guilty–like I had no right to go into an addiction. I thought I was taking someone's spot that needed it more than I did or who deserved it more than I did.*

What Brooke later realized with the help of a counselor is that it was not a matter of deserving to get help or not and that each situation is unique. She discovered that she was worth it and she went after healing all of the reasons she was using. Today, she is no longer addicted to cocaine and has begun working to help others who struggle in life.

If one is really serious about healing an addiction, giving up is not a viable option. You cannot do the healing work when you are dead from an overdose, overwork, or prolonged systemic health issues. Healing requires a no-matter-what attitude. This means learning to harness our consciousness and the power of our will to overcome cravings, well-worn behaviour patterns, and negative self-talk. In the end, our spirit is stronger than our ego identity and will always win. Resistance is futile. Surrender is the sane choice.

I leaned on the strength and power of my Dreamer when I felt the cravings coming on. During a shamanic journey, I had the chance to meet my Dreamer and much to my surprise, she was not broken, sad, mean-spirited, or awful. In fact, she is so radiant, alive, and benevolent that it disarmed me at first. I'd been going through my life thinking that my addict-self was the only part of me there was. It never occurred to me that the addict was only one tiny part of me and that I could draw from the parts of me that were healthy to help me heal. My Dreamer reminded me that at the spirit level, no one is broken–everyone is whole.

When I looked at what was keeping me from feeling whole in the physical realm, I found a general tendency to give up on myself in a way that I would never give up on one of my students or someone I love when they are struggling. This gave me pause for reflection: Why do I do that to myself if I wouldn't do it to another person? I truly thought that I was a horrible person. Every small mistake I made and every sideways glance I got from others seemed to reinforce this faulty belief. I would berate myself for every small thing and then I'd add to that by remembering all the other times in the past that I made mistakes, that someone chastised me for something, or that I was excluded from the group. This deepened my sense of isolation and I really began believing that I was the only one in the world going through this. Of course, the self-pity never helps anything; it is just an indulgent way of keeping us stuck in our inner drama.

The truth is that millions of people all over the world had rough upbringings, struggle with addiction, and live in war-torn areas that are rife with human trauma. Most of us are dealing with ancestral trauma that has been passed on by our ancestors. In fact, there is beginning scientific evidence coming out of New York's Mount Sinai hospital showing that ancestral trauma is held in our DNA. We grew up with patterns that were taught to our parents–even implicitly–by their parents such as: giving up personal power, entitlement, fear of failure, refusal to change, self-pity, self-importance, aggression, passivity, and lack of perseverance. I haven't met anyone with an idyllic upbringing, so feeling sorry for ourselves and others is not the answer. If it were an important part of the healing process, the world would be healed many times over by now!

Family Rules and Keeping Secrets

"Families have codes about what is allowed and what is not. There are rules of communication: who talks to whom, when, and how. There are rules about the demonstrations of feelings: which are acceptable and which are not. And there are rules of conduct: how everyone behaves within the family as well as how each individual is to act outside the family. The rules are not necessarily stated outright, but each family member knows what they are. It is these unspoken rules that generally protect the family secrets and keep the family looking good to the outside world...Children who must decipher and obey strict family codes quickly lose touch with their internal world and become guardians of the family image. This is a spiritual and intellectual boundary violation."

- Megan LeBoutillier from "No is a Complete Sentence: Learning the Sacredness of Personal Boundaries"

I am consciously breaking a fundamental family rule in the telling of my story via this book that has spanned generations. I was taught implicitly and explicitly that what happens in the family, stays in the family; moreover, I was told repeatedly that I could not trust anyone outside our extended family system. I vacillated in writing this book for so long because of that rule; I wanted to appear loyal and loving to my family members because I am. However, the abuse I allowed in my earlier years was a direct result of obeying this rule. Healing my addiction was a process of opening my eyes to see that this piece of my foundation set by my ancestors and accepted unquestioningly by me was rotten to the core. In writing this book, I let go of the vestiges of those early teachings for good.

In fact, what keeps the cycles of abuse going so strongly in lineages is the keeping of secrets. A common saying in Alcoholics Anonymous is: "You're only as sick as your secrets." The unwillingness to seek help from outside the family circle cements these static beliefs because without outside positive influence and image making of what is possible in life, change is almost impossible. I say *almost* because I have great faith in the strength of our souls to persevere through the toughest of obstacles in order to reach for the light that is our birthright as humans.

I love my family. My intent was never to hurt them; I desperately wanted to live my Sacred Dream and I knew that the only way to do that was to step outside the confines they set for me. I know they saw this initially as evidence that I was disloyal, ungrateful, uncaring, and selfish. This has simply never been the case. Today, I see what I could not see in my early life: I have a responsibility to my essence, my ancestors, and to my descendants to live the life I was meant to live and to share what I learned with others in case any of these wisdom nuggets can help them on their life journeys.

Every generation has the opportunity to leave the world in a better condition than they found it in when they were born. No matter what the obstacles plaguing the people in various eras, there have always been human beings who had the courage to fly in the face of conventional "wisdom" to carve out their own pathways and discover new, life-giving ways to be in the world.

I wrote the bulk of this book in 2015. In the warmer months, I like to spend most of my time outdoors in my garden tending to the plants and listening to the messages of the animals that come visit me. A relative had built a beautiful birdhouse that he put up in our fairy garden the previous year. This year, chickadees decided to raise their brood in there after scouting it out rigorously over the winter months. I wondered why they chose our garden and what meaning that might have for me at this point in my life. It turns out that chickadees are the truth-bringers; their medicine is to point out hidden truths that need to be spoken for the benefit of all.

I discovered that these tiny birds are capable of *big* energy and are persistent in their guardianship of the truths in life. When I started to prepare my garden in April, their chicks had already hatched; they were protective and watched me intently as I worked. I spoke to them to let them know I meant them no harm and that they could raise their babies in my garden without fear. They settled after that but they hedged their bets by making sure one parent was going out for food while the other stayed with the chicks. They stayed true to their instincts.

Releasing family secrets and rules that did not serve me deepened my regard for myself and my trust in my own instincts to carry me through life with my integrity intact. In the course of healing my addiction, I had an epiphany: I was the only person I had to be around all the time until my last breath. I could not choose to go spend time with someone else to escape so I better learn to really love myself and be honest with myself in compassionate ways.

It Takes a Village

....

"We'll love you until you learn to love yourself."
                                                    -Alcoholics Anonymous

A while ago, I was having a conversation with an American friend about service to humanity. She told me point blank that she didn't believe there was such a thing as a self-made person. She told me that she was aware that this is part of the "American Dream" of her people but she simply doesn't see how that can possibly be the case when the world depends on service people in order to run. I listened with interest and took in what she was saying; I could hear truth in it.

Imagine what the world would be like without postal workers, janitors, maids, grocery clerks, child-care providers, cooks, assistants, teachers, secretaries, nurses, doctors, and spiritual mentors. How is it indeed possible that someone achieves any measure of success without the support of people dedicated to service? Even the president of the United States depends upon people to cook for him, book his appointments, and get him to where he needs to go on time. It made sense to me, then, that we are really interdependent and the true leaders are the ones who recognize that, value people who are of service, and respond to their needs. In our society, this is all backwards. Service people are often treated as slaves, but that is another topic.

Perhaps it is possible to heal an addiction on your own. I have not personally met every addict in the world to know if that is true or not. However, I do know that the vast majority of addicts I've met needed a good support system around them in order to recover fully. One of the hallmarks of addiction is the feeling of isolation and that they are not accepted and do not belong anywhere. Many addicts do not have a healthy community to interact within. Addicts across the board tend to have weak skills in some areas including: impulse control, self-command, boundary setting, and will direction, to name a few. During the healing phase of an addiction, addicts need to lean on the will of others so they can maintain their sobriety until they've built up enough self-worth on the inside and strengthened their own will.

In my case, my family and friends loved me. I knew that all along. However, their kind of support was enabling me in ways they were unaware of. I chose not to tell my family that I was healing an addiction. I chose to keep it private because I knew they did not have the skills to support me. Many of them were struggling with their own addictions and living their own life dramas.

Thankfully, my Higher Self guided me to a spiritual pathway that is filled with folks who have the experience to work with addicts and wounded people from all walks of life. I, like the president of the U.S., am not a self-made person. My heart is filled with gratitude to all the people in this community that gave of their time and their hearts with compassion and love so that I could continue to heal. They did not, of course, do the work for me; I had to do that myself. Each of them in one way or another were like guideposts for me on my journey. They always accepted me–even at my worst and most ugly. When I was filled with self-pity, they didn't go along with it. They called me on it and this sent me to a place of ownership so I could reclaim my power. When I was self-important, they had gentle ways of bringing me down to Earth. I was always welcome, no matter what condition I was in and that in and of itself means the world to me. They never rejected me and always believed in me–often during times when I didn't even believe in myself.

I know that some people choose to go into rehab facilities and I respect that. Some good work happens in those places. The problem I see is that there is no continued support when people leave the clinics. Without a functional community to go back into and good strategies to draw from, addicts are likely to relapse. Ideally, the community is a place where we learn good coping strategies, where we are supported to grow, where there are elders and people available who can help us get to the root of what ails us and guide us in letting it go of belief systems and habits that no longer serve us.

I agree that these communities are not the norm in our society. However, I am proof that it is possible to seek out these sorts of communities. They do exist. It requires the courage to try something new. It requires being willing to heal. It requires being willing to keep seeking support and never giving up. Perseverance. Patience. Faith. I found my way within a non-denominational spiritual community. Perhaps that is not your way. I pray you can find a way that is a good fit for you. Reach out. It's worth it. You're worth it.

I look forward to the day when societies adopt the strategy that Johann Hari speaks about in his TED Talk "Everything you think you know about addiction is wrong" where he explains that the antidote to addiction is really connection. Addiction has been well studied in the last several decades. There are things we know about how addiction works and what causes it today that we simply did not know previously. This is not an individual problem and it's not the fault of addicts; this is a societal problem we've created collectively and it's one that can only be changed by beginning to shift out of these faulty beliefs and behaviours collectively. Although we've assumed that punishing addicts for their behaviour and marginalizing them is the way to deter addictive patterns, this is actually the stance that encourages addiction to flourish.

Humans regulate themselves, learn, and grow within the context of healthy and secure relationships. In the absence of loving connections and solid bonding with community and family members, humans begin looking for other ways to feel secure, accepted, and safe in any way they can: joining gangs, taking drugs, and becoming fanatical in their beliefs. Because intergenerational trauma is passed down through generations, many attitudes about parenting, relating to others, and messages about how the world works that many of us carry are not life giving.

Someone who grows up in an abusive home or society is less likely to develop safe and healthy bonds with others. Portugal, the land of some of my ancestors, is the first country to decriminalize addiction across the board. Portugal's government has set up social services that are aimed at reconnecting folks struggling with addiction into community by providing professional, financial, and networking support to addicts. The success rate of this strategy is clearly evident in Portuguese society fifteen years after it began.

My Dreamer and Wolf Woman taught me how to dream big, envision a new possibility for my life, and to persevere through challenges until that new dream manifested in my life. They began showing me that there are obstacles to every dream. Results don't happen overnight and it seemed that my dream was close to extinction many times in the journey to success. As I held onto my intent, tried new strategies, and saw it all the way through to completion, I experienced many victories that overshadowed the failures. The dream often did not end up looking like what I'd originally envisioned; I notice that the universe tweaks things along the way to make the dream work better.

Dreaming always involves risk, change, and loss. It's a series of little deaths that need to happen in order for new parts of the dream to come forward. It took me a while to understand that those pieces that didn't serve me needed to die so the energy that was wrapped up in them could return to me. With this extra energy, I began feeling better and that gave me even more strength to go after further pieces that needed to die and begin building new foundations for my life that worked for me. I am glad that I can be an image-maker of this life-giving way of being to my descendants now. This is possible because others were able to provide me with healthy mirrors to look into. This is really how the cycle of addiction changes in society. It takes commitment on the part of the addict and the community at large.

Family Spiral Changes

"There is an expiry date on blaming your parents for steering you in the wrong direction; the moment you are old enough to take the wheel, responsibility lies with you."

-J.K. Rowling

"The process of becoming unstuck requires tremendous bravery, because basically we are completely changing our way of perceiving reality."

- Pema Chödrön

As an educator, I encourage the parents and kids I work with to educate themselves. I've had a lot of experience working with individuals to help personalize their learning so that it is meaningful to them as people rather than simply blindly following along with curriculum set by others. Although I am not against mainstream schooling, I am concerned to see kids being conditioned out of following their natural queries about the world for the sake of spending endless hours memorizing and regurgitating facts so they can pass standardized tests. Through experience working in public, alternative, and homeschooling environments, I've noticed that children who are inspired by adults around them to seek knowledge from many different sources from the time they are young, tend to be more confident self-educating than their schooled counterparts. I'd like to see a shift in public education toward true personalized learning, but that is another conversation entirely!

I am aware that the word "education" may be a loaded one with many triggers attached to it for some readers. Unfortunately, much trauma has taken place in schools, on sports fields, in churches, and other places of "learning." Here in Canada, the Truth and Reconciliation Commission just delivered its recommendations after hearing testimony from thousands of indigenous people who were forced into residential schools in an effort to cleanse them of their culture by the Canadian government in the last century. As hard as it was to hear their stories, I was so proud of each and every one of them for speaking out against the abuse perpetrated by school and government officials.

A real education, in my estimation, is one where we follow our interests and curiosities in ways that help us to grow our characters and help us contribute positively to the world in which we live. This does not necessarily need to take place in a school or a classroom. Nor does someone need to be literate in order to educate themselves. I know that might sound like a funny thing for a teacher to say, but I have experience interacting with illiterate people and cultures. These folks are far from being ignorant! For example, my great aunt Severina was completely illiterate. She knew how to sign her name and could not read in English or in Portuguese. I marveled at what this woman could do as a child. I never could figure out how she could calculate with accuracy the grocery bill as she went along while we were shopping.

Mainstream media is not necessarily representative of accurate information. Much of how addiction is treated by the media is inaccurate, sensationalized, and created more for entertainment than educational purposes. This means that as responsible and intelligent citizens, we need to seek sources of knowledge in books, through conversation with professionals and people who have lived or are living with addiction, on the Internet (provided they are sound sources), through sharing circles, by watching TED Talks, by watching scientific documentaries, studying scientific research, and by taking workshops.

It's wise not to take information at face value but rather to test this knowledge in your own life to see what works and what does not work for you. If it works, keep doing it; if it doesn't, try something else. I've provided a Bibliography at the end of this book of authors who have really impacted my life for the better with their research, their experience, their compassion, their devotion to serving others, and their knowledge. I highly recommend any of these authors to readers wanting to understand more about addiction and healing.

Interestingly enough, even in countries where the Internet, experts, and books are highly censored, folks are still finding ways to get access to accurate knowledge. Where there is a will, there is a way. This is also true of healing unhealthy family and societal patterns. At some point, we each need to take responsibility for how we've created our inner worlds and the effect that is having on our own lives if we are to see true transformations in our lineages.

I remember watching an interview with Nelson Mandela where he was speaking about having been imprisoned unjustly in South Africa for nearly three decades. The interviewer asked him how he survived and kept positive through that experience. Mandela said something to the effect of: you can keep my body behind bars but you can never imprison my mind. He knew that he was in charge of his own education and he was able to take command of his inner world while he was in prison. He went on to become the first black President of South Africa–a testament to his indomitable spirit! I've already begun seeing the positive ripples of my own healing among family and friends. As humans, we can't help but impact each other so we might as well focus on creating more positive image making. If you don't like something about yourself, change it. Only you have the power to do that.

I stand with Dr. Gabor Maté in his assertion that society feeds the illness of addiction. Because addiction is bolstered by social, political, and economic problems, we also must begin to find ways to decrease the external stressors on families that society has created in order to give people a better chance to heal. Dr. Maté outlines a viable plan in his book "In the Realm of Hungry Ghosts: Close Encounters with Addiction" and so I encourage readers to pick up that fantastic resource.

At a party I attended recently, one man exclaimed that there wasn't one person out there without some kind of addiction. I thought it was brave of him to admit this thought in mixed company and agreed. The fact is, we all utilize substances or behaviours to soothe or comfort ourselves when we are under stress to some degree. The behaviours I am talking about here are not to be confused with those that are life-giving and support self-regulation. All addictions take up life force energy that could otherwise be channeled into living our Sacred Dream–the reason we are here on the planet. In this way, there are no small addictions. Some addictions have a bigger impact on ourselves and others, but all addictions indicate a lack of self-command and self-esteem at play. We are all worth the effort of doing the inner work to change these impulsive patterns and no one can do that *for* us.

Some of these are socially sanctioned addictions, such as retail "therapy" or overeating. One person may eat ice cream and potato chips to deal with her depression around her husband leaving her instead of simply admitting she is deeply sad and feeling lost. Another may have a tendency to go on shopping sprees during stressful times. Just because they are considered "normal" by our society doesn't mean they are healthy patterns to run. They all have costs to our energy systems.

As a former addict who has healed an addiction, I've also made a pledge to work with other addicts as a thank you to all those who have come before that helped me to heal. I cannot repay my teachers for their care, patience, presence, and immense time they put into working with me. Each of us who have done this inner work has an amazing opportunity to reach a hand behind us to help someone else up. Most addicts I've talked to, myself included, appreciate working with former addicts more than with folks who have never gone through addiction healing themselves. There is tremendous value working with someone who has had similar struggles and has found ways to reclaim their lives. So pay it forward through the generations, I say. This book is a step in that direction.

Epilogue

....

"The wheel is come full circle."

-*William Shakespeare*

At the end of my addiction healing journey, a year and a half later, I had a Marking Ceremony. This ceremony is undergone to mark major achievements in life. I was surrounded by friends–some of whom knew I had been on this journey. As brothers and sisters who also walk the shamanic pathway in life, there was no judgment of where I had been, what I had chosen, or where I ended up. As I relayed my victories and heard their individual reflections back to me, I felt filled up with joy and hope. I was able to really celebrate all I had come through and take it all in. Before this journey, I'd never accomplished anything in my life that took so much dedication, awareness, and focus. It felt good to say, "Wow. It wasn't easy and I did it anyway. It wasn't always fun and I did it anyway. It wasn't always comfortable and I worked through it anyway."

We all have natural talents and we all have areas in life we struggle with. Those areas of challenge are also where we have a chance to refine our characters and to set free more of our shining. It was so worth the patience of incremental steps. It was so worth not giving up on Life or on myself as a child of Spirit. If I can do it, anyone can. Magic is everywhere. Every moment we are alive provides us for another opportunity to heal. The opportunities never end. We need to be aware of them and willing to grab on to them as they come and follow them into the light where they will inevitably lead us if we persist.

The biggest illusion is that the journey should be easy. Who ever promised that? Ease and easy are not the same. In every hero or heroine's life, there are challenges presented. There are parts of the heroine that must die so that the life-giving parts of her can be reborn anew. The hero learns, eventually, how to look for those healing opportunities. Kahuna Hale Makua gives a big picture view of this in the book, "The Bowl of Light: Ancestral Wisdom from a Hawaiian Shaman" by Hank Wesselman:

> "...[W]e were brought here to enjoy ourselves– to grow, increase, and become more than we were in the beauty of nature on this wonderful world. And...we are to remember our divine origins through the experience of love for one another...This is it...This is what we are here to experience. All the rest, all our work and accomplishments, our successes, and our failures, our families and friends, everything we do and become in our lives is simply the river of experience that carries us, the background against which we struggle or with which we go nalu [go with the flow] as we learn our life lessons and huli [transform] into our once and future selves."

There is no hero or heroine coming to sweep any of us away from the struggles of living. There is no one coming to grant us the happiness we seek. Each of us is our own hero or heroine. Learning to enjoy life is directly linked to our ability to learn compassion and love for ourselves. In doing so, we not only heal ourselves, but create the possibility for those around us to heal as we hold space for their process.

There is a gospel song that states "None of us are free. One of us in chains. None of us are free." I always loved singing that song. It makes clear what the boddhisatvas of the Buddhist tradition know: that until all of us have evolved, we will all continue to experience suffering. We are all part of the same energetic soup. We are all one– inextricably linked throughout time. We indeed are all relations.

I didn't walk away from my Marking Ceremony a forever cured woman in all ways. I left being a slave to addiction behind. A few months after the ceremony, I sprained my ankle and ended up quitting kickboxing. I couldn't do it with my ankle in that condition and I realized that my body was screaming at me to find a form of exercising that put less impact on my joints. I was torn about this because kickboxing was a great way to keep energy running in my body and helped me to reduce stress. I also moved in with my life partner, which meant needing to buy a car to get around the city when I formerly took transit and walked everywhere. Needless to say, it was a hard balancing act at this time to do my life's work as well as exercising as much as my body needed to stay fit. I ended up gaining ten pounds. My ankle took 6 months to heal. I felt like a failure. I realized it was time to start using the tools and strategies I learned. I persevered.

> *"Imagine...you...are a wise elder looking back on your life, reflecting on your legacy, what would you say? What would your story be? What would you like those who come after you to know of your experience?"*
>
> *-Lynn V. Andrews*

Last night, I dreamed that I was in the Downtown Eastside (a Vancouver neighbourhood known for its high-density drug user population). I was at a hotel waiting for my sister to join me. I ended up inviting addicts to stay at the hotel suite I'd rented. I provided food and made sure everyone felt safe. At one point, I was afraid they'd start using in the suite but they never did. Some of them slept off their weariness. Some of them ate. More and more of them poured in and I was afraid I wouldn't be able to serve them all.

A community was forming and I had to go. The place was a mess–paper cups, plates, food wrappers, and serviettes everywhere! I started feeling resentful about either having to clean it up myself or then paying extra cleaning charges on my bill. I wondered how I was going to get everyone out of there. Then I got an idea. I asked each person to pick up some garbage and bring their dishes to the kitchen to be cleaned. Some people volunteered to do the dishes. I thanked them all for coming.

After the cleaning, an indigenous lady brought out a Tupperware container of home made cookies and offered them to us. She and other indigenous ladies sang a blessing song. A feeling of love and care filled the room. We were a true community. I was amazed at how we'd all come together. None of my fears had come to pass. I was conscious that I had to go. One man came forward and offered to shepherd everyone out of the room and return the key to the front desk. I trusted him completely and felt good about handing him the key. I woke up with a good feeling in my heart.

I bet there are seven billion ways to heal from addiction. I hope that sharing the story of the path I chose speaks to some people and gives them faith in trusting Spirit to support their healing journey. Addiction at its core has to do with feeling disconnected and not feeling a sense of belonging. My prayer is that we can all reconnect with the unconditional love the universe has for us and for the miracles that each of us are as creations of Spirit.

Today, I sense with my whole being that I am a part of a universal family. I am no longer an orphan or an outcast. I no longer need to search for ways to escape reality. I no longer call myself an "addict" because that part of my ego personality does not define who I am as a spirit in a human body. I know the addict part of me intimately and I have command over it. At essence, the addict is not who I am; I am Spirit and Spirit lives inside me. I trust in myself and Spirit to navigate whatever challenges Life sends my way. Stress no longer derails me. I belong here on Earth. I am free. I am human. And for once in my life, it's okay not to be superhuman. I can just be me in all my perfection and imperfection. It is good to be alive.

Acknowledgments

···

As I was writing this book, I found myself feeling waves of gratitude for my healing, for my teachers who guided me, and for my blood lineage for giving me my life in human form. Life is so beautiful and rich even with all of the challenges, heartbreaks, and human-generated chaos.

Though he might not know it, my nephew kept me motivated throughout this project. In his childlike innocence and generosity, he made me pieces of art and bookmarks that I placed in the resources I utilized in order to remind me of the legacy I wanted to leave for my descendants.

My niece helped me write this book too. She kept coming to me in spirit form cheering me on, letting me know that this book was important. I wrote through my doubts and fears because of her. She wouldn't let me give up and so I didn't.

I thank my aunt for gifting me my first diary when I was just nine years old. It was a beautiful book with brilliant red fabric, embroidered gold Chinese dragons, and colourful flowers on the cover. I still remember the wonder and joy I felt upon receiving it. My aunt has the gift of being able to see peoples' talents and encourage them. Thanks for always believing in me and supporting my interests.

I send my heartfelt gratitude to my longtime friend, Grandfather Weird Wind, for his unwavering enthusiasm around this book. He showed me how needed this piece is in the world.

Thank you to all my friends who read this book and gave feedback on how to improve it. I send lots of hand massages to Lyreen Dressel for her tireless editing.

A big thank you to all the folks at Balboa Press for helping me self-publish this book.

Thanks to my life partner for asking the question that sparked the creation of this book. You've hung in there with me for years through calm and rough seas; I love you with all my heart, body, and soul.

Glossary of Terms

··

Indigenous- A term to describe a person indigenous to a particular place, the "first people" of a place, if you will.

Aloha- Love is the state of aloha that Great Spirit demonstrates to us unconditionally–no matter what we do, think, say, or feel. In truth, we are never disconnected from aloha; it is *we* who isolate from *it*.

Animal Totems- These are the spirits of animals who dwell in the spirit world. Their function is to act as spiritual guides to humans. Totems know how to navigate the spirit world and can be tasked to bring back information to the human they work with.

Aura- The auric field is the luminous electromagnetic egg that surrounds our body and animates it with life and energy.

Body Types- This refers to the five energetic holding patterns specific to five body types. We each choose two of these body types unconsciously in order to help us "armour up" when we are young so we can survive our childhoods. Wilhelm Reich pioneered the work in the early 1900s.

Ceremony- The word ritual is used interchangeably with ceremony in this book. A ceremony is a simple action one takes with a specific intent in mind aimed to transform a problem or bring illumination.

Consensual Reality- Also called "ordinary" reality. This is the reality we all "agree" on. It is necessary to be grounded in consensual reality in order to live in the physical world successfully.

Dearmouring- A ceremony for releasing body trauma and body type armour (see Body Types). This is important for freeing up trapped energy and bringing more vitality to the body.

Dreamer/Higher Self/Inner Wise One- These terms are used interchangeably in the book. They refer to the essence of our being–the spirit part of us that never dies.

Dreaming- Is an action that harnesses the powers of imagination, love, interconnection, intuition, and Spirit in order to literally re-order the inner reality needed to manifest the outer reality we want to live in.

Dreamtime- Indigenous folks all over the world say that all of life is a dream. In order to change the physical reality we live in, we must be able to travel the dreamtime (spirit world) in order to make impact. This involves understanding the dream symbols that come to us and what they mean. In this book, dreamtime also refers to the sleeping dream and the pure messages we get from Spirit when the ego cannot interfere.

Drum Journeys- Shamans often use the drum beat of four beats per second in order to induce trance states that make it easier for travelers to journey into the spirit world for answers to their questions.

First Nations- The term used to describe some indigenous people in Canada.

Ho'oponopono- A traditional Hawaiian ceremony and process to bring about forgiveness and reconciliation in groups and individuals.

Inner Masculine/Inner Feminine- Our inner feminine is represented by the left side of our bodies; she is our intuitive, dreaming aspect who is very closely linked to our Dreamer. She knows our sacred purpose and knows how to lead the way if we tune into her. Our inner masculine is represented by the right side of our bodies; he is our active element who knows how to stalk out parts of the dream to bring it into form in the physical world.

Intent- The reason one is doing something. Often referred to in this book as a "dream" intent or a "healing" intent. It is the outcome one wants out of an action or ceremony.

Karpman Triangle- A therapeutic map conceived by Stephen Karpman in the late 1960's and used often in psychotherapy as a way to create healthier communication strategies between people. The three roles that people play in unhealthy interactions are: victim, rescuer, and persecutor.

Life Force- This is the energy that animates all of life and runs through all things.

Lomilomi- A hands-on Hawaiian healing modality utilized to work on the body in order to bring harmony to body/mind/heart/spirit.

Medicine Songs- These are songs that come from the spirit world and contain healing energy. They are often sung at gatherings, healings, and ceremonies to support transformation.

Medicine Wheel- An ancient, circular map used by cultures around the world that describes the elements of wholeness as well as how to attain balance in life.

Mesa- This is the South American word for "altar." Altars are often utilized in shamanism in order to support the manifestation of dreams. People pray at altars in order to receive guidance on their journey.

Moontime- This refers to a woman's monthly menstrual cycle. Indigenous cultures recognize the feminine energy of Grandmother moon and her connection to all women.

Neutrality- The ability to stay present to what is going on and to hold space without over- or under reacting. When one is neutral, they are centered and more able to take right action.

Non-ordinary Reality- This refers to dimensions of awareness that are perceivable to those who use all their senses and intuition to glean information from the universe. Shamans go into non-ordinary reality in order to come back with information that will benefit the community (i.e. solutions to problems or curing illness).

Pain Tapes- These are stories we tell ourselves in our minds that keep us in the past or future reliving or recreating painful lessons and states. Pain Tapes are often also stored in body tissue.

Qigong- An ancient Chinese martial art concerned with bringing vitality, balance, and presence to the one practicing. Historically, Chinese warriors practiced qi gong to prepare for battle on all levels of awareness. The focus was on being centered so they only took the necessary actions and did not lose energy.

Recapitulation- A ceremony that supports the healing and quieting of the mind. It is also a term used to describe a process of reflection that stops harmful thought patterns in their tracks so they cannot wreak havoc in one's life.

Reiki- A Japanese shamanic energy healing technique that involves sending universal energy into a living thing or person in order to stimulate wellness.

Sacred Dream- This refers to someone's life purpose; the reason they are here on earth.

Spirit/Great Spirit/God/The Divine- There are many names for God. These are some of the ones used interchangeably in this book.

Spirit World- This is the realm of Spirit that is the matrix of life. This world runs through all of life like a web. Anything that will be made manifest appears in the spirit world before it gains physical form.

Stalking- The ability to take actions in the physical world that move us closer to manifesting our dreams.

Sweatlodge- A sacred ceremony practiced in many different cultures that involves bringing hot rocks into a dome-like space that's been covered in blankets. People enter the lodge to pray and heal. Water and herbs are poured over the rocks to support the purification process.

Tonal- An Aztec word to describe physical reality and the physical world.

Vision Quest- A ceremony that usually involves a prolonged stretch of solitary time in nature where one connects with nature spirits, their ancestors, and spiritual guides (known and unknown) in order to gain perspective and direction in his or her life.

Works Cited

Almqvist, Imelda. *Natural Born Shamans: A Spiritual Toolkit for Life. Using Shamanism Creatively With Young People of all Ages.* Winchester: Moon Books, 2016.

Andrews, Lynn V. *Writing Spirit: Finding your Creative Soul.* New York: Tarcher/Perigee, 2007.

Andrews, Ted. *Animal Speak: The Spiritual & Magical Powers of Creatures Great and Small.* Woodbury: Llewellyn Publications, 2002.

Bear, Sun and Wabun Wind. *Walk in Balance: The Path to Healthy, Happy, Harmonious Living.* New York: Touchstone, 1989.

Beattie, Melody. *Codependent No More: How to Stop Controlling Others and Start Caring for Yourself* (2nd Ed.). Center City: Hazelden, 1992.

Becker, Catherine Kalama and Doya Nardin. *Mana Cards: The Power of Hawaiian Wisdom.* Hilo: Radiance Network Inc., 2002.

Boesveld, S. (2014, April 22). One-third of Canadians have suffered child abuse, highest rates in the western provinces, study says. *National Post.* Retrieved from http://news.nationalpost.com

Brennan, Barbara Ann. *Hands of Light: A Guide to Healing Through the Human Energy Field.* New York: Bantam, Rev. Ed. 1988.

Brown, Brené. *Daring Greatly: How the Courage to Be Vulnerable Transforms the Way We Live, Love, Parent, and Lead.* New York: Avery, 2015.

Brown, Brené. *The Gifts of Imperfection: Let Go of Who You Think You're Supposed to Be and Embrace Who You Are.* Center City: Hazelden, 2010.

Cameron, Julia. *Vein of Gold: A Journey to your Creative Heart.* New York: Tarcher, 2002.

Carson, David and Nina Sammons. *2013 Oracle: Ancient Keys to the 2012 Awakening.* San Francisco: Council Oak Books, 2006.

Castaneda, Carlos. *A Separate Reality: Further Conversations with Don Juan.* New York: Simon and Schuster, 1971.

Castaneda, Carlos. *The Power of Silence: Further Lessons of Don Juan.* New York: Washington Square Press, 1991.

Chödrön, Pema. *When Things Fall Apart: Heart Advice for Difficult Times.* Boulder: Shambhala, 2000.

Coloroso, Barbara. *Kids are worth it! Raising Resilient, Responsible, Compassionate Kids.* Toronto: Penguin, 1995.

Désilets, Saida. (2015, January). Shameless Pleasure: What it is and why you need it. *It's All About Women.* Retrieved from: http://itsallaboutwomen.com

Engrácio, J. (2012, October). Going Mental. [Web log post]. Retrieved from: https://jenniferengracio.wordpress.com

Engrácio, J., Dickie, A., Inksetter, K. *The Magic Circle: Shamanic Ceremonies for the Child and the Child Within.* Vancouver: JAK Out of the Box, 2012.

Engrácio, Jennifer and Carell Mehl (Eds.). *Women's Power Stories: Honouring the Feminine Principle of Life.* Vancouver: JAK Out of the Box, 2015.

Epstein, Mark. *The Trauma of Everyday Life.* New York: Penguin, 2013.

Fleury, Theo and Kim Barthel. *Conversations with a Rattlesnake: Raw and Honest Reflections on Healing and Trauma.* North Vancouver: Influence Publishing Inc., 2014.

Fox, Matthew. *The Hidden Spirituality of Men.* Novato: New World Library, 2009.

Frankl, Viktor E. *Man's Search for Meaning.* Boston: Beacon Press, 1946.

Hari, J. (2015, June). Everything you think you know about addiction is wrong. [Video file] Retrieved from: https://www.ted.com

Harner, Michael. *The Way of the Shaman.* New York: HarperOne, 1980.

Holt, John. *How Children Learn.* Cambridge: Da Capo Press, Rev. Ed. 1995.

Hozi. (2011, October 18). Man with no Arms and Legs-Amazing Story. [Video file] Retrieved from: https://www.youtube.com/watch?v=GSayMXTaQY8

Jim, Harry Uhane and Garnette Arledge. *The Wise Secrets of Aloha: Learn and Live the Sacred Art of Lomilomi.* Newburyport: Weiser, 2000.

Keffer, Marilyn and Gael Carter. *Shamanic Ceremonies for a Changing World.* Gabriola: Shamanic Gateways Inc., 2009.

Kornfield, Jack. *The Wise Heart: A Guide to the Universal Teachings of Buddhist Psychology.* New York: Bantam, 2008.

Kunz, Dora (Ed.). *Spiritual Aspects of the Healing Arts.* Wheaton: Theosophical Pub House, 1709.

LeBoutillier, Megan. *'No' is a Complete Sentence: Learning the Sacredness of Personal Boundaries.* New York: Ballantine, 1995.

Lewis, Mark. *Memoirs of an Addicted Brain: A Neuroscientist Examines his Former Life on Drugs.* Toronto: Doubleday Canada, 2011.

Lion's Roar Staff (2015, July). Pema Chödrön and Jack Kornfield talk "The Wondrous Path of Difficulties." *Lion's Roar.* Retrieved from: http://www.lionsroar.com

Mackinnon, Christa. *Shamanism and Spirituality in Therapeutic Practice: An Introduction.* London: Singing Dragon, 2012.

Maté, Gabor. *In the Realm of Hungry Ghosts: Close Encounters with Addiction.* New York: Vintage Canada: 2009.

McLaren, Karla. *The Language of Emotions: What your Feelings are Trying to Tell You.* Louisville: Sounds True, 2010.

Neufeld, Gordon, and Gabor Maté. *Hold onto your Kids: Why Parents Need to Matter more than Peers.* New York: Vintage Canada, 2013.

Roth, Gabrielle. (2011, May). The Spiritual Power of Dance. *The Huffington Post.* Retrieved from: http://www.huffingtonpost.com

Somé, Malidoma Patrice. *The Healing Wisdom of Africa: Finding Life Purpose Through Nature, Ritual, and Community.* New York: Jeremy P. Tarcher/Putnam, 1998.

St. James, J. (2015, June 7). Your Child Should Never Be Forced to Hug Anyone (Yes, Including a Relative) – Here Are 7 Reasons Why. [Web log post]. Retrieved from: http://everydayfeminism.com

Steindl-Rast, David. *Gratefulness, the Heart of Prayer: An Approach to Life in Fullness.* Mahwah: Paulist Press, 1984.

Tedlock, Barbara, *The Woman in the Shaman's Body: Reclaiming the Feminine in Religion and Medicine.* New York: Bantam Books, 2005.

The Book of Aloha: A Collection of Hawaiian Proverbs and Inspirational Wisdom. Honolulu: Mutual Publishing, 2012.

Thomson, H. (2015, August 21). Study of Holocaust survivors finds trauma passed on to children's genes. [Web log post]. Retrieved from: https://www.theguardian.com

Tsabary, Shefali. *The Conscious Parent: Transforming Ourselves, Empowering Our Children.* Vancouver: Namaste Publishing, 2010.

Villoldo, Alberto. *Courageous Dreaming: How Shamans Dream the World into Being.* Carlsbad: Hay House, 2008.

Wesselman, Hank. *The Bowl of Light: Ancestral Wisdom from a Hawaiian Shaman.* Louisville: Sounds True, 2011.

Zukav, Gary. *Seat Of The Soul.* New York: Simon & Schuster, 1990.

WEBSITES:

Jennifer Engrácio's website:
www.spiraldanceshamanics.com

Dr. Kristin Neff's website:
www.self-compassion.org

Recommended Resources

WEBSITES:

Adverse Childhood Experiences Study
Take the test to see how many "ACES" you have and what that
    means for your overall health and well-being.
www.acestoohigh.com

Energetic Body Types
To find out more about energetic armouring, what your "type" is
    and what it means
www.energeticsinstitute.com.au/psychotherapy-counselling/
    characterology/

Harry Uhane Jim
www.harryjimlomilomi.com

Institute of Shamanic Medicine
Body Power Program
Silent Power Recapitulation Program
www.shamanicmedicine.ca

KiLifestyle Solutions
Reiki Training online and in person.
www.kilifestyle.ca

Sandra Ingerman
Drumming CDs, books, videos and more.
www.sandraingerman.com

Sol Sebastien's The Alchemy of Man: A Mile High Mystery School for Men
www.alchemyofman.com

The Foundation for Shamanic Studies
Michael Harner is the founder of this school.
www.shamanism.org

BOOKS:

Cameron, Brent and River (Barbara) Meyer. (3rd Ed.). *SelfDesign: Unfolding Our Infinite Wisdom Within*. Vancouver: SelfDesign Publications, 2012.

Désilets, Saida. *Emergence of the Sensual Woman: Awakening Our Erotic Innocence*. Wailea: Jade Goddess Publishing, 2006.

Duhigg, Charles. *The Power of Habit: Why We Do What We Do in Life and Business*. New York: Random House, 2014.

Lipton, Bruce H. *Biology of Belief: Unleashing the Power of Consciousness, Matter & Miracles*. Carlsbad: Hay House, 2009.

Roth, Gabrielle. *Sweat Your Prayers: The Five Rhythms of the Soul*. London: TarcherPerigee, 1998.

Somé, Malidoma Patrice. *Of Water and the Spirit: Ritual, Magic, and Initiation in the Life of an African Shaman*. New York: Penguin Books, 1994.

FILMS:

Friesen, Tracey, Cari Green and Harry Sutherland (Producers), & Velcrow R. (Director). (2005). *Scared Sacred* [Motion Picture]. Canada: Independent.

About the Author

Jennifer Engrácio has been a student of shamanism since 2005 and knows that the journey toward healing and wholeness is life-long. She believes there is no need for an intermediary between people and that intelligent force that binds all of life together known by many names (i.e. Spirit, God/dess, Creator, the Divine, Allah, etc.). Her intention is to share shamanic knowledge so folks can tap into the wisdom of the universe in order to grow their own connection with Spirit so they can guide their own personal growth and evolution in a responsible way.

By day, Jennifer is a certified teacher who has worked in many different education settings since 2001. She has a deep passion for working with children as well as great respect and reverence for their magical worldview.

Jennifer is a certified Shamanic Coach and Practitioner, Reiki Master, and Lomilomi Practitioner. She runs Spiral Dance Shamanics, a business committed to supporting the healing and empowerment of others.

Jennifer self-published and co-authored two other books: *The Magic Circle: Shamanic Ceremonies for the Child and the Child Within* and *Women's Power Stories: Honouring the Feminine Principle of Life*.

Jennifer is originally from Vancouver, Canada and now lives in Calgary, Canada with her life partner.

Printed in the United States
By Bookmasters